T0090244

DISSECTING

Secrets of a Medical Examiner

DEATH

Frederick Zugibe, M.D., Ph.D.

AND DAVID L. CARROLL

BROADWAY BOOKS   NEW YORK

*This book is dedicated to my wife, Catherine,
and to our seven children, Fred, Jr., Tom, Cathy,
Theresa, Mary, Matthew, and Kevin, and to their
families, all of whom have been the cornerstone
for all my endeavors and who always provided each other
with love, respect, and caring.*

The Library of Congress catalogued the original hardcover edition as follows:
Zugibe, Frederick T. (Frederick Thomas), 1928–
Dissecting death : secrets of a medical examiner / Frederick Zugibe and
David L. Carroll.—1st ed.
p.   cm.
1. Autopsy—Case studies.   2. Medical jurisprudence—Case studies.
I. Carroll, David, 1942–   II. Title.
RA1063.4.Z84 2005
616.07'59—dc22   2004062889

ISBN 978-0-7679-1880-0

FIRST EDITION

147468846

ACKNOWLEDGMENTS

I wish to acknowledge the early staff of the medical examiner's office: assistant medical examiners Dr. Leo Weishaar and Dr. John C. Petrone; medical investigator James Costello; toxicologist Walter Matusiak; autopsy assistant Tom Zugibe; and forensic secretary Bernadette Abbatecola, all of whose dedication and determination helped me to overcome the many obstacles and overwhelming odds in laying the groundwork that ultimately led to an ultramodern medical examiner system that attained national recognition. I also wish to acknowledge the efforts and loyalty of the entire staff of the medical examiner's office, who always worked together as a team, over the subsequent years: Jimmie Costello, my senior medical investigator, who served with me for over thirty-three years; my medical investigators Mark Breithaupt, Joseph Segelbacher, and Richard Hamilton; assistant medical examiners Dr. Burton Allyn, Dr. Arthur Goldstein, Dr. Richard King, and Dr. John Recht; pathologists Dr. Jim Redner, Dr. Michel Janis, Dr. Eduardo Zappi, Dr. Mark Zappi, and Dr. Hiroshi Nakasawa; forensic odontologists Dr. Arthur Goldman and Dr. Michael Varieur; toxicologists Dr. Jesse Bidanset, Dr. Joe Balkan, Bob Dettling, and Charles Salerno; forensic technician Melinda Szotyory; and forensic secretaries Minerva Olivo, Victoria Affrunti, and Rosemary Russo. My successes would not be complete without mentioning the sterling cooperation received from the investigators and ADAs of the district attorney's office, the county sheriff's department, including the BCI unit investigators and deputy sheriffs, and the detectives and patrolmen from all of the police departments of Rockland County. I also wish to acknowledge the dedication and writing skills of David Carroll, my coauthor, and Stacy Creamer and the staff at Doubleday for their sterling cooperation.

—*Frederick Zugibe, M.D., Ph.D.*

With warm thanks to Stacy Creamer of Broadway Books for her help in overseeing the manuscript, providing insightful advice, and most of all for believing in this project.

With thanks to Tom Zugibe for his time and information.

—*David L. Carroll*

CONTENTS

CHAPTER

1

Of Ice Men and the Lure of Forensics

The great and constant need of those who
investigate homicide and practice forensic
pathology or criminal law is a warm human-
ism.
—RAMSEY CLARK, FORMER U.S. ATTORNEY GENERAL

Seeking truth to protect life.
—MOTTO OF THE ROCKLAND COUNTY MEDICAL EXAMINER'S OFFICE

CORPSE BY THE WALL

NYACK, NEW YORK, IS A HISTORIC HUDSON RIVER VALLEY TOWN FAMOUS
for its antique stores and sensible restaurants. People frequently make the
twenty-mile drive up from New York City to spend a lazy afternoon
drifting in and out of the town's quaint shops, or walking Nyack's network of shore trails that fronts the mighty Palisades. The house of the
painter Edward Hopper is now a museum and a major tourist attraction.
The cottage where the writer Carson McCullers died is frequently visited.

Small Town, USA, but with a lot of polish. Not a neighborhood for
gruesome frolics.

Yet on a warm September day in 1983, along the heavily forested Clausland Mountain Road a quarter mile out of town, Patrolman Edwin Gonzalez, a Palisades Park police officer on morning patrol, spies a woman's blouse crumpled up near an old stone wall along the south side of the road.

Patrolman Gonzalez gets out of his car to investigate.

As he walks toward the blouse he notices an even more suspicious-looking object, a stuffed, heavy-duty garbage bag, the type contractors use to dispose of construction materials. The bag was apparently dumped over the wall, then rolled down a slight incline before stopping between two rocks. It is wrapped with a great deal of tape and rope. It gives off a rank odor and displays bulges where arms and feet and heads might be.

The officer surveys the bag for several minutes, senses trouble, but knows how risky it can be, forensically speaking, to touch a suspicious piece of evidence. Since he is in the Orangetown district of Rockland County, he calls Lieutenant Youngman from the Orangetown Police to come over and investigate.

Lieutenant Youngman is quickly on the scene.

And he agrees, unwrapping the bag would be unsound procedure at this point. Nor is it necessary: circling the bundle, he notices a human foot jutting out from a hole in the bottom of the wrapping.

Lieutenant Youngman calls the Rockland County Medical Examiner's Office. Since I am the chief medical examiner for the County of Rockland, it is my duty to examine the body on site, then transport it to the morgue for autopsy. I drive directly to the scene of the crime.

The first sight that greets me as I approach the foul-smelling sack is a spotted garden snake slithering out from a hole in the bottom. Flies buzz around it crazily, and an army of carrion beetles marches in and out of small holes in the plastic, some carrying tiny packets of decomposed flesh.

Now as most people know from media hullabaloos such as the O. J. Simpson trial, when police and medical examiners arrive at a crime scene the first few minutes spent examining a corpse and collecting evidence can make or break a case. Certainly, this scene is no exception.

This body must be handled gingerly, or important evidence will be contaminated.

Slowly, slowly is the watchword.

STRANGE WRAPPINGS

"Slowly," it turns out, is an understatement.

First, the County Sheriff's Bureau of Criminal Investigation (BCI) arrives and sets to work taking pictures of the bag and of the wooded area surrounding it. As they position themselves here and there, snapping the crime scene from various angles, I stand nearby and study the bag. There is, every official at the site agrees, something puzzling about the way it is packaged.

For starters, when a murdered body is dropped off, it is usually loosely trussed, unceremoniously stuffed into a cardboard box or barrel, then heaved into a deserted corner of the world such as a culvert or secluded woods.

This bag, however, has been handled with extraordinary care. There is even a whimsical quality to the wrapping, almost as if it were a gift package. The person who performed the wrapping obviously did so with a great deal of flair, and this fact already provides clues concerning the perpetrator's personality.

The murderer appears to be a careful, thorough person, who takes a kind of punctilious pride in his work—or perhaps her work; a person with deft hands and thus, perhaps, some manual or artistic skills; a person who knows, as a trained and alert professional killer might know, the importance of small details and the fact that one small, foolish mistake can tip your hand and lead to your arrest.

Since photos are still being taken of the crime scene, it is too soon to touch the evidence or remove the body. It is apparent, though, that inside this bag are more bags, like boxes in boxes. Perhaps a number of them.

Why so many? One bag is usually enough.

And another singular fact. Over the years I have looked into many open graves and closets and metal drums, where there lay corpses in every conceivable stage of decay. The body invariably emits exactly the same noxious stench. Just as cedar wood always smells the same and cow dung always smells the same, so a dead body unfailingly puts forth the same recognizable odor.

But though the stench emanating from this bag is offensive, it is different from the smell of any decomposing body I have ever encountered. Actually, I have never smelled anything quite like it in my entire career.

All very puzzling.

MORE STRANGE WRAPPINGS

The bundle is carefully lifted and driven back to the medical examiner's office, where we lay it out on the table and take X rays.

The pictures confirm what we already know, that the bag contains a human body, entirely intact. They also reveal metallic fragments inside the skull.

We now begin the slow, tedious process of unwrapping. Indeed, there are a number of bags inside the main bag—a staggering *twenty* of them, one inside the other. The inner bags appear older than the outer bags, and each sack has been secured with two-inch-wide plastic tape, then tied with small segments of clothesline. Beetles and other insects emerge from the packing as the plastic is unfolded. I see also that one arm on the corpse is taped tightly to the chest; the other has come loose, probably during the bagging and wrapping. The corpse's hands have been exposed to the elements or to some type of harsh environment, and both are dried and hardened—"mummified," in forensic language.

Finally, the last bag is removed, revealing the body of a heavyset Caucasian male. He is wearing a short-sleeved button-down shirt with "Royal Knight permanent press USA" on the label. Also Haggar slacks and argyle socks. In his right front pants pocket he has $15 and a few coins. We carefully launder all his clothing and meticulously describe each item: its color, size, style, and labels. In the event that someone comes forward in the future to identify the remains, these clothes can be compared with the clothing the missing man was reportedly wearing when last seen alive.

The victim in question appears to be middle-aged. Though his frame is shrunken, he probably stood around six feet tall when alive and weighed 200 pounds or more. While there are a number of forensic inconsistencies in his appearance, external observation suggests that he has been dead for three or four weeks.

He also has a single bullet hole in the back of his head.

THE ANATOMY OF AUTOPSY

Before I describe the autopsy that follows, some background information on autopsies in general is in order: how they provide us with useful information, the sequence of surgical and laboratory procedures we follow, and our pre-established goals. Autopsies have often played an important role, sometimes a central role, in helping me to understand and, we hope, solve a case. For people interested in forensic science and its sometimes esoteric methodologies, knowing a bit about the mechanics of body examination helps.

During an autopsy, of course, a medical examiner's first mission is to identify the corpse on the table. But while our multibagged cadaver does not reveal his secrets so easily, as you will see, eventually his identity becomes the central axis around which this entire bizarre homicide turns.

In general, I attempt to ID a corpse by recording a number of critical physical features that the victim's friends, family, and/or witnesses will recognize. These features include the victim's weight, height, build, sex, age, race, facial features, hair configuration and color, eye color, muscular development, skin color, clothing, jewelry, scars, tattoos, and physical malformations such as a clubfoot or a missing toe. When possible, fingerprints are also taken and matched with those in government and law enforcement fingerprint databases.

Minute inspection of certain body parts often reveals vital information. Weatherworn, craggy hands, for instance, may belong to a laborer, especially one who works outdoors. Pink, smooth hands are indicative of nonmanual professions, often desk jobs. Dirty, unkempt hands tell one story; manicured, meticulously clean ones quite another. A large callus on the first and second knuckles of one or both hands usually belongs to a person who trains in the martial arts, especially karate. Calluses on the fingertips of the left hand mean this person plays the guitar or other stringed instrument; if the calluses are thick, this person may be a professional musician.

If a body arrives in the morgue stripped of its flesh, I often call in specialists such as odontologists—forensic dentists—to examine and compare the victim's teeth against dental photographs listed in databases around the country. We may consult anthropologists adept at using skeletal remains to establish race, sex, age, size, body type, and so forth. When no other method of identification succeeds, forensic sculptors, studying what remains of the victim's cranial architecture, are called on to make clay reconstructions of the mystery person's head and face. Experts in computer-assisted design perform digital facial reconstructions.

The body is first examined while fully dressed.

The clothes are then carefully removed. This process is done by cutting or scissoring, or, better, by unbuttoning and unhooking.

These garments are then laid out near the cadaver so that the location of holes in them can be matched with wounds on the body, allowing examiners to find hidden assault marks and to determine the position of the body when the wounds were delivered. Each item of clothing is labeled, photographed, and marked. If a garment is covered with body fluids it is artificially dried to protect these stains from bacterial invasion and putrefaction.

In some cases forensic pathologists take fingernail clippings from a body and examine them under the microscope for so-called "tattletale" substances such as drugs, earth, and blood (of both victim and assailant), or for scrapings of the assailant's skin. In sex crimes sperm samples are sought in the genital-anal areas and in the mouth. Pubic hairs, both those of the victim and (we hope) the offender, are searched for and examined under the microscope. Any faded or trace markings on the body are inspected under ultraviolet and other forms of spectrographic light to increase their visibility.

The naked body is washed and the wounds are cleaned.

The corpse is then photographed, X-rayed, and fluoroscoped for hidden evidence such as embedded objects, broken blades, undetected stab wounds, and bullet fragments. We take close-ups of wounds and trauma marks. A written description is also made of all visible wounds and injuries, including their placement, shape, and measurement.

Once all this evidence is recorded and set aside for possible further examination, the process of dissection begins.

Each deceased person must, of course, be ministered to in a different surgical way, depending on the apparent type of death suffered, the location of the wounds, and the condition of the body. Each autopsy requires its own specific combination of forensic examination and surgical mechanics.

As a rule, forensic pathologists begin an autopsy at the head and work downward. First, they search the scalp for hidden wounds or artifacts; then they take hair samples. They examine the mouth for tooth damage, tongue lacerations, chemicals or toxic substances, and cuts on the lip and inner mouth. They look for and record any blood accumulations inside the nose and ears.

The inner eyelids are examined for petechiae—tiny blood specks that suggest asphyxiation.

When appropriate, an incision is made in the cranium and the brain is removed, weighed, and scrutinized for injuries. In some cases the cranium is also sawed at various angles to expose the sinuses, jawbone, or other parts of the skull that require scrutiny.

When the head has been thoroughly studied, an incision is made across the chest. The sternum is removed and internal examination begins. Are broken ribs showing? Is blood pooled in various cavities? Are any of the chest organs mangled or torn?

The heart and lungs are removed and weighed; thin slices are taken and preserved for possible future use. Blood is also taken, examined, and preserved, along with fluids from the lungs and pleural cavity.

The abdomen is opened next. Food contents in the stomach are inspected, and the spleen, kidneys, stomach, and intestines are removed, weighed, and given thorough study, especially if they are damaged or wounds are showing. Tissue samples are taken of the heart and other organs for microscopic examination.

The autopsy ends in the pelvic cavity. The external and internal anus and genitalia are inspected, urine samples taken, the bladder removed and studied, and, in cases of sexual assault, vaginal and anal swabs made.

When finished I then write or tape-record a full report describing the procedures and findings in detail. Included in the report is a brief history of the case; a scene description; a list of all persons present at the scene; an X-ray description of the body; descriptions of the clothing, of the naked body prior to dissection, of the condition of the organs at autopsy, and of the wounds; the toxicological findings; and the cause and manner of death.

This report serves investigators as a reference and a thumbnail portrait of the victim's total internal and external physical condition at the time of death.

THE UNKNOWN MAN IN THE PLASTIC BAGS

The first thing that becomes apparent when we begin the autopsy of the man in the many bags is that, although his body is markedly disintegrated, his body tissue is not distended or swollen.

This puzzles me and everyone else on the examination team. A few hours after a person dies, bacteria invariably invade cellular tissue, producing a variety of gases. These gases act something like an inflating pump, causing the face to puff up and the arms, legs, and testicles to swell, sometimes giving the body a balloonlike, Michelin Man appearance. In this instance there are no signs of bloating anywhere.

The surface of the body has a greasy texture that I have rarely seen on a dead person before, and the skin color is an atypical putty beige. Sometimes a drowned body will take on a pasty consistency and color of this kind. But this body shows no signs of drowning.

Most baffling, there is significantly less decomposition inside the body than outside; the gut is not at all distended, and certain inner organs are surprisingly well preserved. Usually, the decomposition that takes place over several days or weeks—and this man may have been dead even longer—is relatively consistent, with body tissue breaking down in predictable patterns and at approximately the same rate. Decomposition of a corpse also invariably starts from the inside and moves outward—which is the opposite of what I see on the autopsy table. Only the outer parts of the cadaver are pulpy and formless. The viscera remain remarkably dry and intact.

Later that day I call several medical examiners in the region, along with several other colleagues, to ask whether they have any experience with this type of inconsistent decomposition. Several speculate that the condition is due to an anomaly in the victim's internal body chemistry. But this concept makes little forensic sense. Basically, my colleagues are as stumped as I am.

Next in the autopsy, we examine the victim's head.

Here we find a bullet hole in the left occipital-parietal region of the skull. Inside the brain, liquefied by now, the bullet itself is lodged in the cranial cavity along with two large bullet fragments. A fracture extends from this wound down to the parietal bone. The nose on the corpse is broken, apparently by violence, and the face has been compressed and flattened by a brown loafer shoe pressed tightly against the face and chin.

At the end of the examination we know for certain that we have the body of a Caucasian male in his late forties or early fifties. The man has a muscular build and heavy frame. His hair is brown and straight, and a partial dental plate is located in his mouth.

Who this man is, how he ended up inside twenty green garbage bags, and, most disturbing of all, why his forensic signs are so peculiar and unreadable, unlike those of almost any known body ever examined in a morgue—all this remains a dark and perplexing mystery.

"HEY, QUINCY, GOT ANY MORE THEORIES?"

For the next several days I find myself thinking a great deal about this unnerving crime.

There is an element of the unnatural. The science is not right. The laws of biology have been tampered with. Evidence is everywhere, yet goes nowhere and makes no sense.

In sum:

We have a body that apparently has been dead for several weeks. Yet it shows none of the typical signs of bloating.

The skin displays a slimy covering rarely seen on any corpse. The body's tissue is rotted on the outside, but a number of major organs remain intact. The very order of the decomposition process has been reversed. The body's hands are hardened and mummified. When hands are mummified, you can no longer take fingerprints.

Basically, we have no idea who this man is, or when and how and why he died. The usual laboratory methods for determining this information prove of limited value given these atypical conditions.

Behind these findings, I can almost hear the perpetrator laughing. I can hear him whispering to me and to everyone else working on the case: "Figure *this* one out, bright boys! It's all right here in front of you. The evidence speaks for itself. Just put the pieces together, use some common sense, and catch me if you can!"

Where to begin?

As always, with the medical examiner's number one axiom: Whenever you are confronted with a forensic puzzle, make no assumptions. Think and observe with the blank, innocent intelligence of a child—the kind of child who sees that the Emperor is naked while others hypnotize themselves into believing he is finely dressed. Think with the imagination as well as with the mind. How has the killer so thoroughly altered the evidence to hide his trail? By what means has he made the remains forensically untraceable?

And the second axiom: While you are thinking outside the circle of ordinary expectation, at the same time go deeper *inside* that circle, to the very point in the center—to the physical and psychological basics.

I think about these matters in the lab and while driving home at night from work. I think about them while watching TV, while talking with my family at the dinner table, and while discussing the case with colleagues on the phone.

The more I think about these strange circumstances, the more I have a gnawing suspicion that evidence in this case has been arranged or choreographed by the perpetrator. In police investigation, we call this process "staging"—that is, altering a crime scene to produce false evidence and wrong leads. Such a stratagem usually has to be recognized by the gut rather than by reason.

What natural force could do such a thorough job of killing off bacteria internally, especially intestinal bacteria, while at the same time allowing outer bacteria to eat away surface flesh, as they would on any corpse?

Perhaps the killer has not flouted the laws of nature at all; perhaps he is actually exploiting them, putting them to work for his own ends, employing one of the most potent preservation methods known to nature: the cold.

This line of thinking brings up an even more intriguing notion. Tomorrow I will go to work on it. The idea is a long shot, I know, and will require some basic science to put it to the test, including data on the little-studied subjects of crystal forms and hand mummification.

I am also well aware that the unorthodox theory I am about to suggest at the Rockland Medical Examiner's Office will be scoffed at by police, politely ignored by my colleagues, and mocked in the press. In fact, some time after this case is brought to a conclusion I am told that during the early parts of the investigation, while I am busy promoting my theory, the police start calling me Quincy behind my back.

Quincy, you will remember, was a TV series whose title character, a medical examiner (played by Jack Klugman), uses ingenious and sometimes highly unorthodox forensic techniques to always get his man.

Given Quincy's brilliance at solving every crime, I am somewhat flattered by the comparison.

THE ICE MAN COMETH

Here is the explanation as I now see it for the strange condition of our corpse: the body of the murdered man found on Clausland Mountain Road has been frozen. Perhaps for a long period; perhaps for months, maybe even years.

This is just a hypothesis so far, but it's the kind of hypothesis that in the forensic world is known as a hunch with a blood trail. The scientific logic goes like this:

1. Freezing kills or alters the growth patterns of decay-producing enteric flora—bacteria that live in the gut—dramatically retarding tissue disintegration, and sometimes almost stopping it entirely. Freezing could definitely have preserved our mystery body.

2. For reasons yet to be established, the body was then removed from the cold, wrapped in plastic bags, and left to rot by the side of a Nyack road.

3. Since the corpse was abandoned out-of-doors, where it was directly exposed to microorganisms from earth and grass, its outer skin surfaces were the first to decompose. The inner parts have taken longer to break down because they are encased in protective layers of skin and muscle. The disequilibrium between outer and inner decomposition now makes perfect sense.

4. During autopsy, I noticed that the victim's head and brain are more decomposed than the rest of his body. This phenomenon, I assume, is due to the fact that the bullet hole in the victim's cranium allows more bacteria to enter and cause decay. Also, if the body were frozen, the head would decompose more swiftly than the trunk because, being smaller, it would thaw faster.

5. Finally, in general, extremely cold temperatures can keep a body intact for long periods of time—months, years, centuries. Mastodons roamed the earth millennia ago, and occasionally fell into pockets of glacial snow, where scientists have found them encased in beds of solid ice, almost totally intact.

Glacial preservation. Long-term refrigeration. Man on ice. It is time to start gathering clinical evidence for my hypothesis.

I begin by leafing through a mountain of forensic textbooks, searching for information on the freezing of tissue. There is little in the literature to go by. Then I remember my own past researches, freeze-drying cellular tissue to preserve it for microscopic studies, information that I subsequently used in a book that I authored, *Diagnostic Histochemistry.* Recalling the astonishing power of cold to fix and preserve human flesh, I decide to fine-tune the focus of my investigation, and to look for signs of freezing and ice crystal artifacts directly in and on the corpse.

Ice crystal artifacts are not the same as ice fragments per se. The term is applied to the deformation of cells that occurs when animal tissue is frozen and then thawed. For example, when a recently dead body is subjected to temperatures below 32 degrees Fahrenheit, the water inside each cell expands as it freezes, just as water inside a plastic container expands when frozen, warping the container's sides. The expanded ice pushes not only against the cell's walls but also against its nucleus, distorting it.

The misshapen nuclei—the ice crystal artifacts—remain long after the cell has thawed. When discovered during microscopic examination, they provide relatively conclusive proof that the tissue was once frozen. So if ice crystal artifacts can be found in the body of our victim, I decide this discovery will go a long way toward proving that he was kept in a state of deep freeze.

I start by taking random tissue samples from various parts of the victim's body, and scrutinizing them under the microscope. Nothing unusual shows up at first—no crystal artifacts. Then I take a tissue section from the victim's heart. Suddenly ice crystal artifacts are everywhere. Samples of tissue from other parts of the body also show signs of freezing.

I inform the police of my findings, explaining that the victim may have been in a state of deep freeze for months or even years—kept somewhere in a cold climate, say, or even hung in a butcher's freezer. As predicted, they chuckle at the suggestion.

To my thinking, however, the freezing makes perfect sense, and the outlines of the murder are starting to come clear. The murderer, my theory now goes, meets up with his victim in a prearranged location for an illicit business transaction. The killer bludgeons his unwary target, shoots him in the head, and then for reasons undetermined transports his body to another location, preserving it in a state of deep cold.

In parts of the Middle East, when a joker wishes to describe another person who makes things difficult for himself, he performs the gesture of lifting his arm and wrapping it behind his head until his hand touches his opposite ear. The implication is that the foolish person eats his dinner in this impossibly convoluted way rather than simply bringing the spoon to his lips.

The around-the-ear maneuver seems at work in this case.

Why freeze a man after you kill him?

Freezing takes a good deal of time and energy. A safe location is needed, and a dependable freezer. Electricity must be paid for, and perhaps rent for the storage space. The evidence must be disguised. The body must be moved. Why not just drop it off a pier? Why go to all this trouble?

Because there is method to the madness. Again surmise, but at this point informed surmise.

The perpetrator, I begin to believe, has frozen his victim, then kept him hidden in cold storage to provide an airtight alibi—making it impossible for a medical examiner to determine the time of death when the cadaver is finally dumped and discovered.

The killer, most likely, also assumed that the frozen corpse would thaw out in a few days of September heat, then quickly break up and leave little traceable forensic evidence behind.

What the killer did not bank on was his own compulsive skill in wrapping. He did such an excellent job of layering the twenty bags, binding them with tape and rope, then securing the fastenings with knot after careful knot, that the corpse thawed and decayed more slowly than he anticipated, leaving enough clues behind in the body's microscopically frozen flesh to provide me with a foothold.

But so far just a foothold.

THE MUMMY'S HAND

The next challenge is to find the identity of the dead man.

At any given time there are approximately 50,000 unidentified and unclaimed bodies in morgues throughout the United States. Finding the identity of anyone in this gallery of lost humanity is to find a needle in the haystack, especially if a searcher is denied the most effective of all tracing techniques: fingerprints.

Fingerprinting ranks as the best and most widely used method for making definitive identification. Its great value lies in the fact that it is backed up by a large centralized file of prints that investigative personnel can consult, producing identifications in many cases where there is otherwise no suspect. Fingerprint identifications can similarly be made in situations where there is a bona fide suspect, but he or she has never been fingerprinted. This trick is done by using latent prints left on objects found in the suspect's home or place of work.

But there is one hitch to this excellent method of "fingering" (slang, derived from the term "fingerprinting") a guilty party.

To obtain a good set of prints, a person's fingers must be in reasonably good condition. Heavily decomposed bodies, fire victims, and especially mummified victims are usually in such a state of disintegration that their fingerprints are obliterated. In the case of our mystery corpse—as the killer no doubt assumed, and perhaps even planned—the hands are so hardened that it is not possible to make a set of prints.

When the word "mummy" is mentioned, of course, people think of tombs in Egypt and of bodies swathed in ghostly winding sheets. Biological mummification is a related but different process, one that takes place naturally when "bridges" of calcium build up in dead tissue, turning what had once been elastic flesh into a material approximating rock or stone. In the process, fingerprints on the mummified hands blur, until they are no longer serviceable as tools of identification. For many years this hardening process was one of the major frustrations of medical examiners. A method for softening mummified tissue was desperately needed by investigators across the country.

Then one day, several years before the present case, it happened that two hikers came upon the nude body of a young woman off a mountain trail in Rockland County. The young woman's remains were deeply pigmented and very dry, and her hands had shriveled and mummified to rocklike hardness. As medical examiner on the case, I determined the cause of death to be manual strangulation.

My initial attempts to soften the girl's fingers and obtain fingerprints using the then popular methods—softening with glycerin, warm saline, oil mixtures, and museum techniques—were all futile. The FBI even referred me to a method using potassium hydroxide in formalin; I tested it on the mummified joint of the victim's hand, where it proved so amazingly destructive to the tissue that I quickly abandoned all attempts to soften the skin.

We tried every means at our disposal to identify the body: dental charting, dental X rays, full body X rays, anthropological studies, hair studies, artist drawings, and descriptive profiling. The gathered information was sent to law enforcement and missing persons agencies, but to no avail.

Since necessity is the mother of invention, I decided to see if I could devise my own de-mummification procedure.

My research took me to the American Museum of Natural History in New York City, where the staff kindly allowed me to use several experimental solvents of my own concoction on an assortment of hands from expendable mummy remnants, to see if the calcium bridges on these ancient fingers could be softened and their fingerprints made visible again. But my experimental solvents, like all other popular tissue softeners currently in use, either failed to work, or if they did work they turned the body tissue into mush and destroyed the specimen.

Not ready to give up, I asked myself whether some totally new approach to the problem might be in order. One of the fundamental elements of mummification is the formation of calcium bridges. Would it be possible to somehow remove these bridges and replace them with a softer substance? After a number of frustrated attempts it struck me that perhaps I should return to the fundamentals of mummification chemistry, and particularly to the basic process known as chelation.

Chelation—the word derives from the Greek *chele,* meaning a claw—involves the isolation of metal ions, usually for the sake of purifying or altering a particular substance. Chelating agents are employed in medicine, for example, to remove lead, which is insoluble, from the tissue of a person with lead poisoning, and to replace it with sodium, which is soluble and is easily excreted from the body. Chelation is also used to remove calcium from the arteries of people suffering from arteriosclerosis.

Now since calcium is *so* insoluble and sodium is *so* soluble, I decided to try to chelate the calcium ions in the dead girl's skin, replacing them with soluble sodium ions that could then be washed out of the tissue, removing the calcium completely and leaving the skin tissue soft and pliable.

After some experimentation, I prepared a chelating agent using the sodium salt of ethylenediaminetetraacetate (commonly known as EDTA) in a solution of detergent, and placed the girl's mummified fingers in the solution for three days. The aim was to replace the insoluble calcium ions with soluble sodium ions, which can be washed away. Sure enough, the calcium bridges began to dissolve, a little at first, then more and more until her hands became flexible and supple, and her obscured fingerprints reemerged.

We took her prints, made the identification, and eventually tracked down her killer.

Now it is 1983, two and a half years after the dead girl was found. Using this newly developed protocol, I reconstitute the skin on the hands of the man in the plastic bags and take his fingerprints. Sending out the findings to databases on the East Coast, we learn that the prints belong to a man from Pennsylvania. His name is Louis Masgay.

The dead man's family is contacted and questioned. The clothes found on the frozen corpse, according to both Masgay's wife and son, match those that Masgay was wearing the day he disappeared two and a half years earlier.

Fingerprints. Clothes. Family descriptions. We have our man.

The family is interviewed further, but aside from telling the police that Masgay was on a business trip to New Jersey the day he disappeared, and that he was scheduled to meet a business associate in a diner, there is not much to help us find the murderer.

THE ICE MAN GOETH

Three more years go by without a lead. It looks as if the freezing ploy has succeeded; not exactly in the way the killer intended, perhaps, but succeeded nonetheless.

Then one day I receive a call from the New Jersey Office of the Attorney General telling me they are holding a suspect named Richard Kuklinski in connection with a number of homicides—including, they believe, the Masgay murder. In return for prison favors, a prisoner named Phillip Solimene, a convicted murderer, testifies to police authorities that he once saw a body hanging in the freezer compartment of Kuklinski's North Bergen warehouse that looked like the newspaper photos he had seen of the missing Masgay.

Shortly thereafter Kuklinski is arrested and charged with several other murders. The FBI has been watching him for years and gathering information on his possible crimes, including the Masgay disappearance. On March 16, 1988, he is indicted on two counts of murder, plus six counts of conspiracy to commit murder and theft. A week and a half later, in return for an agreement by the prosecution to drop weapons-possession charges against his wife and drug- and weapons-possession charges against his son, Kuklinski pleads guilty to two more crimes, one of which is the killing of Louis Masgay.

Mr. Kuklinski, it turns out, is quite a fellow, and a pro at ending lives. Though he works mostly in the New York–New Jersey area, he will murder anyone, anywhere if the price is right. Cyanide poisoning is his favorite modus operandi. While talking to an undercover agent who eventually helped apprehend him, Kuklinski discoursed on the chemical's effectiveness: "It's quiet, it's not messy. It's not noisy. There's a spray mist around too. You spray it in somebody's face and they go to sleep."

Kuklinski told the agent how he tested the speed and effectiveness of cyanide spray. Walking down a busy street and keeping the cyanide canister well hidden, he brushed by a randomly chosen man, gave the innocent a quick, well-aimed spray in the face, and watched with the detached eye of a scientist as the man fell writhing to the ground and expired in moments.

"The best effect is to get them in the nose," Kuklinski explained. "They get it in the nose and they inhale it. Then once they inhale it, he's done, there ain't nothing you can do. You gotta be careful you're not downwind, 'cause if you inhale it, you're done too. . . . So anyway, I told you, I was walking down the street. I went by the guy and made believe I was sneezing. I had a handkerchief over my nose. I bumped into the guy, went past, and kept walking, and this guy—they thought he'd had a heart attack. People milling around him. The way you do it, he has no way of knowing what it is till you're past him. And once he's got it, you know where he's going to go. It's in his system. He's done."

According to Kuklinski, he met Masgay several years ago in a New Jersey diner on the pretense of selling him a large load of pirated pornographic films at a bargain price. Masgay, a businessman in a small Pennsylvania town, intended to sell the tapes at his general store.

At the meeting Kuklinski climbed into Masgay's car and they drove together to a remote location. Here, instead of handing Masgay the tapes, Kuklinski beat him unconscious, shot him in the head, and helped himself to the $95,000 his victim had brought along to purchase the tapes. Then he took Masgay's body to the freezer in his warehouse and left it hanging there two and a half years. Eventually he dumped it in Nyack, where our story begins—and ends.

On May 26, 1988, Superior Court Judge Frederick W. Kuechenmeister sentenced Kuklinski to two life terms, to be served concurrently with a minimum sixty-year term he had already received.

Today, after many more trials and many revelations about Kuklinski, including interviews he gave for several HBO specials, we know that Masgay's killer worked at the top levels of crime. A onetime hit man for John Gotti, the boss of New York City's Gambino crime family, he was responsible for murders all across the country, and had taken the lives of more than a hundred men and women. As it turns out, though, the only victim he ever froze was Masgay. Ironically, this overly cunning maneuver helped lead to his capture and eventual confession. Another admission that Kuklinski made to a wired undercover agent and that helped break the case is especially significant in this regard:

"You sure about all that stuff about fooling the coroner?" the agent asks Kuklinski. "They got all kinds of ways to find out things, don't they?"

"Hey," Kuklinski replies, "you think those guys are smart? Listen to me. They found this one guy, and when the autopsy was done, they said he was only dead two and a half weeks. But see, he wasn't. He'd been dead two and a half years. Those guys got their little nuts twisted on that one."

"Oh, yeah?"

"In a freezer nothing changes, my friend."

"You mean, the freezer maintains—"

"Everything. It's like pulling a steak out of the fridge."

And yet so original was this method of hiding forensic traces—the deep freeze—so clever in conception, so expertly carried out, and in the big picture so unimaginably grotesque and foolish, that Kuklinski continues to haunt the public's dreams today, and to bear the nickname I gave him two decades ago: the Ice Man.

A STORY TO EVERY MORAL

As any experienced medical examiner will tell you, forensic pathology does not stop with fingerprinting and DNA testing. It carries over into realms beyond the quantifiable, into the secret workings of the human heart and the human mind, and especially into the bizarre tricks that human psychology can and often does play on itself—and others. Every forensic investigation is a hall of mirrors.

For this reason, an essential part of laboratory criminal detection consists of learning both the logistic and the psychological lessons that each solved—or unsolved—case reveals, then storing away these cautionary tales and drawing on them when the next case of unexplained death comes along.

Such lessons, found in grim places where others fear to tread, like the interior of a decaying corpse or of a hit man's meat locker, are one of the incentives that drew me to the field of forensic pathology in the first place.

As a child I was always fascinated by courtroom dramas, by mysteries, especially the Sherlock Holmes stories, and by tales of detectives finding clues at the scene of the crime and using them in ingenious ways to smoke out a killer. I was intrigued by the workings of nature and the human body—by how each organ, when studied and examined, tells its own separate tale. In college, I decided to put these interests together.

Starting out my career with a Ph.D. in anatomy and tissue chemistry, I eventually went on to medical school. During my early years as a physician, I had no particular desire to move outside my area of specialization, pathology.

Then several unexpected things happened.

First, I began to feel confined. Greener pastures—or at least broader pastures—beckoned.

Second, and more important, the legal and psychological side of medicine started to capture my imagination. I was attracted not by psychiatry per se, but by the specific mechanisms of motivation and compulsion, and how greed and malice are transformed into crime.

I became fascinated with the ways in which the human mind contrives to commit a violent misdeed, and how another human mind, applying science, law, deduction, and seat-of-the-pants intuition, can read the story of what takes place in the thinking of the felon and in the fragmented clues he leaves behind.

Having studied logic at the University of Chicago, I was also excited by the possibility of participating in a field where reason and objective thinking play as large a part as rote medical procedure does. Though forensic science depends heavily on high-tech methodology, I was soon to find out that it depends to an equal degree on the clarity of perception that investigators bring to a criminal case. An entire criminal proceeding, I learned, can turn on a single observation—or on a single *mis*observation.

THE EYES DON'T HAVE IT

For lawyers in a courtroom, on-the-scene descriptions and eyewitness observations are valuable assets. Lawyers know from experience that the "plausible" testimony of a "credible" witness can make or break a lawsuit. They know that juries are easily swayed by human testimony, and that if what a witness says *sounds* correct, juries usually believe it *is* correct.

Medical examiners, on the other hand, knowing the ambiguity of appearances and the fickleness of the senses, regard eyewitness reports with a good deal less enthusiasm. In their experience, eyewitness descriptions are often the least reliable of all forensic aids, while scientific testing and objective analysis are the two most important crime-solving tools.

One thinks of the famous Japanese film *Rashomon.* The story revolves around an episode in which—or so it seems—a merchant and his wife are attacked by a bandit. The wife is raped and the merchant killed. Three people are involved in the drama, plus a woodcutter who witnesses the event. We see the episode from the point of view of each protagonist, and each story is entirely different from the others. Due to their own fears, lies, blindness, subjectivity—who knows?—the three people describing the crime might as well be reporting three separate murders.

The eyes do not always have it on the crime scene, as the Ice Man killing demonstrates so clearly. Other tools are required besides human perception to get into the mind of a killer and to chase after his mistakes. Here are two cases of mistaken identity I published in the *Journal of Forensic Identification* to prove the point.

Case One

A young man is driving over a railroad crossing when, unaccountably, his car stalls out. The man looks up the track. To his horror, he sees a freight train bearing down on him. He tries to restart his car a number of times. Unsuccessful, he jumps from the vehicle, too late. He is hit by the speeding train.

The man dies instantly, his lower body mangled beyond imagination. Miraculously, his head and face remain intact.

Several minutes later, two police officers arrive at the scene.

As fate would have it, one of the officers recognizes the victim—his name is Bill. The officer quickly contacts Bill's best friend. Would the friend please come to the medical examiner's office right away, the officer asks, and assist in identifying the body?

"Oh, yeah, that's Bill all right," the friend declares mournfully at the morgue, gazing at the corpse's neatly cleaned face. "I can't—I can't believe it!"

Police investigators are a careful lot. So before they reach a definitive conclusion they contact the dead man's family.

Within an hour, the victim's mother, stepfather, and two brothers are standing in front of the cadaver at the medical examiner's office, all nodding in tragic agreement: Yes, this is their beloved Bill. No doubt about it. Bill.

Certificates of identification are signed, and the family staggers home to grieve.

Later that day, a police officer from another department happens to bump into Bill's girlfriend, Jennifer. The officer has heard news of the death over the radio.

"Really sorry to hear about what happened to Bill," he says deferentially.

Jennifer looks at him in a strange way and asks what he means.

"His accident this morning—terrible thing."

The young lady stares at the policeman for a long moment, then giggles nervously. "Bill didn't have an accident this morning that *I* know about. I just left him sitting in my parents' motel ten minutes ago."

Jennifer and the police officer drive directly to the motel.

Sure enough, there is Bill, sprawled out in a recliner, watching TV and drinking beer, very much alive.

Meanwhile, back at the police station accident investigators are receiving the results of a fingerprint search ordered from the county Bureau of Criminal Identification. The prints, it turns out, do not belong to Bill at all, but to another young male of approximately Bill's age, size, and build.

The eyewitness reports were stupendously wrong—even though they came from the supposed victim's next of kin.

Case Two

A nineteen-year-old is killed on a motorcycle going ninety miles per hour while attempting to outrun a police squad car. The victim incurs multiple head and body injuries; but again, his facial features are preserved. He is carrying no identification.

A police tracer is put out on the motorcycle's license plates. Within an hour, the dead man is identified as a disk jockey named Ronny Jax.

As in the previous case, the victim's mother is called to the coroner's office. As in the previous case, his relative looks long and hard at the body and makes a positive ID.

A few hours later, a disk jockey from the local radio station leaves his office, walks to the parking lot, and finds his motorcycle missing. He immediately notifies the police, and in the process he identifies himself as Ronny Jax.

The police inform Ronny Jax's mother that her son is still alive.

But the mother thinks someone is playing a cruel joke on her, and won't believe the news until she gets a call from her son. "Hi, Mom! I'm still here. Motorcycle's missing, but I'm fine!"

Shortly thereafter, fingerprints from the dead man are submitted through the county Bureau of Criminal Identification. They are matched with those of a well-known juvenile offender. The victim, it turns out, stole Ronny's motorcycle, drove it to his death, and was then misidentified—by Ronny Jax's own mother.

So there we have it, two cases of mistaken identity.

But *what* mistakes! A mother fails to know her own son; a brother fails to recognize a brother, a friend a friend. How can it be that sober, reliable witnesses do not know the face of their nearest and dearest, even when the supposed nearest and dearest lies spread out before them on a table a foot away under the glare of giant halogen lights? How is it possible for a person's visual perceptions to play such tricks on their judgment?

Most important, if such mistakes can be made, just how dependable are our powers of discernment?

THE PARTNERSHIP OF MIND AND MACHINE

Up to the early 1960s, most crime-solving bureaus in the United States worked under the old coroner system, a primitive death-investigation structure mainly staffed by pharmacists, laymen, and general medical practitioners rather than pathologists or forensic pathologists. Remarkably, the examination of a dead body was at times even supervised by funeral directors with absolutely no forensic training, and who were considerably more interested in carting the body away for embalming than in evaluating how, when, and why the victim died.

Under this older system, autopsies were rarely performed, and a minimum number of medical tests were available. Indeed, most of the high-tech equipment routinely used in today's forensic labs had not yet been invented. The typical crime lab of the early 1960s, in sum, barely scratched the surface of the biology and physics of murder.

But this state of affairs was soon to change. During the midsixties modern science began its march into the criminal detection lab with trumpets blaring. Quantum leaps in biochemistry and biology helped catalyze groundbreaking research in forensic education. Remarkably sensitive lab tests and equipment were developed for analyzing fingerprints, body fluids, tissue condition, wound structure, trace materials (such as fibers, ashes, hair), and other evidentiary basics. A new generation of high-speed computers accelerated laboratory analysis a thousandfold, and compiled statistical databases of hitherto undreamed of size and scope. Innovative surgical techniques proved useful in the autopsy room as well as on the operating table. By the end of the 1960s, the old coroner model was vigorously evolving into the medical examiner system we know today, with its reliance on forensic pathology, high-tech testing and equipment, and interaction with a range of correlative scientific fields such as botany, entomology, and ballistics.

Stemming from the Latin word *forum* and referring to matters of the law (in ancient Rome the town forum was the place where public trials were held and where justice was meted out), in modern terms "forensic" pertains to legal matters and to activities that occur in a court of law. A secondary definition, not unrelated to the first, defines forensics as argumentation, intellectual dispute, and formal debate.

Almost any science can have its forensics, its statutory and judicial side. Forensic entomology studies insects in relation to crime—for example, knowledge of the sequence in which local species of insects arrive at a decomposing body can help establish time of death. Forensic odontology concerns itself with dental injuries, bite marks, and body identification through the study of jaw fragments and teeth.

The word "pathology" derives from the Greek word *pathos*, meaning "suffering." Medical pathology is thus the branch of medicine that studies the structural and functional changes in body tissue caused by pain-bringing disease. The term "disease" here is applied very broadly, referring to any deviation from normal health—a bullet wound, the Ebola virus, and any other bodily shock that can or does lead to death.

Finally, putting the two terms together, forensic pathology is the field of medicine that concerns itself with the legal aspects of bodily injury and violent death, and that concentrates its attention specifically on the *mechanism, manner, and cause of death and injury.* Combining human scrutiny with scientific inquiry, this remarkable new discipline provides law enforcement facilities with a wonderfully effective mix of reason and science, of creativity and objective analysis, of mind and machine.

And it does more than this, too.

Forensic crime detection is predicated on the notion that for every foul deed committed, aftereffects remain no matter how shrewdly lawbreakers attempt to cover their tracks. It tells us that in every rape, murder, and suicide an archive of silent stories and invisible documentation is left behind that if properly traced and understood leads back to the smoking gun. It insists that for every unexplained clue or circumstance an obvious explanation waits—calls out even—to be deciphered. And it warns that nothing in the room of slaughtered victims or on the pile of broken bones exists in isolation: Every part of the crime scene is connected to every other part, *if* we can but perceive it through an unbiased eye aided by the sweeping searchlight of technology.

This law of connectedness in forensic science has a name: Locard's principle. Edmond Locard (1877–1966) was a brilliant French police officer and a friend of the creator of the Sherlock Holmes stories, Sir Arthur Conan Doyle (Locard considered him one of the true founders of forensic science). Locard taught the investigative generations that followed him that *every contact a person makes with another person or another object, no matter how incidental or inconspicuous, results in an exchange of physical substances.* Today the entire science of criminal detection is based on this simple axiom.

If we pick up a knife, for example, we leave skin oils and fingerprints on the blade. If we brush up against a sofa, infinitesimal fibers cling to our clothes. If we walk through a grassy field, tiny spores, seeds, and bits of earth and vegetation cling to our shoes and clothes. If we shake hands with a friend, each of us leaves microscopic remnants of ourselves on the other person. It has even been suggested—though such speculations can never be proven—that with every breath we take, we draw in microscopic and atomic particles that were once breathed by Julius Caesar, William Shakespeare, and every other human being who has ever lived.

In short, we can have no physical interaction with the world around us or with other people that does not leave behind some evidence of our touch and theirs. The traces we take and leave in this world pursue us as closely as our shadows.

In the art and science of forensics, therefore, the little is the big, the discarded the essential, the trivial the important, the disguised the obvious, and the invisible an entire book that tells a thousand and one tales.

We can run from the forensic pathologist. We can hide from the forensic pathologist. But we can never entirely disappear.

MEET THE PATHOLOGIST/MEDICAL EXAMINER

Situations that fall under the forensic magnifying glass, and that cause a dead body to be brought to a medical examiner's office for examination and autopsy, include the following unnatural circumstances:

- All homicides or suspected homicides
- All suicides or suspected suicides
- Accidental death of any kind, no matter what the nature of the accident
- Deaths whose cause is suspected to be drugs, poison, or abortion
- Suspicious and unexplained deaths; all sudden deaths of apparently healthy individuals in public places
- All occupational deaths
- Bodies that are contaminated and that pose a threat to public health
- Unclaimed bodies

The person who performs the examination and autopsy in such cases is the pathologist or medical examiner. Working with police and homicide detectives, these experts spearhead the investigation of violent and suspicious deaths.

What type of training and knowledge must forensic pathologists possess?

To begin with, they must be medical doctors. Building on this foundation, they must receive training and certification in anatomic pathology, plus subspecialty training and certification in forensic pathology. Training in anatomic pathology includes intensive basic study of disease; training in forensic pathology includes the study of suspicious deaths, violent deaths, deaths by drugs or poison, accidental deaths, vehicular deaths, drownings, electrocutions, lightning strikes, explosions, and surgical deaths.

All this, in turn, requires extensive knowledge of gunshot wounds, ammunition of all types, knife wounds, botany, entomology, toxicology, and numerous other fields associated with sudden or violent death. What's more, a forensic pathologist must be knowledgeable in anatomy, embryology, radiology, surgical techniques, all types of trauma, electron microscopy, phase microscopy, polarizing microscopy, and many other disciplines in science and medicine.

Finally, there is the qualitative part of forensics. A forensic pathologist's intangible, necessary attributes include common sense, curiosity, chronic doubt, acute reasoning skills balanced with an equal portion of intuition, and lastly an unwavering confidence that any crime in the world can ultimately be solved.

The medical examiner, when all is said and done, is an avid Sherlock Holmes fan gone professional, one who loves the spirit of the chase and the challenge of the seemingly impossible, who follows his instincts as well as his science, and who keeps his options, mind, and eyes as wide open as he can.

MATTERS OF LIFE AND DEATH

Considering the scope of this fascinating amalgam of science, logic, law, and psychology, you can, I hope, understand why I was attracted to the field of forensic pathology in the first place, and why I was so anxious to become part of this new era in criminal justice.

It was my good fortune that, just when I was looking for broader horizons in my profession, the job of chief medical examiner became available in Rockland County. The old coroner system was just then being jettisoned in Rockland, and a new bureau was being built from the ground up, with fresh staff and the latest in forensic detection equipment. When I was lucky enough to be offered the job, I took it in a heartbeat, becoming the county's first chief medical examiner. I held the job for the next thirty-three years.

I have never looked back.

Yet I could also say that I have never stopped looking back, never stopped evaluating and reevaluating the cases I have worked on through the decades. The crimes you will read about here are the most fascinating, exotic, and famous of these cases. Each is a kind of crime-solution cameo, showing from an insider's vantage point the mental and technological procedures a medical examiner follows when investigating a violent death.

For the field of forensic pathology, it turns out in the final reckoning, is as much the study of human ways and human life as it is the dissection of death. As Ramsey Clark, a former Attorney General of the United States, once wrote, "A people who will not face death cannot revere life."

In the chapters to come you will see how true this statement is.

CHAPTER 2

Scenes of the Crime
Two Lovely Missing Susans

EMPTY

THE HOUSE IS EMPTY AND STRANGELY STILL.

No set dining table, no signs of activity. The kitchen is uncharacteristically quiet. It is already ten to six. Has anyone started making dinner?

And where is Susan Heynes?

It is October 6, 1975, and the leaves on this quiet street in northern Bergen County, New Jersey, are beginning to turn yellow and orange. Jonathan Heynes is just returning home from his office; he is quality control engineer at British Leyland Motors (Heynes's father is one of the company's founders). He and Susan have been married approximately four months. Ordinarily the newlywed is standing at the front door waiting to greet her husband. But not today.

Jonathan Heynes walks through several rooms, calling his wife's name.

No answer. The house is quiet but not peaceful.

Sensing that something is amiss, he begins to canvass the house in earnest. First he checks the doors: all locked. Then he walks into the living room, thinking that Susan may have fallen asleep in her favorite chair. Empty. No one is upstairs, either.

Checking the garage, Heynes looks inside his wife's yellow Austin. On the front seat he sees a birthday package that she intended to mail today to her mother in England. But the post office is closed now, and the package remains unsent.

Susan Heynes is close to her mother. It is not like her to neglect such a task.

Jonathan Heynes remembers that he gave his wife $40 in cash that morning, and that she keeps a stash of credit cards and her British passport in her purse at all times. He looks around for the purse.

No purse.

Mrs. Heynes is a responsible woman who leaves notes when she is running errands, and who usually carries her purse with her. Irregular absences like these, of course, are not uncommon in daily life. They resolve themselves with simple explanations: traffic snarls, accidental meetings with friends. Mrs. Heynes is a nurse; perhaps she is working late. Jonathan checks her schedule.

She is off today.

THE SEARCH

The minutes pass. The phone remains silent. Finally, at 6:44 P.M., Mr. Heynes calls the police department and reports his wife missing.

Officer Victor Pizza soon arrives and gives the house a thorough looking over. Residents of the neighborhood are questioned. A woman who lives across the street reports sitting in her front yard between 3:30 and 5:50 P.M.

"Nothing unusual today," she declares.

Further searching follows, with no result. Then more local residents are questioned. Now it is learned that Susan Heynes was last seen by her elderly next-door neighbor around 3:30 that afternoon. The two women chatted over a hedge for several minutes while Mrs. Heynes removed clothes from her backyard clothesline. Her whereabouts since that time remain unknown.

It is, of course, a well-known fact that in many murders and disappearances a close relative turns out to be the culprit. Officer Pizza now has the unpleasant job of asking the missing woman's husband some hard questions.

When did he and his wife last speak? the officer wants to know.

Around the middle of the day, Mr. Heynes replies, when he phoned her from Port Newark. During their conversation, he insists, his wife never mentioned that she intended to leave the house.

But there is one thing. Susan Heynes and her husband are both British subjects, newcomers to the United States. That morning, Jonathan Heynes dutifully reports, they argued over the fact that Mrs. Heynes was homesick and wanted to return to England. But Mr. Heynes liked his new job, he told her, and he liked the States. They parted on sulky terms.

Often when a spouse is reported missing the explanation for the sudden absence becomes glaringly apparent early in the game: the husband or the wife has run away, sometimes alone, more often with a lover. With this thought silently nagging at both their minds, Mr. Heynes and the officer decide to inspect Susan Heynes's closet. Here they find her skirts and coats hanging neatly on the pole. They examine her bureau. The contents seem intact (though investigators later discover that her jewelry is missing).

Mrs. Heynes is scheduled to attend a ceramics lesson that night at Bergenfield High School. Being a meticulous person, she has laid out her clothes on the bed, ready to wear to class; they are the same clothes she removed from the laundry line that afternoon while chatting with her neighbor. None of this behavior suggests a woman who is about to run off on a tryst.

During the questioning, Mr. Heynes also reports that on October 4 and 5 he and Susan attended the Grand Prix automobile race at Watkins Glen, New York. Here they met several friends from England who had come to the United States on a chartered airplane to see the races.

An alert is put out, and the departing friends are questioned at the airport by the New York–New Jersey Port Authority police. A search is also made of the chartered airplane. Nothing incriminating turns up. When the airplane arrives in England the next day, the friends are questioned by British security, and again the plane is searched. No clues on this end, either.

New Jersey public transportation and taxi agencies are also queried. Have any drivers picked up a woman meeting Mrs. Heynes's description? No.

The following day there is still no sign of the vanished nurse, and the intensity of the investigation is ratcheted up several notches. A profile of Mrs. Heynes is sent out to police and transportation agencies across the state. The missing woman is described as a white female, age twenty-eight, 119 pounds, five feet six inches tall, with blue eyes, shoulder-length light brown hair, a fair complexion, and a half-inch scar on the right side of her chin. She was last seen wearing a white blouse, a blue denim skirt, blue shoes, and a brown cardigan sweater.

The case is now being treated as a potential abduction—or homicide.

STEPPING OFF THE BUS

Susan Reeve is a single woman, twenty-two years old. She lives in Demarest, New Jersey, a few miles from the home of Susan Heynes. Every day she rides the bus to her job in Manhattan, where she works as a receptionist and secretary at a large advertising agency.

Around 4:40 on October 14, 1975, eight days after Susan Heynes disappears, Susan Reeve finishes work at her New York office and as usual boards the bus home. An hour later, several witnesses see her step off the bus at the corner of Anderson Avenue and County Road in Demarest. Susan lives in this prosperous suburb with her parents and siblings. Her house is about a ten-minute walk from the bus stop.

Today she never makes it home.

Later on, a local engineer tells police that he saw Susan Reeve standing next to a red automobile on a street in Demarest the day she disappeared.

Another onlooker claims that shortly after 6:00 P.M. on the same day he noticed a red car parked on Anderson Avenue. Glancing at the car, he experienced a strange sensation that something was amiss. A day or so later, this same witness heard a radio broadcast announcing that Susan Reeve was missing. He went to the police and drew a picture of the red vehicle.

The search for the vanished woman, the second to disappear from this part of New Jersey in two weeks—and the second named Susan—begins.

So far there is no crime, and hence no scene of the crime. That will soon change.

THE SCENE OF THE CRIME

What, exactly, is the scene of the crime?

Can it be said that the scene of the crime in the Heynes case is established the moment Jonathan Heynes walks into his house, finds his wife absent, searches the premises, calls the police, and testifies to his recent activities that day?

Not really. This is a suspicious sequence of events, but not a site or scene. One could stretch things a bit by saying that if foul play did occur, Susan Heynes was most likely abducted from her home or from a nearby location, making this area a part of the scene by association. But most medical examiners are intolerant of such hair-splitting.

The scene of a crime, they will tell you, is the actual physical location where a dead body lies or a violent offense has occurred—a killing, a robbery, a rape. It is a place in space where the violation of one human being by another occurs, leaving a blot on the social structure that can be erased only by means of criminal investigation and legal judgment.

On occasion a crime has more than one scene—for example, a victim may be killed in one location and the body taken to another. The site of an assault whose victim later dies of the injuries is also a crime scene. A place where incriminating evidence is found also falls under this category.

Most murder scenes are grisly. The scene of the crime, as one medical examiner puts it, is not scenic. Examiners may find a welter of blood, hair, bone fragments, broken teeth, feces. The area may be littered with gruesome artifacts—bullets, shotgun casings, stomped-on eyeglasses, bizarre sexual paraphernalia. If a particularly violent crime is committed, the corpse can be disfigured in ways that most people who have never visited a torture chamber can scarcely imagine. At other times a body turns up that is pristinely, almost magically intact, without visible wounds or discoloration, seemingly carved in wood or wax. It often takes a great deal of testing and probing to determine the cause of such a death.

Sometimes a person's body is found many months or years after he or she was murdered, and in these cases the remains are usually so deteriorated that it is difficult to decipher the cause of death. Sometimes we must work for days in the lab simply to determine the person's sex and their size and weight in life.

At the scene of a crime the body of a murdered individual, especially if it has been enthusiastically manhandled, monopolizes everyone's attention. Silent as a stone, its weirdly inert presence seems to fill the space around it with a dull but irresistible glow. It is difficult to take your eyes off it. Even as the most hardened police detectives and blasé medical examiners do their job they feel the mystery of the motionless figure nearby, a mute reminder of man's inhumanity to man, and even more, of one's own vulnerability.

Professionals in the field of forensic pathology eventually become inured to these displays—but never entirely so. As medical examiners matter-of-factly study the position and bloating of a corpse, as they make sketches and collect blood samples, as they joke with their associates and sip coffee, most are tacitly aware that a human being's life has been prematurely snatched away, and that the mute evidence of this outrage lies several feet from where they stand. Sometimes when I am on the scene of a crime I recall a nineteenth-century tombstone I once came upon in a New England cemetery. It read: "I today, thou tomorrow."

The scene of a crime is always a sobering place.

THE TELLTALE GARROTE

On October 27, the scene of the crime is particularly sober.

It is the day a detective from the Clarkstown Police Department phones to tell me that a young woman's body, severely decomposed, has been found in a wooded area near the town of Valley Cottage, in Rockland County.

Because of a recent police bulletin, the detective has reason to believe that the dead woman comes from Haworth, just across the state line, and that she is a woman named Susan Heynes who has been reported missing for three weeks.

I arrive in Valley Cottage in the middle of the night; a police sergeant lights my way from the parking area down a forest path thick with vines and briars. Reaching a clearing, I see the nude corpse of a white woman lying on her stomach, covered in part with a plastering of sticks and leaves. The half-bare branch of a cedar tree about six feet long lies across her back. Police lights shine eerily on her exposed skin, casting dull reflections.

I examine the body. Decomposed parts of the skeleton are exposed around the head and neck, and the upper areas of the shoulders are seething with maggots. The corpse's face is mummified and the buttocks and genital area have been torn away and eaten by woodland animals. No traces of clothes can be found in the area.

No traces, that is, except one: a pair of pantyhose.

This bedraggled piece of hosiery is tightly corded around the victim's neck in the area of the fourth and fifth cervical vertebrae and is twisted around a thick branch that has evidently been used to tighten it in the manner of the strangulation device known as the garrote.

A killing tool with a long history, the garrote was commonly used in the dungeons of the Spanish Inquisition, where it was looped around the victim's neck and the stick given a turn every ten or fifteen seconds until the question-and-answer session proceeded to the inquisitor's liking. In nineteenth-century India, the cord and stick were employed by a cult known as the Thuggees to assassinate British soldiers and subjects (hence the word "thug"). Today this instrument is still used to execute criminals in Spain and in several South American countries. If you remember the scene from the film *The Godfather* in which rival mobsters garrote Luca Brasi, the Godfather's right-hand man, you will recall that the job is done with a garrote-like wire loop, in this case without the twisting stick so intrinsic to the pantyhose device.

After I finished up my on-site inspection, we transport the victim's body back to the medical examiner's office, and here we begin the autopsy. Classic signs of violent strangulation immediately become apparent, specifically a fracture of the thyroid cartilage and of a horseshoe-shaped bone, the hyoid, located in the throat near the thyroid gland.

Now, a pair of pantyhose can easily cause suffocation when pulled tight around the throat as part of a garrote. But no matter what force is used to tighten it, pantyhose do not have enough tensile strength to actually *break* the bones and cartilage that support this area of the neck, especially in young people. Doing a bit of research, I learn that the hyoid bone is fractured during a ligature strangulation—that is, a strangulation using only rope or wire—less than *1 percent* of the time.

Something is peculiar here.

Though I formally determine that death was caused by "asphyxiation due to ligature strangulation," the fractures in the throat, I think, are telling me something extra. Their presence, I conclude, indicates that while the murderer was busy twisting the pantyhose with one hand, he was pressing the thumb of his other hand over the victim's hyoid bone with enough force to snap it.

To generate such compression, the neck must be held at just the right angle, and the squeezing must be done by a person with extraordinarily strong hands. The killer is most likely a man, and a powerful one, too. Breaking a victim's neck bones with one hand while tightening a garrote at the same time also requires a rather difficult coordination of two separate movements. Such an unusual method of strangulation is what police call a signature or calling card, a factor that may lead to further clues.

Finally, there is the inevitable question: Was the murdered woman raped? We cannot tell. During the autopsy, I find the lower parts of the woman's body so decomposed that it is impossible to say whether sexual activity has occurred. Though the uterus is amazingly resistant to decomposition and is usually the last of the soft organs to decompose, there is simply not enough tissue structure left in this part of her anatomy to study or test.

Still, my gut and my experience strongly suggest a sexual killing.

MISSING SUSAN TWO

The news of two beautiful young women with the same first name vanishing weeks apart from the same affluent region of Bergen County has an irresistable public appeal. For weeks, reports on the women's "evaporation"—media speak—are constantly on the TV news. Even the austere *New York Times* runs an article or two on the case. Citizens of Bergen and Rockland Counties are continually implored to report any sightings of the missing women, and local newspapers carry photographs showing "the two lovely missing Susans," as one tabloid refers to them. Despite their different hair colors, the two women do, in fact, look enough alike in these pictures to be related. This is an interesting fact, as predators often select their victims on the grounds of similar appearance.

A few hours after bringing the dead woman back to the medical examiner's office, the electronic arrival of dental records from England and South Africa confirms her identity. She is indeed Susan Heynes.

NESTLED IN A BED OF REEDS

Then, less than twenty-four hours after the first gruesome discovery, I find myself squatting next to the nude body of a second murdered woman, found by two rangers in Tallman Mountain State Park in Rockland County.

The victim is lying face up, her legs spread wide apart, and a pantyhose is pulled tightly around her neck, complete with the familiar knot and wooden garrote stick. Speculation is strong that this second body belongs to the second missing Susan—Susan Reeve.

Shortly thereafter, members of my forensic crew arrive at the scene in Tallman, and at this point the entire burden of examining the body and overseeing the search for evidence automatically falls on my shoulders. This is how the chain of command works in the first hours at the scene of a homicide. The medical examiner must do it all.

In compensation for this crown of thorns, all authority at the site also belongs to me, the medical examiner. Under this banner of dominion, I must reign with the right of kings, giving irreversible orders, making all decisions as to when and how the body should be handled, and cracking the whip with just enough snap to make certain that every worker and every agency operates at maximum effectiveness. For as everyone on the scene knows, without scrutiny by a medical examiner, both on-site and later in the lab, a legal finding of the official cause of death cannot be made. Even if a victim is found dead from a gunshot wound, and every-thing at the scene suggests murder, the shooting may ultimately prove a suicide or accidental death. The victim may even have been shot *after* death. Nothing, however obvious it seems, can be taken for granted. Only the medical examiner can make the final determination.

The bed of tall, graceful river reeds that cloisters the dead woman before us this sunny morning is located in a swampy section of the park running parallel to the Hudson River. Offering a host of bike trails, picnic grounds, and quaintly crafted stone houses constructed in the 1930s by the Works Progress Administration, Tallman Park is also used with uncomfortable regularity as a "drop site" for bodies by the Mafia and assorted professional hit men. But these remains do not strike me as the work of either. In this case, I think we see the efforts of a lone wolf.

My job now is as follows: Create an overall forensic story, complete with words and pictures, as well as I can, from beginning to end, of the mechanism, manner, and cause of this young woman's death. The more accurate this story proves to be, experience tells, the faster the investigation will proceed, and the more apt we will be to track down the bad guy.

GETTING THE PICTURES RIGHT

We cordon off the area.

The ironclad rule now is: Do not touch the corpse until all necessary photographs are taken. When photographers record the appearance of a murder victim, the body must be lying *exactly* as it was found—slumped to the ground, fallen off a cliff, burned in a fire. By no means can it be moved, dragged, turned over, searched, or even touched by law enforce-ment personnel or anyone else until all photographs have been taken and the medical examiner has given it a thorough inspection. Premature han-dling alters the corpse's original position, however slightly. It leaves alien fingerprints, disturbs the organs, and changes the balance of the body's inner fluids, all actions that automatically degrade its forensic credibility. The photographs taken of a corpse disturbed in this way will, as a result, be counted as unreliable and, worse, misleading. Since the centerpiece at the scene of any homicide—the body—has been altered from its original condition, a medical examiner's photographs may be inadmissible evidence at a trial. On certain occasions such photos even provide defense lawyers with an argument for a mistrial.

Knowing all this, I call on the technicians I most trust to do the job right: the investigators from the BCI—the Rockland County Bureau of Criminal Identification. These men and women are specialists—they must be, for criminal photography is a delicate art—and I allow no one else, not the press or even the police, to take pictures in this situation. Conditions at a crime scene change with surprising rapidity: body fluids evaporate, bloating alters facial expressions, parted branches in escape routes return to their full height. Professionalism is essential if a prompt and accurate pictorial record is to be made.

As they work, the BCI investigators follow the first principle of crime photography. Moving clockwise, they photograph the scene from the wide to the narrow, from the general to the particular; that is, they start with long-distance views that encompass the entire crime area. They then gradually work inward toward the corpse until, shot by shot, they narrow down the focus to the woman's body alone. If bystanders happen to be in the focal area, photographers will intentionally include them as well. Murderers are notorious for lurking in the shadows before and after a killing and for returning to the location when crowds start to gather. More than one killer's face has shown up in random photos taken at or near the scene of his crime. Think, for example, of the famous photograph of Jack Ruby standing among a group of reporters at the Dallas Police Department the night before he slipped into the same building and gunned down Lee Harvey Oswald.

Once the large-to-small sequence of photos of the scene is completed, close-up shooting begins in earnest. The emphasis at this juncture is not only to record descriptive physical details of the corpse, but to capture the relationship of the body to objects in the immediate environment. At the scene in Tallman State Park, BCI investigators start by taking a close-up sequence of the strangled woman from four sides, then from different angles: from above, from the side, from eye level, and from ground level. They record the victim's leg position, her torso, her open arms and unclenched palms, her face, and especially the ligature markings on her neck. They finish up with photographs at various angles of the surrounding landscape.

The complete collection of photographs is then dated and described in a photo log.

The first stage of on-site inspection is now complete. The body can now be handled; I begin my preliminary inspection. Prominent on my list of things to look for are body size and estimated weight, the dead person's likely age, his or her sex, race, skin tone and coloration, hair color and style, the condition of the clothes (or, as here, the lack thereof), and any apparent vomit, sputum, semen, foreign hairs or fibers, blood, scars, signs of disease, rope, wire, mud, soil, grass, and leaves. I take note of whether the body is lying on dry or wet ground or on a bed of leaves.

Also important is evidence of how many hours, days, or weeks the person has been dead. Rigor mortis, insect eggs in body cavities, body temperature, the degree of cloudiness or opacity of the eyes, and many other timeline indicators are used in these dating procedures, most of which are later completed in the lab.

I look as well for telltale items nearby—weapons, bottles, wrappers, bits of clothing. I inspect any punctures, bullet holes, lacerations, or bone fractures; I check for obvious alcohol traces, signs of drug abuse, and the presence of industrial chemicals such as glue or tar. I make note of jewelry (bracelets, rings, watches) and revealing body decoration, such as piercing and tattoos.

Then there is the matter of decomposition, which is generally considered one of the *least* reliable methods for measuring time of death. The rate at which a body decays is subject to a variety of changeable factors including temperature, weather, light conditions, environmental influences, insect infestation and bacterial infection, the weight and age of the deceased, and preexisting conditions within the body, such as chronic disease.

If a body is found in a house during the winter, settings on the home thermostat can sometimes provide important clues, allowing me to figure out how much decomposition generally takes place at this specific degree of heat. In one case I was called on to investigate a double murder where the body of the first victim was lying in a cool cellar while the second was stuffed under a bed in a heated attic. Though both bodies had been dead for approximately forty-eight hours, the coolness in the basement preserved the first victim, making her corpse appear almost lifelike. The second victim, exposed to heat in the attic for several days, had turned a mottled green and purple in the same amount of time.

Finally, after my preliminary examination of the girl's body, I tell investigators that, judging from my experience of similarly decayed bodies in similar settings, this young woman has probably been dead for approximately two weeks.

I also report that her body has been moved here from the place where she was murdered, and that there may have been a stop between. Several factors point in this direction; the first is known as lividity.

BLOOD POOLS AND POOLS OF BLOOD

Because a dead person's heart is no longer pumping blood and all circulation is stopped, whatever blood remains in the veins and vessels follows the path of least resistance, surrendering to the pull of gravity, and "falling" to the lowest regions of the body. Referred to in textbooks as *livor mortis* or, more commonly, *lividity*, this process causes a person's skin to turn a dark pink or purple in the areas where the blood has pooled. This discoloration, in turn, provides vital clues as to when and where the person died.

For example, if a man is shot dead and falls flat on his face, a large volume of blood will immediately flow to his abdomen, his face, and the front of his legs. The blood settles here, causing the skin in these regions to turn a reddish or pinkish purple.

Now if this person is turned over within five or six hours, his blood will still be liquid enough to flow into his back areas. But if more than five or six hours are allowed to elapse, his blood will lose its fluidity and will congeal permanently in the front parts of his anatomy.

The same principle also holds true in reverse. If a victim is shot and falls on his back, his blood will pool in his back. If he is left in situ for an hour and then turned over, the blood in this man's body will flow back into his front parts. But if he is allowed to remain in a supine position for, say, nine hours, and is then turned over, the man's blood will remain permanently frozen in his back areas.

Due to this simple principle of physics, thousands of crimes have been solved.

For example, the body of Susan Reeve—the autopsy and dental X-ray records soon establish her identity—is found lying on an incline, her head at the top, her feet at the bottom. However, lividity has settled in the back of her head and in her upper back; there is no lividity in her legs or buttocks. This pattern indicates that before her body lay in its present position, it lay on its back for more than six hours with legs at the *top* of an incline and head at the *bottom*.

From the on-site examination I conclude, first, that Susan Reeve's body has been decomposing for approximately two weeks, which means that she was murdered close to—or on—the day of her disappearance, October 14. This assumption is later confirmed by microscopic study of cells from the dead woman's endometrium, the inside lining of the uterus. Her family reports that her last menstrual period was approximately two weeks before her disappearance, and the microscopic findings correlate fairly well with my estimate of her date of death.

After Susan Reeve was killed, her body remained at the original site for more than six hours while the lividity settled in her head and upper torso and congealed there. She was then moved to a new site in the state of New York—perhaps she was moved more than once—in an attempt to create the impression that her murder occurred elsewhere.

Several pieces of the puzzle are fitting into place; the next question, an all-important one, is whether a relationship exists between the two killings. That the same unusual killing instrument and choking technique were used in both slayings, that the murders occurred around the same time and in the same area of the same state, that the victims are young, pretty, Caucasian women who resemble each other strongly suggest a single killer. But these facts do not offer incontrovertible proof. Ultimately it will be a collection of small, seemingly inconsequential bits of plant matter that provides the definitive answer.

THE YELLOW LEAVES FALL

In examining Reeve's naked body I notice a number of long, pointed yellow leaves embedded in the upper parts of her chest and abdomen.

From my own training in botany and studies of plant life in Rockland County, I recognize that these leaves belong to the weeping willow tree *(Salix babylonica)*. Because they are set so deeply in the dead woman's skin, I know she was lying facedown on a stretch of ground replete with these yellow leaves for at least several hours.

I walk around the immediate area and look for their source, but there are no weeping willow trees to be found. None within several hundred feet of the body; none within several hundred yards. The two park rangers who found the body have an impressive knowledge of the park's plant life. No, they tell me, no *Salix babylonica* trees grow in this area of the park.

At this point I inform the police of my findings and conclusions: The lividity reading demonstrates that the body first lay on its back, with the head at the bottom of an incline. Next, the body lay facedown in a spot near a weeping willow tree—lay there long enough for leaves to stick to its skin. There is no willow tree at the site where the body was found. Therefore, I tell the police, I believe that Susan Reeve's body was moved *twice* before being dumped in Tallman Park.

The police take over from here, and the investigation is launched.

Many months later, while testifying at the trial of Susan Reeve's accused killer, I am shown a photograph and asked to tell the court what I see. I reply that the photo depicts the site in Valley Cottage where the body of the first Susan, Susan Heynes, was found. I also remark that there is a willow tree in the photo.

What conclusions do I draw from this?

First, because blood is congealed in Susan Reeve's upper torso, though her body is discovered on an incline with her head higher and feet lower, I conclude that she was murdered in Location A or dragged there in the first few hours after her death. After lying in Location A for more than six hours so that the blood congealed, she was moved to Location B, under the willow trees in Valley Cottage where Susan Heynes's body was discovered.

Finally, after an indeterminate period of time, Reeve's body, with its telltale willow leaves and lividity, was moved once more, to its final destination at Location C in Tallman, most likely to create the appearance that the deaths of the two women are unrelated.

Here is a perfect example of how attempting to confuse the evidence at a crime scene simply creates a new path of evidence that leads back to the criminal's own doorstep.

If the perpetrator had simply disposed of Susan Reeve's body near where he killed her, and not trucked it around with, no doubt, a number of unspeakably gruesome side effects, no lividity studies would exist to prove she had been moved, and no matching willow leaves would have been found to tie the two crimes together under one murderer's roof.

Remember Locard's principle: A killer always leaves something at the scene of a crime; or always takes something away with him. Here the killer literally takes the body away with him; and in so doing sets wheels in motion that lead to his arrest.

THE CLINCHER

There is one more critical match to make. The fact that both murdered women were originally deposited in the same location is strong evidence that a single assailant is responsible for both crimes. But medical examiners are fussy about tying up loose ends and want to amass as much evidence as a case can hold.

We place Susan Reeve's body in a body bag and transfer it from Tallman to our lab in Pomona. When the van arrives and the body bag is opened, an unpleasant surprise awaits us. Susan Reeve's corpse, in remarkably good condition at the scene of the crime, has now markedly disintegrated. This rapid decomposition is caused by heat buildup inside the body bag, and the consequent growth of bacteria. Both these factors foster rapid breakdown of tissue, releasing gases that cause a body to bloat and become grossly distorted. Susan Reeve's corpse has gone from human to unrecognizable in the time it takes us to drive from the crime scene to the medical examiner's office.

Fortunately for our lab team, the evidence I am seeking at this point is not dependent on organ or skeletal condition. Rather, I am most concerned with examining the victim's neck and the pantyhose noosed around it.

This procedure I wish to perform demands a delicate dissection. To avoid accidental breakage of bones or cartilage, as well as the accidental introduction of unwanted artifacts such as sand or hair into the incision, I normally use the so-called Prinsloo method of dissection, in which the initial incision is made in the back of the neck rather than the front. First, I drain the head and chest of residual blood to reduce all pressure on the neck. Then an incision is made starting behind the earlobe, cutting an arc all the way round to the suprasternal notch at the base of the neck, just above where the two sides of the collarbone meet. This incision creates a flap that can then be lifted, giving me access to the throat area without the direct frontal incisions that might damage or disturb the hyoid bone and the thyroid cartilage.

As I probe this area, it becomes apparent that Susan Reeve was choked to death in exactly the same way as Susan Heynes. The same signs of neck gripping, suffocation by pantyhose garroting, and a snapped hyoid bone—our "calling card"—are present.

As part of the autopsy, we also examine the corpse's pelvic area and vagina. Though no semen is present, we find a "denuded" area within the vagina. Denuded or highly rubbed areas in the vaginal regions are, in most instances, caused by friction due to forced or prolonged penile activity on a living victim. Almost certainly, this woman was raped before she was murdered.

Everyone involved in the investigation is now satisfied that Susan Heynes and Susan Reeve were killed by the same man.

THE OVERPOWERING URGE TO RAPE

Approximately two weeks before the homicide of Susan Reeve and Susan Heynes, a woman phoned a public prosecutor at the Bergen County Prosecutor's Office. In a distraught voice she described the following events:

One night that week she and a man named Robert Reldan were drinking together and smoking pot in her apartment; one thing led to another, and soon they were fondling and embracing. Suddenly, without warning, Reldan dropped all pretense of romance and became violent. Within moments his hands were wrapped around the woman's neck and his thumb was pressing hard on the front of her throat, causing great pain.

The woman cried out for him to stop.

He continued.

She looked at his face, where, she said, she saw a diabolic glare beaming from his eyes that she instinctively knew was murderous. Appropriately terrified, she screamed louder.

Her cries attracted attention from a bar located below her apartment. Several men of her acquaintance came running up the stairs to see what was going on, and Reldan quickly exited the premises.

At the time of the conversation, the prosecutor later tells me in a taped discussion, he did not worry himself a great deal over this account. The woman was known around town to be unreliable and an alcoholic, which is one reason her testimony was never used at Reldan's trial. "Anyway, we get hairy calls like this every week in our office," he insists. "You treat each one as a potential murder and you drive yourself nuts."

Well and good.

But after the Heynes and Reeve killings, he learned that in both cases the assailant not only strangled his victims, but broke their hyoid bones with his thumb, the prosecutor remembered his conversation with the distraught woman, and he decided to find out more about this Robert Reldan.

What turned up amazed him.

Looking through a list of sex offenders recently paroled from prison, the prosecutor learned that Robert Reldan spent the late 1960s in jail for rape. During this time, a pioneering project known as the Sex Offenders Rehabilitation Program was launched in prisons across New Jersey. Educated and articulate, Reldan volunteered; he starred in the group's therapy sessions and became the first inmate to graduate from the program. When his course of rehabilitation was finished, prison psychologists unanimously declared him cured.

As poster boy for this new psycho-criminological breakthrough, Reldan was chosen to make a guest appearance on William F. Buckley's Show, *Firing Line,* a popular TV interview program of the time. Holding his own with the show's host, no small feat with a man of Buckley's intimidating erudition, Reldan described how his rehabilitation had rid him of all ugly criminal urges toward women.

A year or so later, in 1971, Reldan was released from prison on parole.

Within three months, he launched a sexual attack on a woman in Metuchen, New Jersey. He followed the woman to her car, where he ripped her clothes and then tried to choke her. She fought him off and attracted the attention of nearby police by leaning on the car horn.

Reldan was arrested and returned to prison. He was released again in 1975, a few months before the two Bergen County women disappeared.

THE HALF-MILLION-DOLLAR BAIL

Reldan's life has been a strange concoction of coincidences, macabre twists, and lucky breaks.

To begin with, he is not a dollar-store garden-variety criminal. Smart and charismatic, he was born Robert Nadler. Somewhere along the line he morphed into Robert Reldan by reversing the letters of his last name. From a wealthy, prominent family, he is heir to a sizable fortune (from which he is eventually disinherited). He is also the beloved nephew of Lillian Booth, widow of one of IBM's founders. In his teens he took flying lessons, rode horses, traveled through Europe with his aunt, and ran with a group of wealthy jet-setters. He also commited a string of petty crimes such as joyriding and shoplifting. Family influence helped sweep these offenses under the rug. But as he moved into his twenties, Reldan escalated to felonies, including car theft and burglary. Still, there were no serious consequences.

Finally, in Teaneck, New Jersey, in 1967, Reldan's true demons emerged. Disguised as a laundry deliveryman, he followed a woman home, overpowered her at the door, dragged her into her living room, and raped her on the floor.

He was quickly apprehended, convicted, and sent to prison.

When describing her ordeal to the police, it is later learned by the Bergen County Prosecutor's Office, the violated woman reported that during the rape Reldan grabbed her by the throat, placed his thumb over her Adam's apple, and gripped her neck in a particular way, completely immobilizing her.

The woman Reldan tried to rape in Metuchen told the police that her attacker used the same choking technique.

Now it is 1975, a few months after Reldan was released on parole.

The prosecutor at the Bergen County office knows that Reldan is a convicted sex offender, that he has recently tried to strangle a woman, and that two women have, in fact, been strangled in the area. He decides to call the ex-con down to his office for a chat. Several days after that meeting, Reldan is caught breaking into a private house in Closter, New Jersey. Suspecting that Reldan is involved in the Reeve and Heynes cases, and wishing to keep him in custody while they do more homework, the prosecutor's office demands a whopping half-million dollars for his bail.

Learning about this outrageous bail request in a simple breaking-and-entering case, several reporters, their blood already up over the disappearance of the New Jersey Susans, surmise that Reldan may be more valuable to the New Jersey authorities than anyone is letting on. Digging into his records, they quickly learn of his sexual offenses. Soon articles appear in local newspapers, fingering the ex-con and known rapist as a suspect in the murder of the two women.

Meanwhile, another investigative front is opening up, purely by chance.

A PERFECT MATCH

During the 1960s and 1970s, many large New York City department stores not only sold jewelry to the public but bought it from them as well. Strict rules designed to protect department stores from purchasing stolen merchandise governed these transactions. Careful records were kept at every jewelry counter, and after each purchase sales personnel filled out a ream of paperwork and placed it on file.

Now, as luck would have it, around this time a clerk at Macy's is reviewing the previous day's jewelry purchases. Thumbing through records, he comes across a name that rings a bell. Who is this person? Why do I know this name?

It hits him.

That morning the clerk happened to be reading an article in the *New York Times* about a man named Robert Reldan, and his possible involvement in the murders of two New Jersey women. Now here is that man's name on one of yesterday's jewelry purchase slips.

The clerk calls the Bergen County Prosecutor's Office.

The description of the four pieces of jewelry Reldan sold to Macy's—remarkably, he used his real name when peddling the goods—is compared with the description of the jewelry stolen from Mrs. Heynes's collection: a white gold wedding band, an engagement ring with a large diamond and fifteen diamond chips, a solid gold Omega lady's watch, and a solid gold chain and pendant.

The matchup is perfect.

Further research shows that Reldan sold the jewelry to Macy's on October 20. He was then interviewed by the Bergen County Prosecutor's Office the next day. Sensing the walls closing in and wishing to obliterate whatever footprints he'd left, on October 22 he returns to Macy's and repurchases the jewelry.

Such behavior, in legal terms, is said to show "consciousness of guilt."

Further incriminating evidence is added to the docket against him, and soon Reldan is formally charged with the murders of Susan Heynes and Susan Reeve.

TRIALS AND MISTRIALS

A detailed description of what happens next is beyond the scope of our forensic interests. The general outline, however, is so bizarre and unexpected that it is worth telling in a nutshell.

At the first trial, in 1979, Reldan is charged with first-degree murder in the death of Susan Reeve, because the evidence shows that she was sexually assaulted. He is charged only with second-degree murder in Susan Heynes's death, because by the time the victim's body was discovered it was so badly decomposed we could not determine whether Heynes was sexually assaulted.

The trial begins with a waterfall of damning disclosures: Susan Heynes's blood has been found in Reldan's aunt's garage, a few miles from where Susan Reeve disappeared (this garage, most law enforcement officials agree, is where both women were strangled); search dogs sniff out hairs, fibers, and blood belonging to both women in Reldan's automobile; there is damaging testimony from a number of credible witnesses. Yet despite this collection of pointing fingers and guilty behavior on the part of the accused, legal technicalities cause the first trial to end in a hung jury.

A second trial is held in February 1982, and the verdict is soon in: guilty of second-degree murder, one count, and of first-degree murder, the second count. During this trial, a strange incident occurs.

Reldan sits alone with a police guard each morning while the trial is in session; one day, out of the blue he turns in his chair, faces the guard square on, and without a word sprays him in the eyes with Mace. He then jumps from the third-floor courtroom window, and flees in a car parked for him by an unknown person on the street below.

An hour later, the Bergen County Prosecutor's Office phones me. During this second trial, my testimony concerning the lividity, the willow leaves on the moved body, and the matching methods of strangulation has weighed heavily against Reldan. Before his escape that day, the prosecutor's office informs me, Reldan announced he had some "unfinished business" to take care of in Rockland County. Since I live in Rockland, and since my testimony has been so damning, the prosecutor suspects I may be the business he is talking about.

Whether this was so remains a mystery to this day, as Reldan is caught before reaching Rockland. He is then brought back to finish the second trial, which ends in a conviction.

A sigh of relief goes up in northern Bergen County. But amazingly, his conviction is soon overturned on appeal.

More legal technicalities.

A third trial follows, in 1986. Before it begins, Reldan complains to the court that he has received substandard legal representation in the past two trials. At the last minute he asks permission to drop his public defender and hire a private attorney. The judge denies the request.

Reldan then announces he will serve as counsel in his own defense.

Since every lawyer knows the saying, "He who represents himself in court has an ass for an attorney," this plan seems perfectly engineered to crash and burn. The prosecution is delighted. But the moment Reldan sets to work addressing the jury, it becomes clear that he is thoroughly conversant with courtroom procedure and well versed in the intricacies of New Jersey criminal law. A man of enormous cunning and intelligence, he has made a thorough study of jurisprudence over the past ten years, perhaps—who knows?—for just this moment.

During this third trial Reldan cross-examines a number of witnesses, including his own past rape victims. The height of the drama comes when Jonathan Heynes, now living in England, returns to the United States especially for the trial. Newspaper reporters fill the courtroom, hungry for fireworks. "A tense silence fell over the courtroom when Reldan approached the witness stand . . ." reported the Rockland County *Journal News* on February 11, 1986. "Heynes turned away from Reldan, his lips quavering, his hands shaking. Asked by Superior Court Judge Frederick W. Kuechenmeister whether he wanted to recess, the witness declined and said, 'I want to get on.' Throughout the cross-examination, Heynes avoided looking at Reldan, and was struggling to maintain his composure. When Reldan, wearing a blue blazer, didn't express himself clearly one time, Heynes snapped 'Are you asking me a question!' The scenario repeated itself with Barbara Reeve, mother of the second victim. When cross-examined by Reldan, she avoided looking at him, and answered tersely."

"I knew it would be difficult," Reldan said in a telephone interview with the *Journal News* after the questioning. "I didn't want to make it any harder on them.

"But you know," he added, in the manner of a well-trained lawyer anxious not to tip his client's hand, "while in their minds they might think that I was the person that did away with their daughter and wife, we're on trial here to determine that."

A few weeks later, that determination is made.

Despite Reldan's remarkable performance in court, he is found guilty of both murders. This time there is no mistrial.

DIRECT FROM JAIL

Because the two pantyhose murders took place in 1975, seven years before New Jersey reinstated the death penalty, the maximum sentence Reldan can receive is life in prison plus thirty years. Once behind bars, he quickly finds the harassment by fellow inmates psychologically unbearable. Suffering a breakdown, he is moved to the mental health facility at New Jersey State Prison in Trenton—from which he promptly escapes. Guarded more closely after his recapture, he now gives up any notion of escape and starts to work with serious intent on becoming a writer. Before long his works are being published in literary journals and on the Internet.

Today Reldan carries on an active correspondence with prison reform advocates, as well as with established writers, novice writers (whom he counsels), and fans of his poetry. This strange man's writings concern themselves primarily with loneliness, the horrors of prison life, and, perhaps ironically, romantic love. Between the lines of certain poems, the mind occasionally gets a hint, an unconscious one certainly, of a distant, dreamlike encounter with two innocent young women murdered and abandoned in dark woods long ago.

CHAPTER 3

The Corpse in the Leather Mask

We soon determined he was not the infor-
mant but the murderer.
—ROCKLAND COUNTY CHIEF DISTRICT ATTORNEY
KENNETH GRIBETZ

THE EMPTY HOUSE ON THE HILL

A DEAD BODY DOES NOT ALWAYS EMIT A LOATHSOME SMELL. UNDER THE
right circumstances it releases a mild, inoffensive odor; or it may have no
odor at all. This happens most frequently when a cadaver is burned to
cinders, or stripped to the bone, or both.

In the case of the murdered youth lying in the darkness of a cavelike
eighteenth-century smokehouse some forty miles from New York City,
the lack of overpowering and hence criminally suspicious smell is the reason why so many days pass before his corpse is discovered.

The smokehouse—some say it was actually a root cellar—measures
five feet wide by four feet deep. Dug into the side of a grassy hill, it is
lined with brick and squares of stone, and its ceiling is just high enough
to allow a small man to stand up without bumping his head.

Running nearby is a leafy path that winds downhill to the site of a Revolutionary period inn, the Erie Hotel. The only traces of this onetime ren-

dezvous for General Washington and his staff are its foundation stones plus several outbuildings, most of them overgrown in a tangle of berry bushes and thicket. These picturesque ruins, occasionally a site of pilgrimage for Revolutionary War buffs, sit half hidden on the grounds of a private estate located near the town of Tompkins Cove in northern Rockland County.

Even today this area of Rockland remains gratifyingly rural, reflecting in a distant mirror how New York's lower Hudson Valley must have appeared to landscape artists and venturesome picnickers exploring these grounds in the mid-nineteenth century. Bordered by almost three acres of manicured garden and lawn that slope in flowered terraces to an enclosing wood, the main house sits on the rim of a hill gazing down on the Hudson below. From this vantage point you can see Sing Sing Prison to the south across the river, and to the north the bend in the river that leads to the islands fronting West Point.

This beautiful piece of landmark property was acquired several years earlier by John P. LeGeros, a native of the Philippines, who runs the Division of Audit and Management Review for the Third World Development Program at the United Nations. He and his wife visit the estate as a summer getaway. Most of the year the house sits empty except for occasional weekend visits by the LeGeroses' two sons, David and Bernard, both of whom are living the high life as bachelors in New York City. Recently, Bernard has been coming quite often.

THE HIKERS

On an afternoon in late winter of 1985—St. Patrick's Day, in fact— five teenaged hikers are cutting across the deserted LeGeros estate on their way to a nearby trailhead. Aware that they are trespassing but not seeing anyone around, one of them notices the smokehouse hidden behind some shrubbery.

The boys decide to sneak a look inside. Partially removing a heavy dead tree that bars the opening, the teenagers squeeze around it and through the smokehouse door. When they see bones of a large creature lying under a wooden frame, they assume it is a dead animal, a big dog or a deer. A moment later someone yells, "It's a body!"

One of the hikers switches on a flashlight.

In the center of the stone chamber they see a shrunken corpse lying curled up on a bed of charred wood and dead embers. Though the cadaver is mostly a rack of blackened, partially burned bones, the tip-off to its human identity is a black leather mask pulled over the upper part of its head, fitting as snugly as a ski mask.

Varieties of this piece of extreme bondage equipment are sometimes used in sadomasochistic sex. The mask on this body is complete with a zippered opening across the mouth to assure silence or enforce pleasure, and slits for eyes and nose; one of the teenagers later describes how finely tailored this piece of leatherwork appeared to him, skillfully stitched on the sides and neatly formfitting. "Must have cost somebody a lot of money!" he exclaims.

By some unfathomable quirk of physics and fate, this ominous hood has remained entirely intact, without a single burn mark to betray that not so long ago it was circled by flames in the midst of a blazing funeral pyre. The bottom of the victim's face has fared less well: only a charred, gaping jaw is left in place, along with a set of gleaming white, perfectly formed teeth, the bottom row of which has somehow worked its way free of the muffling mouthpiece.

As soon as the boys realize what they have stumbled on, they head for the police. The curtain now rises on one of the most lurid, Byzantine, and high-profile murder cases of the cocaine-snorting, trickle-down, disco-dancing 1980s.

THE PRESERVATION AND THE RUINATION

My crew and I—along with an investigator from the Bureau of Criminal Identification (BCI), complete with his cameras and photographers—are brought by the police to the smokehouse, now cordoned off.

First, we finish the job of removing the tree from the door of the smokehouse, taking pictures at each stage. Inside we find a broken screen door covering the body. This object is carefully lifted away, along with more debris, giving us full access to the corpse.

The south wall of the smokehouse is coated with soot, and scattered on the earth floor are burned pieces of wood, glass fragments, a sock, and a blackened boot. This last is near the entrance. The faint smell of gasoline or kerosene lingers.

The skeleton itself lies parallel to the south wall. It rests on its left side with legs flexed at the knees and drawn up into a fetal posture. Its right arm is fanned out from the body. The left is flexed inward.

A thin carbonization covers most of the skeleton's surfaces, and the flesh on the victim's left hand is carbonized and shriveled. The sooty residue was clearly produced by smoke and flames. The right hand and radial bones are missing, along with both feet. Most significantly, the body is bare of flesh from the jaw to what remains of the legs. Examining the embers, we estimate that the fire burned itself out several weeks ago, and that the corpse has been lying in its grim crypt all this time.

At the time of the body's discovery, the leather mask covering its face is in "open" position, with zipper pulled to the left. At the back of the mask are a line of metal grommets tightly laced with a leather tie, but through a small space between the back edges tufts of wavy blond hair emerge. Hair sticks out of the eye slits at the front of the mask, too. Examining these strands of hair, and noting the perfect preservation of the mask, we begin to hope that when we remove the mask during autopsy at least some remnants of flesh will be intact.

After photographs are taken in various stages of discovery and our preliminary studies are made and written up, we take the body to the morgue.

We begin the autopsy by gently removing the leather mask.

What we find beneath it produces an astonished gasp from just about everyone present in the examination room: above the parched and burned remains of jaw and mouth, just at the line where the bottom of the mask crosses the upper gums, the perfectly intact face of a strikingly handsome young man stares up at me, his physical beauty and remarkably well-preserved facial features contrasting in a bizarre way with the rest of his remains.

The youth's blond hair is parted neatly on the right side; his cheeks are round and well-fleshed, his lashes and lids are unsinged, and his blue eyes are intact, though clouded and opaque. Indeed, the young man's visage has a pristine quality, smooth-skinned and strangely serene and naive. Neither flame nor the ravages of decomposition have reached into the secret places beneath the leather covering. As I stare down at him I have the fleeting impression that his eyes may move at any moment. Rarely in my career as medical examiner have I seen a body that displays such an uncanny combination of utter ruination and an almost supernaturally perfect state of preservation.

THE WOUNDS

Once I begin to examine the top and back of the victim's head, I gain quite a different perspective on his appearance. Bloody material is lodged in the young man's right ear canal and covers most of the outer skin surface of his ear as well. A mass of caked blood extends over the bridge of the nose to the opposite cheek, and the hair on the back of his head is stiffened with clots of blood.

We find three wounds on the back of the head, all of which are consistent with bullet holes. Wound A is a relatively large hole located in the lower or mid-occipital region of the victim's skull. The inner walls of this wound are coated with gunpowder, but the area surrounding the entry hole shows no evidence of powder burns, tattooing, or stippling—signs that a weapon has been fired in direct contact with the skin. The bullet that causes Wound A is never found.

Wound B, located below and to the side of the first wound, has a "stellate" or starlike shape. A small piece of lead is dug out from under the scalp in this wound, demonstrating that it is an exit hole for the bullet that caused Wound A.

Wound C is lower on the back of the skull than Wound A. It has the same overall appearance as the two other wounds, with an absence of powder burns. Probing shows that the bullet in C has blasted through the second cervical vertebra and shattered the victim's upper spine. His spinal canal and the areas surrounding it are filled with blood. A small part of the jacket of a bullet is found near the neck region. The remainder of the bullet is never located, though the police search for it diligently for some time.

The hooded murder victim in the smokehouse, we conclude, was shot twice in the head from close up: Wounds A and C. Bullet A passed through the central part of the man's brain, and Bullet C shattered his spine. Wound B is the exit hole for the bullet that caused Wound A.

Was the victim alive or dead at the time he was shot in the head?

The answer to this question will in due time determine a verdict in a court of law.

THE SKELETON

With the exception of the young man's upper head area, miraculously protected by the tightly wrapped mask, his body is stripped of flesh.

The sternum and a number of ribs are missing, which is odd—where did they go?—and a large, loose, leatherlike segment of skin containing hair fibers is separated from the remains, as if violently ripped away. This is peculiar, too: fire rarely does such things.

Most of the dead man's bones are lightly blackened by carbonization; here and there, small pieces of flesh have fused onto the bones, forming hard, black nodules. The bones show evidence of tooth marks and are mostly picked clean.

In this early stage of the investigation, the police and their colleagues, using a commonsense approach, suggest the following reconstruction of the crime:

First, the young man is murdered somewhere on the LeGeros estate.

Second, his remains are carried to the smokehouse.

Third, wood and branches are piled beneath him, gasoline is poured over him, and his body is torched.

Fourth, the fire burns away all his flesh, leaving only bones behind; the murderer has purposely made it difficult for investigators to identify the corpse and the manner of death.

My own reconstruction is rather different. In my experience, burn cases are among the least understood of all homicides. The problem, in a nutshell, is that nonforensic pathologists credit fire with a great deal more destructive power than it actually has, at least at the relatively low temperatures generated by a bonfire. This misconception is so common that Vernon J. Geberth, in his classic *Practical Homicide Investigation*, warns readers:

> Practically, the average investigator lacks the expertise to thoroughly investigate crimes of arson. However, most arson-related homicides are very amateurish, and it will be obvious to the investigator that there is something wrong . . . meaningful interpretations of these clues, however, must be left to the experts, since arson investigation is highly technical and complex.

Forensically speaking, the burning of a human being is defined as the destruction of cellular tissue due to contact with flame. In cases where a person is burned while still alive, autopsy exams reveal a large amount of inhaled carbon monoxide in the blood, along with charred, darkened areas around the base of the nostrils where the struggling victim has breathed in hot smoke. Unburnt skin on the wrists and ankles may indicate that a victim was tied up and made helpless before the fire was set. An unburned strap-width ring around the victim's neck indicates that the person was first strangled, then burned.

In many cases of burning, the body is found lying in the so-called pugilistic attitude. This colorful term derives from the fact that in the midst of a blaze the muscles tighten and contract, shrinking the body into the crouched, raised-fist pose commonly adopted by boxers. The crumpled-up fetal posture of the burned youth in the smokehouse is a variation on this theme.

Most important for understanding the forensics of the smokehouse murder, it is necessary to realize that, as Geberth warns:

> Most incidents of arson are perpetrated to destroy evidence or conceal the crime by destroying the body. However, the body does not burn as easily as most people believe. Instead, the body resists the destructive forces of the fire with amazing durability, allowing the pathologist to make determinations from the remains.

Over the years I myself have seen burned bodies removed from airplane crashes, theater fires, chemical explosions, even suicides soaked with gasoline and self-ignited. The remains from such firestorms tend to all look more or less the same: baked and charred, but mostly intact. It is only at the superhigh temperatures produced inside a crematorium, say, or at a steel smelting plant that fleshy matter is completely reduced to dust.

There are some exceptions. The body of a one- or two-year-old child will be reduced to a few ounces of ash in several hours. A newborn may vanish entirely in flames in little more than an hour. A clothed body burns more rapidly and completely than a naked one (a fact that the killers in this case would have been fortunate to know), and obese individuals are consumed more thoroughly than lean.

Bodies incinerated in small closed spaces burn more efficiently than those burned out-of-doors. For example, at the end of World War II, when Hitler's personal entourage cremated his remains on a Viking-like pyre as the Russians closed in on Berlin, they mounted a tremendous blaze that lasted, some experts theorize, for days. The fact that this fire was lit outside, however, impeded its full annihilative power, and allowed scientists to identify the German dictator by studying his dental records against his unburned teeth.

Such details notwithstanding, the fact is that human tissue is tough, resilient stuff, and it takes a furiously large amount of heat, pressure, chopping, dissolving in acid, blowing up, and the like to liquidate it quickly—a fact that has been the undoing of more than one incautious criminal.

In the case of the smokehouse homicide, the perpetrators, believing that a corpse can be reduced to ash by a simple wood fire, set the body ablaze, then leave the premises, confident that nature will finish the job.

What actually happens at such relatively low temperatures, however—around 1200 degrees Fahrenheit—is that instead of disintegrating, the corpse's flesh roasts much in the manner of, if you will forgive the gruesome analogy, meat on a backyard barbecue.

From your own kitchen experience you probably know that if a cut or chop from the butcher counter is left on a flame for many hours, the meat does not turn to ashes. Quite to the contrary, it forms a hard, crusty shell that keeps the core of the meat intact. Ironically, burning flesh over a wood flame does not destroy it. It cooks it, protects it, and most of all, preserves it.

THE ANIMALS

Then the animals come by: small woodland creatures, rats most likely, plus raccoons and possibly feral dogs. These suburban prowlers tend to nibble away small pieces of flesh rather than bite off huge chunks of skin and gristle the way a fox, coyote, or mountain lion would do. The missing ribs, feet, fingers, and torn-off pieces of skin have almost certainly been dragged away to a hole or cave nearby.

At the autopsy we see the small animal bites quite clearly. The entire sternum and the ends of several of the victim's ribs display row after row of small animal teeth marks. Straggly, frayed fibers characteristic of nibbling are also present along the surface of the skeletal structure: the spine, shoulders, ribs, and thighs. The loose flap of hairy skin found near the body is similarly marked on its edges with irregularities consistent with small animal chew marks. A leatherized piece of skin on the body's left forearm has small tooth marks running up and down its edges.

We learn another critical fact, too.

Recall that when the dead youth was first discovered his skeleton was lightly coated with carbon. Since we know that the original fire seared his flesh, and that this hardened tissue was devoured by predators over a period of weeks and perhaps months, leaving the bones picked white and clean, we conclude that what remained of the body was burned a second time. Forensically speaking, only a second fire can account for the sooty, blackened bones.

What could possibly drive a killer—or killers—to return to the scene of the crime, perform such a risky act, perhaps call attention to the long-abandoned smokehouse, and in the process increase the chances of being discovered? An educated guess would suggest that sometime after originally burning the corpse, the killer, anxious to know how well the fire did its job, returns to the scene of the crime. Here he finds the remains of a bare white skeleton.

Thinking—mistakenly—that the victim's flesh has been neatly crisped away by the wood bonfire, and once more overestimating the demolitionary force of fire, he decides to eliminate all remaining evidence by burning up the leftover bones.

The result?

A light covering of black soot deposited on an otherwise mostly in-tact skeleton.

Bone does not burn easily.

THE MAN IN THE LEATHER MASK

Who is this man? At first it seems that identifying him will be diffi-cult at best. Fingerprints and organ tissue samples are, obviously, unob-tainable. No young blond males are missing in the area. The best we have to go on is dental castings, but these do not match up with any dental plates on record in the United States.

Then, as often happens, the mystery solves itself by time and circum-stance.

It begins when friends and fellow students of Eigil Dag Vesti, a twenty-six-year-old native of Oslo, Norway, and a senior at the Fashion Institute of Technology in Manhattan, notice that he has suddenly stopped coming to classes. This is unlike Vesti, who is an ambitious and highly motivated student.

Last seen on February 22 by two friends who drop him off at his apart-ment in Chelsea around one-thirty in the morning, the young Norwegian abruptly goes incommunicado. Calls to him are unreturned. Ringing his downstairs buzzer gets no response. When concerned friends enter his apartment, they see no signs of recent use.

Finally, after a good deal of grassroots searching on the part of friends, the police are informed.

Posters of Vesti are soon placed on poles and bulletin boards all over lower Manhattan. On March 17, an article about his mysterious disap-pearance is published in the *New York Daily News,* along with his photo-graph. A few days later the same story appears in the newspapers in Oslo. Vesti's two sisters fly to the United States from Norway to help in the search.

Working with our team at the medical examiner's office, the sisters provide us with the address of their brother's dentist in Norway. We send him the dental plates, and confirmation is quickly returned. At the morgue, Vesti's sisters also identify their brother's face over closed-circuit

TV. The skeleton found in the Tompkins Cove smokehouse, we are now certain, belongs to Eigil Dag Vesti.

What do we know of this young man? A considerable amount, really.

He was tall, thin, with square-jawed, model-handsome features, and laden with continental charm; his fellow students at the Fashion Institute were in awe of him. "Vesti was the talk of FIT," his classmate Tamela Spangler tells the *Daily News*. "He was so good looking, so fashionable, you couldn't help noticing him. He blew everybody away."

With good looks and sweet disposition, Vesti soon made his way into sophisticated branches of New York café and disco society. At the famous Limelight disco he was granted entry to the elite VIP room, a wood-paneled lounge packed each night with the likes of Mick Jagger, Truman Capote, and assorted other glitterati. One of the friends who dropped him off at his apartment on his last night is the adopted daughter of the actor Richard Burton. "He was ambitious enough to know that in the fashion world," remarks a friend, the fashion consultant Dennis Hand, "it is wise to be seen in the right circles with the right people."

Vesti was also proudly homosexual, with a strong, some say extreme, masochistic bent. He made the gay club circuit several nights a week, and frequently visited male S&M bars. He was also a familiar presence on the New York City art scene, where many of the artists and art dealers knew him by name and reputation. He often posed nude for photographers.

In short, the murdered man was a man about town.

The police begin to compile records of Vesti's friends, and of friends of his friends; on the list is a young man named Bernard LeGeros.

THE BAD BOY

Bernard LeGeros is a bad boy.

The son of the Philippine diplomat who owns the estate where Vesti's body is discovered, LeGeros has been in and out of trouble since the age of fifteen.

Nurturing a fascination for violence, weapons, and death, and attempting suicide several times (once he was talked down from jumping off a roof; another time, he swallowed cyanide), the twenty-two-year-old tells friends that as a teenager he frequently sneaked into the pathology laboratory at New York University Medical Center, adjacent to his mother's dental research office, and spent hours "playing" with the corpses.

Currently a card-carrying cocaine user, a wannabe jet-setter on the New York art and disco scene, a friend of drug dealers, gun runners, and small-time-hood graffiti artists from the Bronx with names like Dax and the Leak, Bernard is renowned for his sulkily good looks and for off-the-wall claims of his own wickedness. To those who are not tired of listening, he brags of being a hit man, a bodyguard for the Mafia, a narcotics officer, a CIA operative. He likes to dress up in a dark blue police uniform, complete with handcuffs and billy club, and walk around his parents' estate. Several times he offers his services as an assassin to friends for $3,000 a hit.

An acquaintance testifies that LeGeros is fond of styling himself the "Keeper of the Gates of Hell." According to a photographer friend, after the Vesti homicide, LeGeros tells a shadowy group of late-night drug takers that he killed Vesti, and that he and his accomplice cut open Vesti's body after they shot him, scooped out a cup of blood from his abdomen, and drank it. The blood was pulpy, he adds, and he spat it out. LeGeros notes parenthetically that he intends to start a scrapbook of this murder and of other murders he will commit in the future. A man should kill another human being, LeGeros proclaims, without emotion, as casually as he lights a cigarette or drives an automobile. At the time he hears these psychopathic claims the friend takes them with a grain of salt and cocaine, being accustomed to LeGeros's psychopathic dreams, and to the fantasies that coke users so often spin. "He had Rambo-like fantasies," one acquaintance quips of LeGeros, "long before there was a Rambo."

Though he claims to be heterosexual and though he frequently dates women, Bernard's face and name are well known at the most prominent hard-core sadomasochistic homosexual clubs in New York City, including the Mine Shaft, the Badlands, the Hellfire Club, and the Anvil.

These "bar and dungeon" hangouts, many of which are housed in warehouses along the lower Manhattan waterfront, are enormously popular in the early and mideighties until the AIDS epidemic and several seamy murders diminish their appeal.

In their back rooms, and in the rooms behind their back rooms, LeGeros is present at extraordinarily violent sexual rituals such as the piercing of male genitals and the hanging of male volunteers by their scrotums. ("There is," a forensic psychiatrist friend of mine once noted, "a type of man who, if he inflicts homoerotic pain on another man, enjoys watching it, or if the other man performs acts of homosexuality on him, this man sees no contradiction in always considering the *other* man the homosexual, never himself.")

These antics eventually find their way to the grapevine and occasionally into the gossip columns. Soon it is no secret that handsome, rich Bernard LeGeros, seen most often at gay bars in the company of a wealthy and powerful forty-year-old art dealer named Andrew Crispo, is welcome at any hotspot you can name in New York City's leather-and-chains subculture.

Crispo, it should be added, is himself notorious for his frequently nonconsensual sadistic exploits.

It is reported that he has long kept a leather mask, chillingly similar to the one found on Vesti, displayed on a mannequin in the foyer of his multimillion-dollar country house. Police say they remember seeing the mask when responding to an accidentally tripped burglar alarm. "I noticed it in the corner," one unidentified member of the police reports to a New York City newspaper. "The thing that struck me as funny was that there was a shiny zipper on the mouth. It was on a mahogany mannequin, the type you'd keep a woman's wig on."

Word on the street is that LeGeros, who works at Crispo's art gallery where he often poses as the dealer's bodyguard, has been initiated into all the sadomasochistic secrets by his mentor. According to witnesses quoted in the police report on the Vesti case, the two men often work as a team, inviting unsuspecting men to Crispo's gallery or apartment where they beat them up or force them to perform bizarre sex acts, then threaten them with death if they go to the police.

But one of these victims does go to the police.

In the fall of 1984, half a year before Eigil Vesti disappears, Crispo and LeGeros are accused of kidnapping a very unwilling young homosexual and torturing him in Crispo's apartment. Crispo is subsequently charged with rape in this incident, which can carry a sentence of up to twenty-five years. "The man was whipped," an accomplice at the scene of this crime tells a reporter from *Vanity Fair,* "[he was] pissed on by Andrew. . . . I also hit the man with a whip . . . at the end the guy thanked Crispo for not killing him . . . he was scared."*

This case is awaiting trial at the time of Vesti's murder.

So, given where LeGeros is known to pass his hours from late night to early morning, given his violent quirks and murderous claims, considering that he and Eigil Vesti frequented the same bars and ran in the same circles, and considering that Vesti's corpse with the S&M leather mask attached to it is found in the LeGeros backyard, it is only natural that the police would like to have a word with this young man.

THE STORY

The first interview with LeGeros takes place on March 18, almost a month after Vesti disappears.

At the initial meeting, LeGeros tells a police detective that he last weekended at his family estate in early February with a girl named Josephine. Josephine works for a phone sex service, he explains. He met her at the Limelight.

When did he make his last trip to the country house? the interrogator wants to know.

On February 21. To pick up some clothes.

By this time the police have learned that Bernard owns an AR-7 .22-caliber rifle, and that he keeps it in different locations around his country house, including under a removable floorboard in his room.

Does he know where that rifle happens to be right now?

No, LeGeros replies. It disappeared. Perhaps the police should check the grounds around the house. Perhaps the killer stole the rifle from his father's house, used it on Vesti, then tossed it into the woods.

The topic turns to the many men LeGeros knows who might be inclined to perform such a sadistic killing. LeGeros helps the detectives compile a list. The interview then comes to a close.

Over the following week, LeGeros persistently calls police investiga-

---

*"Will Crispo Walk?" *Vanity Fair,* September 1988.

tors and gives them his theories about homosexual behavior, the disappeared rifle, who killed Vesti, why, when, how.

The more he regales them with his notions—sometimes he calls in the middle of the night—the more suspicious his behavior appears.

LeGeros, for example, suddenly thinks he remembers where he put the rifle. Then he forgets.

Perhaps the murderer is a chicken hawk—an older man interested in sex with adolescents. Probably he's a psycho who hangs around gay bars and is prepared to kill.

Perhaps the murderer has killed before. But probably not.

I think he moved the body. Why? I'm not sure, just a hunch. Anyway, I think I know who did the shooting! No, no, probably not. Not him. Somebody else. Maybe it was a woman. But nobody local. Somebody from upstate, probably. Somebody who . . .

The more LeGeros presses his speculations on the police, the more unhinged he seems. Finally, during a twenty-eight-hour marathon interview, he unwittingly reveals several self-incriminating pieces of information, going so far as to place himself near the nightclub where Vesti was last seen on the night of the killing.

The police read him his rights.

"The twenty-eight-hour interview with Bernard, that was probably the most challenging individual effort of my career," Detective Sergeant William Franks, chief investigator on the case, later remarks. "Bernard wasn't going to give it up easily, but I think he enjoyed the whole thing, the attention."

In the station LeGeros talks. But obliquely.

He had nothing to do with the actual murder, he assures interrogators; but yes, he was there when it all took place.

Here's the story, he says.

On the evening of February 22, he and an old prep school friend from LaSalle Academy in New York City, Billy Mayer, meet Eigil Vesti and invite him to a "wild party" upstate.

Vesti agrees.

Using the elder LeGeros's Oldsmobile station wagon, the three young men travel north over the George Washington Bridge and up the Palisades Parkway. On the way, Mayer starts belittling Vesti and exercising mastery over his new "slave," pretending that he is a Nazi interrogator, calling Vesti a "Jew fag" and a "Jew-loving cocksucker."

Vesti is apparently unbothered by this abuse, and perhaps accustomed to it. Along the way he blithely remarks, "Maybe I should have brought my skis. This is nice up here. Where are we going?"

Mayer retorts, "You're going to Norway—in a fucking box!"

Though Vesti apparently takes this threat as part of the role-playing Nazi interrogation, it is at this moment, according to LeGeros, that he realizes Billy Mayer really does intend to kill his young male slave.

The car races on through the night, arriving at the Rockland estate a few hours before sunrise.

According to LeGeros, the three men walk into the living room of the family house, where Bernard entertains them by showing off his collection of knives, swords, and rifles, including the .22-caliber AR-7.

Billy Mayer then leads Vesti downstairs to the basement, where the two men indulge in heavy-duty sadomasochistic games while LeGeros sits upstairs listening to the victim's shrieks. After a while, LeGeros asserts, the sounds of strapping and yelling become so loud he turns on the radio to drown them out.

After almost an hour, Mayer returns to the living room, leading a naked Vesti by a metal chain. The apparently still willing victim is naked, and is now wearing a black leather hood.

Knowing that Mayer intends to murder Vesti, LeGeros takes his friend into another room and asks that he do the dirty work outside. LeGeros does not want to be a party or witness to the crime.

Agreeing, Mayer snatches LeGeros's .22 rifle, and pulling his captive by the leash out the front door, vanishes into the night.

After several minutes, frightened but fascinated, LeGeros changes his mind and follows them.

Shadowing the twosome down an embankment, across a tennis court, and along the trail to the smokehouse, LeGeros watches as Mayer binds Vesti, forces him to his knees, and makes him perform various sex acts. LeGeros then watches as Mayer raises the rifle to the back of Vesti's head and, aiming downward, pumps two bullets into his brain.

Noticing LeGeros standing in the shadows on the hill above him, Mayer shouts out, "Now we have to take care of this mess!"

Fetching pieces of wood and a container of gasoline from the garage, the two men return to the smokehouse, set Vesti's body on a pile of sticks and branches, and light it. Then they leave the residence, driving along the river and stopping once at the Hudson's edge to throw the .22 rifle into the water. They dispose of the victim's clothing somewhere in the woods along the Palisades Parkway. Finally, back to New York.

For eight days, the body of Eigil Vesti lies silent and undetected in the smokehouse. Then Bernard begins to worry: Have the remains been thoroughly destroyed? Did the fire do its work?

His anxiety becomes so strong that he returns to the scene, where he finds Vesti's cadaver entirely skeletonized.

In an attempt to further expunge the evidence, he adds fresh boughs and twigs to the pile of charred wood beneath Vesti's bones, douses it with gasoline, and burns the leftovers for a second time, leaving the scene while the fire is blazing. What LeGeros does not know is that, as the autopsy indicates, Vesti's skeleton will remain almost entirely intact in the flames, showing only a light coating of ash and soot by the time the flames go out.

Satisfied with his work, LeGeros sits and rests for a moment. Then he walks over to the main house and picks up Vesti's hat from the couch still unmoved, "a gray felt with a broad brim," as he describes it. He drives home to his apartment in New York City wearing the hat at a jaunty angle, referring to it as his "souvenir."

Here LeGeros's confession comes to an end.

As the DA remarks, "We soon determined that he was not the informant but the murderer."

But there is more to this story than the first round of admissions indicates. A few hours later LeGeros calls his interrogators back in. He has not been entirely honest with them.

How so?

"Well, first of all," LeGeros replies, "*I* was the one who shot Vesti. Not Billy Mayer."

"Where was Billy Mayer, then?" an officer asks.

"He wasn't there at all."

"Not at all?"

"No."

"So everything you're telling us is a lie?"

"No!" LeGeros shouts. "Everything I told you is true. Except for the fact that I shot Vesti. And that the other guy who was there, it wasn't Billy Mayer. It was the guy I work for. The art dealer. Andrew Crispo. He made me do it."

THE TRIAL

The trial of Bernard LeGeros takes place in September 1985, approximately six months after Vesti's death. In many ways it casts a spotlight more on Andrew Crispo than on LeGeros, though it is LeGeros and not Crispo who is standing trial.

For though LeGeros maintains a low-level celebrity in disco society and now in the newspaper headlines, his is the celebrity of the child hoodlum and the crazy rich kid. Crispo, on the other hand, is a friend of rock stars, politicians, museum directors, tycoons. He is a serious player; at least, the world has viewed him this way so far, and has rewarded him in kind.

Abandoned by his mother at birth and raised in a Catholic orphanage in Philadelphia, Crispo arrives in New York City at the age of eighteen without a college education and without a dollar to his name. Immediately he begins to bootstrap himself from stockboy at a Fifth Avenue department store to one of the most learned and internationally celebrated contemporary art dealers in the United States.

Currently at the pinnacle of his career, he now sells Motherwells and Georgia O'Keeffes to film stars and Swiss billionaires. He also maintains long-standing relationships with art museums both in the United States and abroad.

Yet even at the pinnacle of his power and reach, even while making millions of dollars setting trends in art merchandising, even while he has a Southampton house next door to the socialite Gloria Vanderbilt and the artist Roy Lichtenstein, the shadows surrounding Crispo's personal life darken as his not-so-secret sadomasochistic escapades begin to close in on him.

Already indicted for the torture of the young homosexual who filed suit against him, sworn testimony in a New York City courtroom from LeGeros now places him at the smokehouse on the night of the 22nd. It identifies Crispo as the killer, and as the Svengali-like mastermind of Vesti's death.

LeGeros himself never takes the witness stand during his trial. But according to his testimony at several pretrial interviews, the February 22 meeting with Eigil Vesti takes place at Crispo's apartment; a police report chronicles, "Bernard [LeGeros] states that they met Andrew Crispo at Andrew's apartment later that night of the 22nd, and when he entered the apartment he observed a person he later identified as Eigil Vesti sitting on the couch. Bernard said that Vesti was stark naked, and he was masturbating. . . . Bernard stated that he took the whip and struck Vesti several times himself with the handle of the whip. . . . Bernard said that when Andrew came out of the bathroom they had a conversation and decided to take Vesti to Rockland County to his parents' residence and kill him."

Then the moment of truth, according to LeGeros's confession.

"We left the main residence that night, and walked to the grotto where Vesti and Crispo again engaged in sadomasochistic acts. Andrew Crispo told me that Vesti wanted to die. 'Get him ready,' Crispo says. Crispo forces Vesti to kneel down, then suddenly stabs him twice in the heart, and after that tells me to shoot him in the back of the head with a .22 caliber AR-7 rifle."

THE FIFTH

Is Crispo the real killer? Should *he* be standing trial?

Certainly the police reports on him are brimming with terrifying testimony. Several witnesses overheard him planning the murder of a bartender at the Limelight the night of Vesti's death.

One man reports that after he had S&M sex with LeGeros and Crispo at Crispo's gallery, Crispo threatened to kill him for "not being a man," announcing that from now on he is going to kill every gay man he finds.

One woman that LeGeros dates tells police that "Crispo seemed to be in control of Bernard the whole time she knew him. Bernard would do anything to please Andrew Crispo." Crispo himself is quoted as telling a friend, "With a few drinks in him Bernard will do anything I tell him."

Once, taking a guest on a tour of his Southampton estate, Crispo points to a contemporary block sculpture in the middle of his lawn, and announces that underneath this monument is the place where "he buries the bodies" of the people he kills.

A man identified as Mr. White describes walking down the street one night with Andrew Crispo near the Badlands bar. In the middle of their conversation Crispo points to a nearby pier and exclaims, "That's where I have most of my burials at sea."

Crispo goes on to relate that once, as he was having sex with a woman, he ordered Bernard to kill her. They wrapped chains around the woman's body, Crispo says, and threw her off the pier into the river. Other women victims then followed. Crispo, according to several reports, enjoyed binding, beating, and torturing women as much as he did men.

This list of murderous boasts goes on and on. If half of them are true, Crispo is a serial killer. Yet none of the stories in the police casebook are relevant at this trial. Crispo is not being charged with Vesti's murder; indeed, he has never even been a suspect. How could he be? The killer has already confessed.

Also, the prosecution would not be allowed to use any of LeGeros's statements against Crispo at trial. There is no evidence to corroborate what LeGeros says, and because he is an accomplice to the murder his testimony standing alone cannot convict Crispo.

Finally, when Crispo (who once retained the notorious Roy Cohn as his private attorney) is subpoenaed as a witness in LeGeros's trial, he comes to court but refuses to testify. Put on the stand, never once glancing across the courtroom at his onetime pupil and current accuser, he takes the Fifth to all the prosecutor's questions—refusing to answer on the grounds that to do so may incriminate him. (In the United States, people cannot be compelled to testify against themselves: this is provided by the Fifth Amendment to the Constitution.) Crispo has already admitted to the Rockland DA that he was present at the LeGeros estate on the night Eigil Vesti was murdered, just as LeGeros stated, and that he indeed had S&M sex with Eigil Vesti that same evening. Crispo even admits to helping LeGeros carry logs and gasoline from the house to burn Vesti's body, and to helping him dispose of the dead man's clothes. In pretrial hearings, Crispo's lawyer insists that his client may be guilty of certain crimes, such as tampering with evidence and obstructing governmental administration. But he is clearly not guilty of murder.

For it is LeGeros, and LeGeros alone, Crispo's lawyer emphatically states before the DA, who pulled the trigger, and who brought the blood. LeGeros has confessed to the killing. And where, the lawyer asks, is there a single shred of evidence to show that Crispo stabbed Vesti, as LeGeros claims, or even that he played a supportive role in the shooting?

There is none.

Crispo is charged with several violations, such as accessory to a crime and assault, but the charges are dismissed for lack of evidence. He never does face charges in Vesti's murder.

THE KILLING OF THE DEAD

LeGeros arrives in court brandishing a strange legal strategy.

Soon after his arrest, his lawyer claims that his client is mentally unfit to stand trial. Meanwhile, LeGeros will not enter a plea. But though LeGeros may be psychopathic—that is, overly aggressive and without a sense of right and wrong—he is clearly not psychotic.

Once judged psychologically fit to stand trial, the accused killer then enters a plea of not guilty, a strange about-face for a man who has already admitted to Vesti's murder in front of the police, and who has signed a written confession identifying himself as the shooter. But there are reasons.

These become clear during the trial when LeGeros's lawyer reiterates his client's claim that moments before Vesti is shot, Crispo pulls a knife and stabs him in the chest, killing him on the spot.

It is, the lawyer for the defense argues, only moments *after* the stabbing that LeGeros, now high on large amounts of cocaine forced upon him by Crispo, and blindly obeying Crispo's command in his drugged state, empties two bullets into the victim's skull; just to make sure, Crispo reputedly tells him.

Finally, the lawyer shows where he is going with this line of reasoning.

Yes, it is true that LeGeros shot Vesti in the head.

But if Vesti died from knife wounds to the heart moments before the shooting, then he was *already dead* when the bullets entered his brain.

Since you cannot slay a dead man, LeGeros did not kill Vesti. And LeGeros, therefore, is not guilty of murder.

THE LIVING OF THE DEAD

After listening to this remarkable claim, I am called to the stand to give my pathologist's opinion on the matter, which is quite clear-cut.

Setting up several large color photographs of Vesti's dead body plus his three head wounds, I call the jury's attention to the fact that there are no marks on Vesti's ribs where a knife might have penetrated. Sometimes—not always—stab wounds to the heart leave cuts, nicks, and slices along the rib cage.

Was any stabbing done at all? Perhaps yes, perhaps no.

Pointing to a photograph showing the back of Vesti's skull, I call the jury's attention to Wound A. Let us work backward for a minute, I tell the jury. Let us assume for the sake of argument that a person is already dead when he is shot in the head.

When the scalp is removed and the skull bone is exposed during such a person's autopsy, you will see no sign of blood infiltration into the bullet hole and the areas surrounding it. In a dead person, a bullet passes neatly through the skull, leaving a gaping but clean, unbloodied, even pristine hole behind.

There is no bleeding, because the heart of the dead man is not pumping when the bullet pierces his skull. Consequently there is no pressure in his circulatory system to force blood up through the veins and into the wound.

But in the photograph of Wound A in Vesti's head, I point out, significant amounts of blood can be seen infiltrating the tissues surrounding the entry wound. So much leakage can mean only one thing in forensic terms: at the moment the victim was shot, his heart was still pounding vigorously. Eigil Vesti was clearly alive at the moment the .22 rifle discharged its bullets into his brain.

AFTERMATH

Without a forensic leg to stand on, LeGeros's case collapses. He is found guilty of second-degree murder, and is given a prison term of twenty-five years to life.

In 2003, he files a postjudgment motion against the County of Rockland, alleging that his conviction was procured by duress, misrepresentation, and fraud on the part of the prosecutor—that the prosecution intentionally "mischaracterized" the medical findings to support its theory that the defendant was the sole killer, willfully distorting forensic evidence in the process to support their claim.

His motion is denied. He remains in state prison today.

Andrew Crispo, on the other hand—despite federal tax evasion convictions, lawsuits galore by angry customers, a bank seizure of thirty-nine of his best paintings, bankruptcy proceedings, legal judgments by auction houses and art dealers, five criminal indictments on behalf of assorted victims of rape and/or torture, and even a term in prison—despite these and other vicissitudes of fortune, Crispo remained in the art business for many years, and sold many more fine contemporary master paintings. Some of them hang on the walls of museums you may have visited.

CHAPTER 4

The Slashed-Face Murder

Well . . . they flew away.

—FREDERICK ZUGIBE, M.D., PH.D.,
CHIEF MEDICAL EXAMINER OF ROCKLAND COUNTY

THE ERRANT SOCCER BALL

THE PARKING LOT BEHIND THE HOLIDAY INN IS THREE-QUARTERS EMPTY.
The only activity that might divert a guest gazing down at this undistin-
guished stretch of concrete is several workers from the motel kicking a
soccer ball back and forth.

It is one of those crisp, azure midfall days in Nanuet, New York, and
the men's spirits are high. As their enthusiasm builds, one of them puts
too much spin into his kick and the ball careens off at a sharp angle into
the woods bordering the back of the lot. The leaves in this area of southern New York State have not yet fallen from the trees. The forests are
thick with foliage.

The kicker jogs into the woods to fetch the ball, only to run up
against a wall of thorny bushes and creepers. The going is slow. It takes
him several minutes to penetrate twenty or thirty feet through the un-
dergrowth. Finally he sees the ball lodged in the middle of a small
thicket. At the same moment he notices a large disordered pile of—
what? Clothes? Refuse?

He pushes his way through the weeds to investigate and soon realizes that the errant soccer ball has led him to the body of a dead woman. She is lying on her back, fully dressed, with her arms neatly folded over her head. Her face, decomposed enough to show bone along the mouth and jaw, gapes up at him with death's primal grin.

Staring speechless at this horror, and overcome by the odor of putrefaction, the man turns and runs. Before he bolts he notices one especially ghastly feature: the victim's face has been slashed several times, and each slash is filled with crawling maggots.

INCIDENT, SCENE

The police are called in, and I am dispatched to the scene in back of the motel. Here I study the corpse for some time, take samples, and make appropriate notes.

What follows is part of the official description in my autopsy report.

INCIDENT

Death of a black female behind the Holiday Inn on Route 59, Nanuet, New York, on October 11, 1984. She was pronounced dead at 5:20 P.M.

SCENE

A black female was found lying supine at the base of a short, gradual sloped embankment at the northeast corner of the Holiday Inn motel approximately thirty feet, six inches from the road surface. The body was positioned with feet in a northwest direction, and head in a southeast direction. The upper arms were extended upward, then flexed at right angles at the elbows, the hands being level with the top of the head. There was some facial decomposition and skeletonization. The jaw and left facial area were bared to the bone. Both upper and lower teeth were fully exposed. The skin surrounding the bared areas on the face showed sharp incisions or slash marks, most likely from a sharp instrument. There was also evidence of animal bites.

The rest of the body appeared unremarkable. The body was fully clothed, and did not appear to be in any disarray. The deceased was wearing a raincoat that appeared stylish, grayish in color, slacks, and a sweater. A stab wound was noted in the left chest area over the heart, and rotation of the body revealed grass stains on the trench coat with marks vertically placed consistent with drag marks. The woman appeared to be in an age range between 29 [and] 35.

Swarms of journalists, investigators, and local gawkers quickly converge on the crime site. The next day, reports of the murder are broadcast on the nightly news. Rockland Chief District Attorney Kenneth Gribetz announces that a Rockland police alarm describing the murdered woman has so far brought no response. Gribetz also informs the press that the victim has been dead for an unknown number of days, that she may have been throttled in the parking lot of the Holiday Inn, then dragged into the woods, and that "identifying her body will prove difficult, as her face is badly decomposed."

As the case continues to break, the press, already sensitive to the fact that a brutal murder, as yet unsolved, was committed at this same Holiday Inn less than a year ago, buttonholes the motel's manager, Richard Weiss, and pressures him for a scoop.

But Weiss keeps mum. "Other members of the Holiday Inn will not comment either" is his only comment.

Not to be so easily rebuffed, one reporter pokes around the parking lot on her own and soon discovers that several video cameras, used for parking lot security, are still perched on the corners of the two-story motel. For reasons that no one can explain, the cameras are pointing away from the parking lot, not at it. If properly aligned, they might well have caught the entire murder sequence on tape. From then on, the case would have more than likely solved itself.

But fate decrees otherwise. The hunt is on.

STALLED IN THE WATER

Establishing the identity of the woman with the mutilated face is easier than District Attorney Gribetz supposed.

At the autopsy we take fingerprints and dental imprints and send the records out to a number of police agencies and medical centers in the metropolitan area. At the same time, Detective Janice Rogan, an early investigator on the homicide, makes a vital connection. "I remember reading about a missing black girl from New York City the week before," Detective Rogan says, "and seeing her picture in the *New York Daily News.* And I said, Hey, we found one in Nanuet, they're missing one, let's check it out."

When our dental plates and fingerprints are compared with those of the missing woman, it is established that the body behind the Holiday Inn belongs to Marie Jefferson, a thirty-two-year-old resident of the Bronx who was reported missing by her family a week and a half before she is found. Divorced for two years, Jefferson lives in an apartment with her thirteen-year-old son. She works as an administrative assistant for the New York Telephone Company on West Fiftieth Street in Manhattan.

There is even a suspect in the murder, Marie Jefferson's ex-boyfriend and ex-fiancé, Samuel McCullough, a thirty-nine-year-old short-order cook who works at a coffee shop in the Bronx. Police soon learn that the two broke up several months before the murder. McCullough has been persistently harassing his ex-girlfriend to resume their relationship, and she has been persistently refusing. It is also established that McCullough was the last person to be seen with Marie Jefferson on the day of her disappearance. Phone company employees noticed the couple together in front of the phone company building around four o'clock that afternoon, October 3, 1984. But according to onlookers, McCullough and Jefferson met in an amiable way, and the two of them walked down the street arm in arm; there was no shouting or struggling, no attempt to run or cry for help.

Investigators also learn that a car resembling McCullough's white Lincoln Continental was noticed by motel guests in the Nanuet Holiday Inn parking lot around sunset of that same day. But interviewed guests later disagree about the color of the car, and whether its windows are tinted or light. Several motel guests talk of hearing screams. Probably just a boisterous teenager, they thought at the time; or a lovers' quarrel, druggies, a disturbed woman from the neighborhood venting too loudly. And who is to dispute these surmises? One woman even reports seeing a large black man who fits McCullough's description climbing into a car and driving out of the lot. But when shown pictures of the suspect, she cannot make a positive ID.

Aside from these unhelpful and contradictory observations, there is nothing substantial for the DA's office to sink its teeth into. Nothing definitively ties McCullough to the scene of the crime. A car resembling his Lincoln was noticed in the lot. Okay. But descriptions of it vary. There are no witnesses to the killing, and the overheard screams could have come from any number of sources.

As for the fact that Marie Jefferson was seen with McCullough in Manhattan the day she vanished, witnesses insist that she went off with her ex-boyfriend willingly. What's more, police investigators do not know whether the victim was actually murdered the day she disappeared. The fact that Jefferson was last seen with McCullough is by no means proof that he murdered her. As the case matures, this question of which day, exactly, Jefferson was murdered becomes increasingly critical.

Finally, during his police interrogation McCullough shows great expertise at politely stonewalling his questioners. No lies or hostile refusals. Mostly just playing dumb with shrugs, blank looks, and a lot of "I don't remember."

Not much to go on for the assistant DA. After reviewing all the findings in the case, he decides that there is simply not enough hard evidence on board to indict. The assistant's boss, Chief District Attorney Gribetz, agrees. No district attorney's office ever likes to lose a case in court.

The inquiry goes on hold, and remains in a state of suspended animation for several months.

PROFILING A KILLER

Let us now go back to the scene of the crime, and to the day, October 11, 1984, when Marie Jefferson's mutilated remains are discovered.

At the murder site her body is examined, photographed, and tagged; then it is transported to the medical examiner's office for autopsy. In the morgue it is weighed and photographed, X rays are taken, and the body is placed in a refrigerated room for the night. The next morning, the autopsy begins.

We start by removing the dead woman's clothes and examining each article piece by piece. Though the garments are fully intact, there are vertical grass stains on the raincoat, indicating that she has been dragged some distance along the ground. This dragging apparently took place after the killing, for the stains run evenly lengthwise in the same direction, indicating that the victim was not squirming and struggling at the time. We also find bloodstains darkening two holes in the dead woman's raincoat and blouse, blood from knife wounds most likely.

Otherwise, the clothes tell us little. We examine them for semen (none), bullet holes (none), telltale objects in the pockets (none), rips and tears (none), foreign fluids and chemicals (none), vomit and mucus (none), drugs (none), blood or fluid belonging to someone other than the victim (none), and twigs, leaves, or natural residues (none). Finally, we begin the dissection, opening the front of the body from the neck to the abdomen with a Y-shaped incision.

The dead woman's organs are located in their normal anatomic positions from the bottom of her rib cage down to her groin, and they are all unremarkable—a medical term meaning normal or undisturbed. The respiratory, digestive, endocrine, nervous, and other major body systems all appear unaffected by the attack. There are no signs to suggest sexual molestation.

Still, Marie Jefferson's killer went about his business in the most calculatedly savage way. Not only has the dead woman been stabbed twice in the chest, but her face is crisscrossed with three slashing wounds, including one directly across her eyes. There is also a final slash to the kneecap. The viciousness of these wounds is itself a clue. It helps me compile a portrait of the murderer's behavior *plus* a profile of his state of mind in the heat of the killing.

Here are the inferences I draw from the external condition of the victim.

First, when found at the scene of the crime Marie Jefferson's body is fully clothed. There are no rips or tears on her clothing other than those at the wound sites, and no clinical indication of sexual activity. Rape is not a prime mover on the killer's agenda.

Second, the fact that the two knife wounds penetrated the victim's sternum and the heavily plated parts of her rib cage tell me they are inflicted by a person of size and strength, almost certainly a man.

Third, in the course of my career I have observed that professional killers and those who kill in the course of a robbery rarely waste time tormenting their prey. They are more concerned with making their victims dead than with watching them suffer. This is not out of mercy but because they know that the longer they toy with a victim, the more likely they are to be caught and to leave added evidence. Time is of the essence.

Jefferson's assailant, on the other hand, obviously took his time and was clearly not driven by anything as rational as money. The gratuitous slashes on Marie Jefferson's face and limbs are intended to disfigure and degrade, to draw out the agony rather than to immediately silence the victim. They are too cruel and targeted to have been inflicted at random. The stab wounds to the chest are likewise made with the ferocity of a man in a paroxysm of rage. Such focused sadism, my assistants and I agree, seems inspired by pure malice and wrath, possibly—even, I would say, probably—by the desire for revenge.

So far, the evidence indicates that this killing started with slow, purposeful knife torture and ended with a fast, finish-it-off-and-get-out-of-town coup de grâce. The woman on the autopsy table, I believe, was murdered by a man she knew. Probably by a man she knew quite well.

THE ART OF READING STAB WOUNDS

Since the lower parts of the victim's body are intact, my attention now shifts to the two stab wounds to the chest and the three facial slashes.

The former, described in the autopsy report for this case as Chest Wound A and Chest Wound B, are slit-shaped, deep, and not abraded at the edges. They caused a good deal of internal bleeding but churned up little external blood, signs that the knife was sharp.

As you might guess, when examining stab markings during an autopsy, examiners must use their knowledge of the different types of wounds made by different types of cutting instruments. Large, blunt instruments such as a fireplace poker tear ragged, splitting edges into the flesh and produce a great deal of bruising around the entry hole. Broken glass digs out irregular, jagged wounds that are rarely deep enough to invade major body cavities. Chopping instruments, such as cleavers and machetes, make huge, gaping, blood-spattered, horrifying holes. They are among the easiest wounds to match up with weapons, and to identify.

Dull-tipped pointed weapons, such as a screwdriver or closed scissors, produce small, round, deep incisions with a puncturelike appearance. Ragged edges characterize the points of entry, along with internal bleeding and broken bones.

Interestingly, because bones are constructed of such hard, densely calcified material, they retain the imprint of a pointed instrument a good deal better than skin or soft tissue. In some instances it is possible to tell what type of weapon was used in an assault, and to deduce its size and structure, simply by studying the mark it leaves on the bones. The size, blade width, and dimensions of a knife wound may even be so clearly imprinted on the bones that they can be measured at autopsy as accurately as if the blade had been stuck in a block of balsa wood.

Another critical point to note about knife wounds is that they appear open and gaping, or tight and narrow, depending on whether they run parallel to the grain of the skin—the "cleavage lines of Langer"—or against it.

The cleavage lines of Langer, arranged in approximately the same patterns on every human body, are natural creases or bands of tension formed by the direction that the elastic skin fibers take on different parts of the anatomy. Surgeons, as you might expect, are well versed in these patterns. They know that if an incision is made parallel to a line of Langer, the mark heals into a tight, thin line. If they cut transversely across these lines, as they sometimes must do, an unsightly, discolored, and even deformed scar results. In terms of criminal detection, a stab wound that cuts across the lines of Langer generally produces a gaping hole. A wound that runs parallel to these lines often appears as nothing more than a slit.

Both Chest Wound A and Chest Wound B on Marie Jefferson follow the grain of the skin, creating incisions that are relatively smooth all the way through—further indication that the wounds were made by a metal blade, probably a finely sharpened one, that entered and exited the body with a minimum of turning or twisting.

Finally, the edges of Marie Jefferson's two chest wounds are smoother on the right side than on the left. This tells me that the knife has a single cutting edge. It also suggests that the killer is most likely left-handed, as the natural tendency when gripping a knife is to point the cutting side inward.

MEASURING THE FATAL CUT

Opening the chest area wider, and further examining the stab holes, I observe that in Wound A the killer's knife penetrated the clavicle just above the second rib and went on to pierce the upper lobe of the left lung.

In Wound B, the knife slid into the left pectoral muscle between the third and fourth ribs. From here it cut through the left ventricle of the heart and out again, eventually piercing the tenth thoracic vertebra.

I note that while both injuries caused relatively little external destruction to the victim's chest surfaces, they did catastrophic organ damage, enough to end Marie Jefferson's life quickly, almost certainly in no more than a few minutes. I can name the cause of death with reasonable confidence: hemorrhaging—more technically, exsanguination.

Next, I attempt to establish the length of the murder weapon.

Since it was not found at the scene of the crime, I must learn all I can from the traces that the blade left behind. If a suspected weapon happens to turn up under a pile of sod or in someone's dresser drawer during the investigation, knowing the actual weapon's dimensions will aid in making a matchup.

Using the depth of Wound B as an index, and taking into account the markings on the victim's ribs, I determine that the knife blade is approximately fourteen centimeters—or about five and a half inches—long.

Estimating the length of a knife from the depth of the wound it makes can be tricky, because different parts of the body have different degrees of elasticity or give. Abdominal tissue, for instance, is springy, so that a three-inch knife plunged into the gut can be driven all the way back to the spine, producing a six-inch-deep stab wound.

At most autopsies, a trained forensic eye will take tissue flexibility into consideration and compensate appropriately in estimating incision depth. On occasion, however, medical examiners forget to take account of this variable and as a result overestimate the length of the killing instrument, sometimes by several inches. In the course of my career I have examined stab wounds that measure six or seven inches deep but were inflicted by nothing longer than a penknife.

Stab wounds delivered to the chest do not usually cause such miscalculations. Owing to the hardness of the ribs and the sternum, this area tends not to cave in when struck, even by the point of a dagger. In some cases, it is true, a rib cage will collapse under the pressure of a powerful jabbing thrust. I see this most often on the soft bones of children and the brittle bones of the elderly. But in a robust, healthy adult, the durable plating of the rib cage and sternum acts as a suit of armor, cracking and scarring but usually not breaking against the force of the lance.

SEQUENCING THE DEATH SCENE

Putting together the medical data I have gathered so far from Chest Wounds A and B, and taking into account the psychology implied by the sadistic wounds, it appears likely that the sequence of Jefferson's homicide runs in the following way.

First, the killer slashed Marie Jefferson's face and knee to punish and torment her. This segment of the attack continued for five to ten minutes. After watching his victim writhe and scream in agony, and feeling that she has been adequately punished, the killer quickly finished off the job with two swift knife blows to the chest.

The similar entry trajectories of the knife in these wounds, and their nearness to each other, indicate that the blows were delivered in quick succession and that the same person inflicted them. The remote possibility that two persons were involved in this butchery is essentially ruled out.

Lastly, several of the arteries around Marie Jefferson's heart were severed in the stabbing process, and massive damage was done to her heart. After the face slashing this led to what we assume—and hope—was a mercifully speedy death.

FISHING FOR TIME IN THE EVIDENCE POT

Examine the victim's clothing, organs, and wounds.

Profile the hypothetical reasons for the assassin's determination to slice and mangle in such a grisly way.

Establish the cause of death.

Propose a likely sequence or staging of the actions that took place during the assault.

Finally, taking these findings into consideration, and putting them into one big pot, I must next deal with a major "must-know" in any forensic examination: On what specific day—or at least in what week or month—was the victim murdered? Without this knowledge it becomes extremely difficult to pin a suspect to the scene of a crime, or to match witness reports with actual events. Knowing the time of a victim's death helps prove or disprove an alibi. It eliminates suspects or includes them, matches a killing method (such as a slow- or fast-working poison) to a murder, and in certain instances, shows whether a person died from homicide or suicide. It is used in court to support method and means, and in civil cases to determine whether a particular clause in an insurance policy is valid under the circumstances of a death. Knowledge of the time of death is equivalent to the basement of a house; it helps investigators build a case on a solid circumstantial foundation.

We have all been reared on scenes in TV programs and crime novels in which the furrow-browed medical examiner stands over the corpse of a slaughtered victim, performs a perfunctory check, and announces that the aforementioned was shot to death the day before yesterday, probably in the afternoon, most likely around 2:30 P.M.

Brilliant work!

The problem is that any such scene is based on pure dramatic license.

In the real forensic world, gauging time of death with any accuracy in a homicide is one of the most complex, challenging—and, more often than I would like to admit, insurmountable—tasks. Attempts to establish time of death are frequently plagued by difficulties: lack of witnesses; moved bodies; variable weather, moisture, and temperature conditions; evidence that has been tampered with or that was poorly collected; alterations intentionally made to a corpse (such as freezing or dissolving in acid); and, most common of all, extensive decomposition.

To make matters worse, no entirely dependable medical tests or lab procedures exist for pinpointing time of death after the first few days have passed. For this reason, forensic scientists rarely speak of "time of death" at all. They prefer to hedge their bets and cover their flanks, referring instead to "*estimated* time of death."

In some homicides, of course, the time of death is self-evident, delivering itself to police and medical examiners on a golden plate. Eyewitnesses provide a fair approximation of the hour, say, or at least the day a crime took place. Victims turn up who have not yet gone into rigor mortis, indicating that they have probably been dead for less than six hours. Or, in a medical examiner's joking fantasies (as it might be in a *Perry Mason* episode), a stray bullet from the murderer's gun strikes a wall clock, stopping the hands at the precise instant the victim is shot.

There are no such free rides in the Jefferson case. At the medical examiner's lab, I will do everything I can to accurately determine the time of death. That is my mandate. But I cannot make any promises.

THE ANATOMY OF DECOMPOSITION

Looking over the victim's remains and the amount of tissue breakdown that has occurred so far, I make an educated guess that Marie Jefferson has been dead from six to ten days. This guess would carry little weight in court. There are so many variables involved in decomposition—temperature, moisture, age, size, clothing (or lack of it)—that a good lawyer can easily make a medical examiner look incompetent for presenting time of death estimates based on visual examination of decay alone.

Still, there are indications that, though far from foolproof, serve as a plausible guide to a body's steps of decay. To better grasp the challenges involved in staging this process, a short lesson in the mechanics of decomposition should help make what happens next in this case more understandable.

"Decomposition," in brief, is a blandly neutral word for a universally abhorrent and unpalatable reality: rotting; or, to be even more graphic, being eaten. We are eaten when alive by assorted flora and fauna; and we are eaten by species of the same bacteria when dead. This microscopic feast, referred to as "putrefaction," is substantially helped along by fermentation produced by enzymes that are already inside our bodies.

In a living person, for example, enzymatic digestive juices in the intestines reduce solid foods to essential nutrients. After death these same enzymes continue their reductive ways, but now they work on the cellular structure of the body itself, especially the lining of the gastrointestinal tract, which over a matter of days can be dissolved by enzymes to the point of implosion. In warmer climates, a significant contribution to body breakdown is also made by fungi. Since these tiny organisms require robust supplies of oxygen to thrive, they propagate on exposed skin surfaces only. Fungi are rarely if ever found on corpses enclosed in tightly sealed coffins or tombs.

Tissue disintegration can be accelerated or delayed, depending on the type and number of microorganisms at work, and on weather conditions surrounding the body, especially temperature. At 70 to 100 degrees Fahrenheit, putrefaction proceeds at optimal speeds. But when temperatures dip below the 50-degree mark, decomposition slows. The lower temperatures then go, the more gradual decomposition becomes, until the point of deep-freeze is reached, and a body goes into a state of suspended animation similar to the condition of the corpse hanging in the Ice Man's industrial freezer.

Most of the bacteria active at the beginning stages of decomposition already reside inside the body, particularly in the bowels. In a living person these bacteria perform needed digestive tasks. Once death comes, they turn predator, breaking free of intestinal quarantine and invading a majority of body cavities. Here they devour flesh at amazing speeds, soon reducing cellular tissue from a solid state to a liquid. These foragers are soon joined by legions of organisms from the outside environment. Even a few hours after death, the inside of a corpse becomes a teeming sea of scavengers, including such common types of bacteria as *E. coli,* streptococci (strep), and staphylococci (staph).

Despite the swarms of microorganisms that begin digesting flesh almost at the moment of death, under normal conditions two to three days pass before the visible results of putrefaction start to appear. Though subject to endless variables and exceptions, the following sequence is a usable model for tracking the stages of tissue breakdown and decomposition.

Beginning. The first indications of observable decay begin when a person's stomach and genitals turn green or greenish-red. These color transformations take place on both dark-skinned and light-skinned persons.

In this early period, dark blue interlacing vein lines appear; this network mottles the person's neck, shoulders, and groin in a process known as marbling.

During these first several days of decomposition, given optimum weather conditions and absence of destruction by animals, a medical examiner can still estimate the date of death with some accuracy. Observing the greenish-red colorations along with the web of veins that is slowly emerging on the skin, examiners will tell you that this body has most likely been dead from forty-eight to seventy-two hours.

Early middle. The greenish-red discoloration begins to spread across the abdomen, chest, and thighs, and in due course it covers most of the figure. Estimating the time since death is more difficult now. Still, such body discoloration, as a rule—and again, given optimum conditions— tells forensic specialists that the victim has been deceased for around a week.

Middle middle. For up to a week, a dead body looks more or less like what it is, a complete if discolored human body. In the period two to three weeks after death, however, physical transformation and tissue putrefaction accelerate dramatically. The skin now becomes pocked with watery blisters. The rectum voids, and fluids empty from the lungs and stomach, channeling up and out through the mouth and nose. Decay dramatically modifies facial features, turning them into monstrous masks and making facial identification more difficult. The skin darkens from reddish green to purple and then finally to black. Internal gases are released by fermentation, causing the trunk and limbs to puff up; the corpse looks inflated or bloated.

The volumes of gas generated by a cadaver at this stage are immense, and some say dangerously volatile. Unsubstantiated legend has it that putrefying bodies occasionally accumulate so much fermentation gas that they explode in their coffins. The body of Queen Elizabeth I is rumored, with little basis, to be a case in point. In his memoirs, the Duc de Saint-Simon, soldier and courtier during the reign of Louis XIV, describes the corpse of a dowager countess lying in state, and swelling to such an enormous size that it finally bursts open, covering mourners with a shower of flesh. Better attested are reports of some forty coffins exhumed by medical professionals in Huddersfield, England, during the 1960s. Several of these containers bulged at the sides, presumably from gas buildup. The lead linings of the caskets that showed no expansion were all corroded, leaving tiny holes along their rims that presumably served as an escape valve for the explosive gases.

Late middle to early end. After three or more weeks pass, a body starts to come apart in earnest. Soft organs such as the kidneys, brain, and liver liquefy, while hair, nails, and skin come loose from the physical frame. In a well-decayed body, slippage is so total that skin sometimes slides off the hands and feet intact, maintaining a glove shape, a phenomenon called glove configuration.

Occasionally, I have found these skin gloves so well preserved that I can use them to take fingerprints. First I put on a pair of thin surgical gloves. Then I slide my hand into the glove of loose human skin. I ink up the fingers and roll them on a blotter, ending up, as a rule, with a fine, clear set of the dead person's fingerprints.

Many months and many years later. Even as dissolution inexorably advances, muscular organs such as the heart and uterus remain more or less intact for some time. When a body is buried in a coffin or entombed, several years or even several decades sometimes pass before all its tissue dissolves.

Under certain conditions, moreover, especially in extremely dry climates, a corpse's skin can become highly resistant to decay. In the Saharas and Gobis of the world, one occasionally comes upon an abandoned unfortunate who has died long ago, but who has been naturally mummified by dryness.

A BATTERY OF TESTS LEADING NOWHERE

The above staging of decomposition, it should be emphasized, is textbook style. In real life a bloated, blackened body, especially one that has been worked over by insects, forest animals, and vermin, is so altered that it is difficult not only to identify the person, but to tell what color, race, and even sex they once happened to be.

Still, there is the mandate: Use every scientific means available to find out everything possible, especially time of death, even if you know in advance that the value of these tests is limited. During the autopsy of Marie Jefferson we thus run through a number of standard forensic routines to determine as best we can the time of her demise.

First we note that by the time her body is found, it is out of rigor mortis. This lets us know she has been dead for more than thirty-six hours. No surprise. Her lividity comes up negative, meaning that if the victim was moved it happened no more than several hours after her death. Interesting, but not a point of much value in this case.

Around eight to ten hours after death, the pupils of the eyes take on a milky or cloudy appearance. This remains for several days and can be used as a time index. But Marie Jefferson's corpse is clearly more than several days old, so this test is irrelevant—besides which, the victim's eyes are too decomposed to assess in this way.

Occasionally, time since death can be broadly gauged by using a rectal thermometer to measure body heat. A living person's internal temperature is about 98.6 degrees Fahrenheit. The moment we die we begin to cool, as a rule of thumb at approximately 1.5 degrees Fahrenheit every hour for the first six hours. Weather and location affect the cooling rate, of course.

After eighteen to twenty-four hours, our body reaches the local ambient temperature, and there it stays, growing cooler or warmer as the ambient temperature waxes and wanes. Thus, by using body temperature readings taken within a day or less after a person has died, the time of death can sometimes be estimated with fair accuracy. Again this test is no help with Marie Jefferson's body, which has long since cooled to the ambient temperature.

We next perform a vitreous potassium test, extracting a sample of vitreous humor from what is left of the victim's eyes, and measuring the amount of potassium it contains. The vitreous humor is the transparent gelatinous mass that fills the eyeball, behind the pupil's lens. Because potassium levels in the vitreous humor increase at a predictable rate after death, the vitreous potassium procedure was once heralded as the test of tests. At last we had a procedure that could establish time of death to plus or minus five hours, an amazing leap forward in forensic pathology.

But laboratory experience and follow-up studies soon rained on the parade. First, it turned out that the usual margin for error in this test is ten hours plus or minus, not five, and this only during the first day. As time passes, the range of error becomes larger and larger. And, the slightest elevation in temperature surrounding a body further skews the potassium readings.

Other tests based on the same principle—that certain bodily substances, such as glucose, cholesterol, serum calcium, enzymes, and cerebrospinal fluid, increase or decrease at a fixed rate after death—have all been put through their paces in the lab; and all, for various reasons, have failed to perform as stable indicators of time since death, especially after several days elapse. Indeed, of all the laboratory tests now in use, vitreous potassium, despite its limitations, is still the best we have.

Using this method, we derive a value for Marie Jefferson, which tells us she has been dead for at least six days—plus or minus several days.

This is very useful information. But not definitive. How many more days past six has the victim been dead? Seven? Twelve? Twenty?

We seem to have hit a brick wall.

Then I remember something.

REMEMBERING BERGERET

The strange and remarkable science of forensic entomology uses insect reproduction cycles, insect nesting habits, and insect eating patterns to help solve homicides. A relatively new field, forensic entomology has grown steadily in importance over the past twenty or thirty years as it continues to dawn on pathologists that a harvest of forensic information can be reaped by observing the living and dying habits of the humble beetle, wasp, and fly.

The first known modern instance of forensic entomological investigation involves a certain Dr. Bergeret—that is all we know of his name—who in 1850 discovered that two bricks had been removed from the chimney of a boardinghouse and that the dead body of a newborn child had been stuffed into the space behind them.

Bergeret noticed that a number of moth larvae were breeding in the infant's remains, and in a moment of inspiration he decided to take samples of the larvae back to his lab, breed them, and study their growth patterns. Perhaps, he reasoned, he could learn exactly how many days it would take the moth larvae to grow to the size of those in the infant's body, then use this day count to work backward in time and learn the approximate time of death.

Here is an instance, one imagines, of the intellectual quantum jump that is sometimes made in science, usually without precedent, usually without standing on the shoulders of giants, and often by a person who is never given credit and who soon fades into obscurity.

Sure enough, after observing one full life cycle and learning the number of days it took the larvae to reach the size of the specimens found on the infant's body, Bergeret was able to estimate the day on which the child was interred in the chimney wall. His work soon bore fruit: a young woman in the neighborhood was known to have roomed in the boardinghouse at the estimated time of the infant's death. She was known to have been pregnant, but after the delivery was never seen carrying a baby. She was duly charged with murder.

At the trial, it was impossible to prove that the woman actually murdered the infant, which indeed was her own. She claimed that the baby died from natural causes, and that she buried it in the chimney for lack of funds to pay the gravedigger. This account could not be disproved and eventually she went free—whether guilty of infanticide or not, we will never know.

Over the following decades, the hatching cycles of insects were studied sporadically by criminal investigators both here and in Europe. Still, until the 1970s, discussions of forensic entomology were rarely included in textbooks on medicolegal investigation. Even in the early 1980s, information on the science of insect detection is absent from most medical curriculums.

It is thus providence, with a dollop of luck, that the very week Marie Jefferson's body is found and autopsied I happen to be reading several studies in a farm journal on the hatching patterns of a species of flesh-eating flies. This subject has long intrigued me. As I read, and as I think over the circumstances of the Jefferson killing, I remember Bergeret—his work is not entirely forgotten after all—and decide that perhaps I can use fly hatching cycles to establish the time of Marie Jefferson's death.

During the on-site examinations I collected a number of maggots from the slit wounds on the victim's face—the same maggots that so horrified the soccer player who discovered her body.

I preserved some of these creatures in an alcohol solution. Others I brought back alive to the lab. My intent at the time was to simply study their life cycle and perhaps write a paper on the subject one day for a forensic journal. In this regard, precise measurements were made daily throughout the cycle.

But now my interest becomes more than academic. I already know from entomological literature that flies are genetically fine-tuned to detect the odor of putrescent flesh, even from long distances. Once they home in on a carcass they immediately begin to feed, boring through flesh like miniature augers until they are glutted.

The females then lay eggs in the open wounds. If no open wounds are present, they deposit the eggs in any available body orifice including the eyes, ears, mouth, and nose. Soon these eggs hatch into maggots, which live off the muscle tissue surrounding their fleshy cradle. After growing to a certain size, they enter an inactive stage, known as the pupa. A butterfly, for instance, is in the pupa stage when it sleeps in its cocoon.

Finally, the pupa reaches maturity and a full-grown fly emerges. This fly then eats and lays its eggs on whatever carrion it finds, and the fly reproductive course continues through endless generations.

At this point in my inquiries, the most significant fact is that the fly's hatching and growth cycles always require the same number of days to complete themselves. Just as a hamster needs sixteen days to reach full development in its mother's womb, and just as a human being ordinarily has a nine-month gestation, so the period of time from the moment a given species of fly is hatched to the moment it matures is constant.

Taking these facts into consideration, it seems a relatively simple matter to run tests in my lab with live larvae, and to measure the growth of these larvae as each day passes. On Day 1, I reason, the larvae will reach x length; on Day 2, y length; on Day 3, z length; and so on.

When the live maggots reach the size of the preserved specimens from Marie Jefferson's facial slashes, I will have, in theory, a fairly accurate reading, plus or minus a day or so, of how many days have elapsed since the time of her murder. It is clearly worth a try.

COUNTING OF DAYS

As it turns out, the maggot specimens I collected from the victim's eyes at the scene of the crime belong to one of the most common and irksome of flies; the blowfly (genus *Calliphora*).

In the South, this creature is known as the bluebottle or bluetail fly, the one that bites the master's pony, makes him "run and jump and pitch, and throw the master in a ditch" (from the folk song "Blue Tail Fly"). When you are out hiking in the woods or enjoying yourself at a picnic, it is this loud buzzer that circles your head relentlessly, divebombing your eyes and ears. Whether you are alive or dead, the blowfly's only goal is to take a bite out of you.

During the warm months between April and November, blowflies arrive on a body within minutes after death and start laying their eggs immediately. Ordinarily it takes several days for other insects, such as beetles or mites, to infest the same wounds. Flies are fast workers; especially the blowfly. From a forensic perspective, this means that if only blowfly eggs are present in a wound, the corpse will be a day or two old at most. In the Jefferson case, other insects have clearly invaded the wounds, so the victim has been dead for more than two days. This, of course, is not news.

Next, I gather weather data for every day in the past two weeks. The weather has been temperate during this time, with no cold snaps, so the maggots in Jefferson's eyes grew under textbook conditions (at low temperatures they would have grown more slowly). I also learn that blowflies do not lay their eggs at night, on rainy days, or before noon. Looking back over the past two weeks, I note it has rained only once. I add all these facts to the mix.

Finally, I focus on the precise number of days it takes a newborn blowfly to grow from a larva into a pupa and then into an adult fly.

Using the preserved maggots taken from Marie Jefferson's body as size constants, and simultaneously growing control colonies in my own lab, I observe that the blowfly matures according to the following schedule:

Blowfly eggs hatch into larvae—maggots—24 hours after they are laid.

In two days, the maggots reach a length of 3 to 4 millimeters.

In three days, they grow to 5 or 6 millimeters in length.

In four days, they reach 7 or 8 millimeters.

In five days, they are 10 to 12 millimeters long.

In six days' time, they measure 13 to 14 millimeters.

After six or seven days the larvae turn into pupae. They remain in that stage for approximately seven days, finally emerging as full-grown blowflies.

Now I assemble the pieces. The preserved maggots from Marie Jefferson's wounds average around 13 to 14 millimeters in length, so they are six days old. Next, measuring the maggot samples in my test colonies, I find that maggots of this length are also around six days old.

Some pupae were also collected from the victim's wounds at the scene of the crime. They have been in the pupa stage now for several days, based on the growth of my live samples. And as larvae they would have matured for six or perhaps seven days before turning into pupae. The pupae on the victim's body thus hatched seven to nine days before I collected them.

Analyzing this information, and taking weather and temperature into account, I reach an estimate of the date of death that satisfies everyone on the forensic team. Marie Jefferson, the sum total of evidence shows, has been dead between seven and nine days.

We file this fact away with the rest of the autopsy data. The case is cold right now. Perhaps the time of death we have established will be useful at a future date.

NOT SO SILENT GRUMBLINGS

As it turns out, we do not have to wait long.

Over the several months during which the Jefferson case lies fallow, grumblings are heard among police investigators and at the DA's office. Several detectives working this case are especially bothered, in particular Detective Janice Rogan, who helped identify Marie Jefferson's body from the article in the *New York Daily News*.

Rogan tells her colleagues that witnesses have not been pressed hard enough to reveal everything they know, and are reporting what they saw in an incorrect or incomplete way. Rogan also believes that her team is unearthing substantial evidence against the suspect, Samuel McCullough, but that this information is not being given serious consideration by the DA's office and by District Attorney Gribetz. She becomes especially chagrined when Gribetz announces that the DA's office feels it does not have enough good evidence to win the case. In Rogan's estimation, as well as in the opinion of other investigators and even of the chief of police, this decision is premature.

As the months pass, she continues to badger the DA, lobbying for reactivating the case. Much of the evidence concerning McCullough suggests his guilt, she insists. Some is quite obviously incriminating. It is all circumstantial, true, but enough circumstantial evidence still wins cases. And there is much more evidence to be found, she and others believe, if the DA's office will just agree to restart the investigation.

Finally Rogan sets up a meeting with Thomas Zugibe, first assistant district attorney of Rockland County and, I should add, my second-born son. At that meeting, Detective Rogan, the chief of police, and several investigators explain their findings and their misgivings about the way the homicide is being handled. They show Tom their paperwork on the case. Then they ask: In his estimation, given the facts presented, is this case prosecutable?

At the time Tom is in trial with another case, so he is reluctant to get involved, although he too has heard the complaints about the way the Jefferson inquiry is being handled. "At first I'm kind of half-interested and too busy for all this," he tells me later that day. "So I just sort of sit back and let them hold forth. The more I hear from these guys, though, the more intensely I go over the records they show me, the eyewitness reports, the data that's included in the reports—and, just as important, the things that are being left out, overlooked, misinterpreted—the more I see that this really is a triable case. Plenty of incriminating stuff."

The next day, Tom visits Gribetz in his office.

There's a case here, he announces. A strong one. We can win it.

After quizzing Tom on the details for several minutes and listening to his arguments with increasing interest, the DA is convinced. "Okay, my boy," he tells him, "since you want it so badly, it's all yours."

The collaboration that follows between the Rockland chief medical examiner and the Rockland first assistant DA is, I would imagine, one of the few occasions in the history of forensics when a father-and-son team work together to solve a crime.

RESTARTING THE LEGAL ENGINE

Tom goes to work immediately, examining records, going over past testimony, reinterviewing witnesses, visiting the phone company office and the Holiday Inn, re-creating situations, probing, pushing, all the time assembling fragments of evidence into new and revealing scenarios.

After several weeks, here is what he learns:

In the months before Marie Jefferson disappeared, Samuel McCullough was not simply harassing her. He was *stalking* her, calling her at work and at home dozens of times every day, tracking her on the streets and in the supermarket, standing in front of her apartment building at odd hours, and, most alarmingly, threatening her with bodily harm. Her friends go on record one after another, telling investigators that in the weeks before her death Marie Jefferson was so frightened by McCullough's violent attentions that she took alternate routes to work and hid in the shadows of buildings when she thought he was nearby.

Investigators also learn that McCullough physically attacked Marie Jefferson on two occasions. Four months before they were to be married, in 1983, he menaced her with a baseball bat, striking her on the flanks. Though she never reported the assault, she did call off their engagement.

One wonders why she continued to keep company with such a dangerous man. But sure enough, four months later McCullough and Jefferson were vacationing in South Carolina when one morning McCullough attacked Jefferson with an ax. A mutual friend restrained him, but even on the day his murder trial begins, McCullough is subject to an outstanding warrant for assault.

None of this information was brought out in the preliminary investigation.

Marie Jefferson's son (who went unquestioned in the first round of inquiry) reveals that the day before his mother disappeared McCullough accosted her in the park. According to the thirteen-year-old, his mother kept shouting, "It's over, don't you understand, Sam! It's over!" McCullough, in turn, replied with the ominous retort "Well, if I can't have you, no one will!"

Then there is the matter of what really took place in front of the phone company on the day the victim disappeared. When first pressed for further description, phone company employees who witnessed the meeting between Jefferson and McCullough stick to their original story: McCullough took his ex-girlfriend by the arm, and the two of them walked quietly away from the office.

Tom then asks for a demonstration, using himself as the guinea pig.

"Take my arm as if it was Marie Jefferson's arm," he directs the employees. "Show me the way McCullough held it that day. Show me the exact way he escorted her down the street."

Several witnesses respond by taking Tom's arm, forcing it up and tight behind his back, and pushing him forward as a police officer might a prisoner. Surprised at this aggressive reworking of what they thought they saw that day, Tom explains to the witnesses that his questioning technique is often used in police work. It is based on the fact that our physical and visceral centers often remember what we see better than what our minds recall. When a witness physically re-creates events and translates their memory into real body movements, the recollections self-correct, becoming sharper and more accurate.

The phone company witnesses subsequently amend their testimony, affirming that Marie Jefferson was forcibly abducted, not "gently" ushered down the sidewalk that day. The witnesses likewise remember that a few minutes after the couple walked away from the phone company office they saw McCullough's white Lincoln drive past them. Marie Jefferson was sitting in the front seat. McCullough had his arm tightly wrapped around her. After this brief view no one ever saw her alive again. For some reason, this information did not raise major red flags in the early parts of the investigation.

Finally, in the late afternoon of this same day, a Lincoln Continental similar to the one owned by McCullough was observed by guests in the Holiday Inn parking lot. In the first round of questioning, as you may remember, there were conflicting reports of the car's color—white or tan?—and of whether the windows were dark or clear.

To get to the bottom of the matter, Tom has McCullough's white Lincoln taken out of impoundment and driven to the Holiday Inn lot. Here he parks it in the same spot it was seen on the day of the abduction and has it photographed from the two rooms in the motel where the sightings occurred. These photographs are taken at sunset, which is approximately the time of day that the motel guests witnessed the Lincoln pulling out of the lot.

It quickly becomes obvious to Tom and his investigative team that the discrepancy between the two accounts of the car's appearance is due to the angle at which the setting sun strikes the surface of the car at the moment of observation. As the photographs demonstrate, an observer in one room will see what appears to be a tan or cream Lincoln Continental with dark tinted windows. An observer standing in the second room, where the light from the setting sun hits the car directly, would easily see that the Lincoln is bright white and that its windows are clear.

In a word, the same automobile looks like two different vehicles from two different vantage points. Both witnesses actually saw the same car— a white Lincoln Continental exactly like the one owned by Samuel McCullough.

Then, as a bonus, during the session in the parking lot Tom Zugibe discovers a knife slash running across the Lincoln's vinyl roof. In the first report witnesses at the hotel did not mention this mark. Tom finds these witnesses and brings them to the car. He sets up a tall ladder, and has each witness mount and look down on the vehicle from above at an angle approximating his or her original line of observation. One of the witnesses immediately shouts out from atop the ladder, "Yeah, yeah, I remember seeing that slash there! I forgot about it."

This cut mark could, of course, have been made at any time in any way. Yet taken in the context of the killer's method, and considering the knife slashes found on the victim's face and knee, its presence is another straw weighing on the camel's back.

THE FINAL STRAW

The evidence against McCullough is massing. Is there now enough to convict him in a court of law?

Perhaps. Perhaps not. What is needed is a clincher, some form of confirmation that directly places Marie Jefferson and Samuel McCullough together on the day she is murdered. After all, on the afternoon they met in front of the phone company, McCullough may simply have taken Jefferson for a car ride, browbeaten her, even done her physical harm, and then gone on his way. Jefferson could have been murdered subsequently, four or five days after their meeting.

It is at this point in the case that Tom comes to see me in the medical examiner's office, telling me that establishing the day of death is now such a crucial point of focus in the Jefferson case that without it the DA may not have a strong enough case to win.

And Tom knows of what he speaks. When I first started out as medical examiner and had no other help, he spent his summers and holidays off from college helping me investigate crime scenes; he sat in on more than a hundred autopsies. He knows from experience how difficult it can be to pin down the time of death in a heavily decomposed corpse. He also knows how relevant this single piece of information can be to solving a crime.

Do I have anything, *anything at all,* he asks, on how long Marie Jefferson's body lay in the woods after she was murdered? Three days? Five? Ten?

Did her death coincide with the screams heard eight days before at the parking lot in the Holiday Inn?

Did it overlap with her abduction eight days earlier in front of the phone company?

Smiling, like the genie from the magic lamp, like the wish-granting elf, I walk over to my files and proudly pull out a folder full of my blue-tail fly studies. Tom looks them over for a minute and begins to grin—bingo! Dead for seven to nine days. Eight days elapsed between the afternoon Jefferson was seen in New York City with McCullough and the afternoon her body was discovered in Nanuet.

Here we have it: if not a smoking gun, then commanding circumstantial evidence that the two protagonists were together on the fated day at the Holiday Inn parking lot where Marie Jefferson's life was ended.

This piece of information, the approximate time of death, is added to the already swelling pot of evidence unearthed by Tom. The case against McCullough is now substantial and persuasive. The DA smells conviction.

AT THE TRIAL

Up to the time of his trial, McCullough plays dumb concerning his comings and goings on the day of Jefferson's disappearance. But before the jury his amnesia vanishes, and he assures the court he was not with

Jefferson at all that afternoon. The two of them had broken off their relationship several months earlier, he declares. On friendly terms. He has not seen or talked to her since.

"Where were you around the time she disappeared?" Tom Zugibe asks McCullough while he is on the stand.

"Right outside of Atlantic City. Visiting my cousin."

When a string of phone company workers subsequently testify to seeing McCullough in front of their office that day with Jefferson, the defendant's Atlantic City alibi falls apart. And then the cousin testifies: throughout McCullough's visit—he obviously drove straight to Atlantic City immediately after the murder—he acted in a suspicious way, jumping when the phone rang, staring nervously out the window, behaving like a man pursued and possessed. McCullough told his cousin over and over that if anyone asked, she was to insist he had been staying with her for several weeks.

Next follows the testimony of a parade of witnesses for the prosecution. One phone company employee climbs off the witness stand and in front of the jury demonstrates on Tom Zugibe the behind-the-back armhold the suspect used on Marie Jefferson.

Another witness, from Waterford, Connecticut, informs the jury that she was just arriving at the Holiday Inn when the commotion in the parking lot began. "I had the door key in my hand, just about to put it into my motel doorknob, when I heard the screams." The screaming was so loud, the witness says, she felt "like it was coming through the walls." She ran to the window and saw "a black guy getting into a big white car." In the twilight his facial features are indistinguishable. But he is plainly husky, tall, and overweight.

When asked why she did not immediately notify the authorities of this incident, she replies that she thought the man was a pimp (complete with Lincoln Continental) beating up one of "his" women. She did not want to get involved.

Still another onlooker at the motel, a sales representative from Cedar City, Iowa, testifies to hearing screams so loud they drowned out his TV. "I heard distinctly a female voice in distress calling for help," he reports. "They go: 'Help me, help me, please!' Then at the very height of the cries I heard the words very distinctly 'Oh no, oh my God no!' "

Hearing this, the man dressed and ran down the stairs into the parking lot. By now the screams had stopped, but he saw a car pulling out. He wrote down the license plate number, went back upstairs, and put the note in his briefcase. A few days later, he was cleaning the briefcase out and found the note. Since he had heard no reports of foul play at the motel, he discarded it. Three days later, the police called.

Other pieces of damning testimony are likewise presented by the prosecution.

An officer from the Rockland County Bureau of Criminal Identification explains to the jury how strands of hair belonging to an African American woman, and consistent with those of the victim, were removed from the trunk of the defendant's car. Testimony is also offered concerning blood found on the carpet inside McCullough's car. DNA matching has not yet been developed, so it cannot be definitively said that the blood belongs to Jefferson, but blood types match.

RE-CREATING THE CRIME

In the end, Tom tells the jury, summing up his case, the probable circumstances in the Jefferson murder story go something like this:

Angry because she broke up with him and would not come back, Samuel McCullough abducted Marie Jefferson on the street after work and forced her into his car.

During the hour-long drive to Nanuet, Marie Jefferson tried to escape from McCullough's vehicle several times. To keep her subdued, McCullough probably stopped the car somewhere along the road and forced her into the trunk: hence the hairs found on the trunk door.

Next, McCullough drove his Lincoln to the Holiday Inn parking lot in Nanuet.

It was quiet there. Nobody seemed to be around, and it was getting dark. Not a clever or vigilant man, and blinded by his fury, McCullough thought himself unnoticed as he opened the trunk, toyed with his victim

for a few moments, sliced her face several times as she lay there screaming, then stabbed her to death.

Finally, he removed the body from the trunk, dragged it thirty feet or
so into the woods behind the motel, and left it there, not even taking the
precaution of covering it with underbrush.

The evidence strongly suggests that some version of this sad and
bloody sequence unfolded that afternoon in October. McCullough, insisting on his innocence to the end, is found guilty of second-degree
murder and given the maximum sentence, twenty-five years to life. He
dies in prison.

AND BRUSH AWAY THE BLUETAIL FLY

One last twist.

During the trial, Tom, the prosecuting attorney, puts me on the witness stand, where together we go over my entomological data: I explain
to the jury how studies of the fly's life cycle can help establish time of
death in a homicide, and how by growing sample flies in the lab we were
able, within standard margins of error, to determine the day of Marie Jefferson's murder.

After Tom finishes his questioning, the lawyer for the defense begins
cross-examination.

Befuddled, I think, by the entomological information I have just
presented, and somewhat uncertain how to rebut this strange but
scientifically convincing evidence, the defense attorney begins questioning me on the details of the blowfly's life cycle, asking for more
and more technical information, much of it redundant or off the
point.

Finally he says, "Dr. Zugibe, you claim to have studied samples of
Calliphora pupae and the larvae, the dead flies. But what about the live
flies? What happens when these insects come out of the pupa stage?
Could you explain to the court what you did with these fully grown flies?
Did you save any of them?"

Baffled by this irrelevant question, I simply shake my head no.

"Then, might I ask, just what happened to these adult flies?"

I take my time before answering.

"Well," I finally reply with all the gravity I can summon. "They . . . flew away."

It takes several minutes for the jury and spectators to stop laughing, and for the judge to restore order so that the trial can proceed.

CHAPTER 5

Conviction Is in the Details
The Brinks Robbery

The federal Brinks conspiracy trial became
a political science lecture hall Monday as
defense and prosecution attorneys and witnesses debated how one man's bank robber
and murderer might be another's righteous
revolutionary.

—ROCKLAND *JOURNAL NEWS*, AUGUST 16, 1985

DEATH IS IN THE DETAILS

DURING THE INVESTIGATION OF A CASE, THE HUNT FOR THE MURDERER, and the trial and conviction that (we hope) follow, forensic science plays a number of roles that can fit both high and low on the ladder of legal importance. At the top rung is forensic evidence and testimony that definitively clinch the prosecution's case; at the bottom is an opinion or finding that sheds light on a small but relevant detail.

Such a detail might, for example, include whether a fracture of the ribs on an emergency CPR recipient is due to an inherent weakness in the person's bone structure, or to overzealous pushing by the resuscitator. In another case, forensic testimony can help a jury decide whether the crisscrossed abrasions on the calf of a woman run over by a motorcycle are from the vehicle's tires, or from pressure exerted by these tires on the mesh stockings the victim was wearing. The outcomes of a vast number of cases, both criminal and civil, are built on an understructure of such fine points.

In the infamous 1981 Brinks robbery (not to be confused with the 1950 "Great" Brinks robbery, in Boston), evidence I offered at the trial far from broke open the case. At the same time, my staff's forensic contribution added a foundation stone to the prosecution's case—a case that opened a new page in American sociological history. For the Brinks robbery, it can be seen in retrospect, was a good deal more than just a deadly shootout between cops and robbers. It was, social commentators now agree, one of the first instances of organized terrorism to occur within the borders of the United States of America.

The robbery takes place in Rockland County, at an unassuming suburban mall in the town of Nanuet. That day, my staff and I are called on to perform autopsies on three law enforcement professionals who have been shot down in two major gun battles during the robbery and escape. Later, my colleagues and I give evidence at several Brinks robbery trials concerning the nature of the gunshot wounds. This evidence, as I say, does not solve all the mysteries. It *does* answer several central questions and thus shows how important fitting just a single forensic piece into the larger circumstantial puzzle can be for helping law enforcement agencies understand the greater hows and whys of a catastrophic crime.

In the case of the Brinks robbery, moreover, the revelations that came out during the trials shocked the nation. For those with an interest in human behavior and in how easily good intentions can turn to fire and brimstone, these trials rendered transparent a peculiar psychological mechanism, found in revolutions from the French to the Russian, by which a sincerely dedicated idealism transforms itself into a cruel ideology complete with tyrannical leadership, then into a berserk frenzy, ending finally with a devastating slaughter of innocents.

RATTLING THE WALLS

It is difficult to say exactly when the story of the Brinks robbery begins.

Though the climactic incident takes place at the Nanuet Mall on October 20, 1981, some criminologists date the first spinning of the wheel that sets the other wheels into motion to March 6, 1970, eleven years earlier, the day a brownstone in New York's Greenwich Village blew to kingdom come.

It happened out of the blue. A woman was walking her dog, a father was leaving his house to pick up his twin daughters from private school, a sanitation man was lifting bags of garbage and loading them on the truck, when an enormous explosion rocked the entire block, and the town house at 18 West Eleventh Street burst into flames.

The dog walker, dad, and sanitation man ran for cover as chunks of the building toppled to the street, crushing several parked cars. Adjacent brownstones, including one owned by the actor Dustin Hoffman, shook and swayed dangerously. Acrid black smoke, the kind normally produced by chemical fires, engulfed the area, and flames blew out of every window at number 18, giving off what one observer later described as "a frightening incandescent glow."

In the midst of this pandemonium, a strange thing happened.

From a tunnel of smoke and flame, two young women staggered out of the building in a daze and wandered onto the street. Both women were covered in soot and one was totally naked: the explosion burned the clothes off her body.

A neighborhood resident, Susan Wager, ex-wife of the film star Henry Fonda, came to the rescue. She led the two survivors to her brownstone, dressed their wounds, and gave them fresh clothes. The women were trembling and bleeding, Wager could see, but neither appeared to be seriously injured. They remained silent when Wager asked their names and queried them on the explosion.

They were in shock, she assumed.

A good Samaritan, Wager left her two wards in the care of a housekeeper and went back out to look for other victims. Soon, the truncated bodies of two young women were pulled from the wreckage. (A third body, that of a young man, would be discovered the next day.)

A half hour later, Ms. Wager returned home. The housekeeper informed her that the girls had left the house some time ago to find a drugstore and, in their words, "to purchase some first aid supplies."

Susan Wager never saw either of them again—except, some years later, on the nightly news.

COMES THE REVOLUTION

In one of Bob Dylan's most famous songs, he tells us that if you are hanging out on the mean streets—especially East Fourth Street which is, despite the serious, income differences, only seven blocks from West Eleventh Street—you don't need a weatherman to tell you which way the wind is blowing.

The year that song is released, Dylan fans ponder the meaning of the weatherman line, trading esoteric interpretations and wondering how closely it connects with the songwriter's implicitly revolutionary lyrics from "Blowing in the Wind."

One group of avid student activists, a number of whom are members of Students for a Democratic Society, the SDS, decide to make this phrase their own, and to raise the stakes in the process. Breaking away from the SDS, which they now agree is too pacifist, and forming a more militant arm of the student movement, the new organization titles itself the Weathermen after Dylan's lyric.

Immediately, this fledgling movement issues manifestos announcing the revolution. They help the LSD guru Timothy Leary escape from jail. They tout the cult leader Charles Manson as a hero for opposing the establishment ("Dig it!" Bernadine Dohrn, antiwar activist and card-carrying Weatherman, tells an enthusiastic audience of radicals, "Manson killed those pigs, then they ate dinner in the same room with them, then they shoved a fork into a victim's stomach").

During the "Days of Rage" at the 1968 Democratic presidential convention in Chicago, Weathermen use dynamite to blow a huge statue of a policeman off its pedestal in Haymarket Square, causing chunks of the statue's leg to fly onto a nearby expressway. A hundred windows in the neighborhood and several storefronts are blown out by the impact. Weathermen members also home in on riling up antiwar protestors, an act that leads to injuries on both sides of the police line plus hundreds of arrests, and eventually the infamous trial of the "Chicago Seven."

Most important, the Weathermen agree that waving placards and dialoguing with establishment lackeys at peace protests will do nothing to solve America's most urgent social problems. Gandhi's way, and Martin Luther King, Jr.'s way, is too slow and uncertain for them now. The only efficient means of changing the social order, they insist, is guns and bombs. During the late 1960s they engineer a series of dynamite blasts at Harvard University, at various corporate headquarters, and at several federal buildings, all of which go unsolved.

Then on March 6, 1970, several members of the Weathermen, emboldened with the success of their anonymous hit-and-run strategy and growing ever more sophisticated at bomb building, are busy in the basement at 18 West Eleventh Street assembling fuses and dynamite concoctions to blow up a local police precinct.

It is surmised—no one knows for certain—that in the process one of the demolition experts crosses the wrong wires; the bombers blow themselves up instead. The two young women who wander out of the conflagration, Kathy Boudin and Cathy Wilkerson, are Weathermen members. Both have been in hiding and on the run from the law since jumping bail several years earlier on charges of assaulting police officers at the Chicago convention.

Raging at the state, at the plight of African Americans, at the Vietnam War, at the condition of the poor and disenfranchised, at other inequities both real and perceived, the predominantly white Weathermen change their name to the Weather Underground (so as not to appear sexist), and then, as the 1970s dawn, drop off the map entirely.

Planning their revolutionary strategy in seclusion from the early 1970s up to the early 1980s, they perform eighteen "armed expropriations" of banks and armored cars, in the process helping themselves to more than a million dollars in booty from these jobs. They also break notorious terrorists out of prison and set up safe houses across the country stocked with explosive materials, assault weapons, blueprints of police headquarters, plans for burning down power stations, sophisticated equipment for counterfeiting official documents and IDs, and lists of prominent politicians and businessmen targeted for assassination.

During this entire time the scope and intentions of the group go unrecognized by police and FBI intelligence, who believe the attacks are isolated incidents and thus remain oblivious to the fact that they are dealing with a growing and highly sophisticated terrorist conspiracy. Authorities are unaware that during the 1970s the white Weather Underground is likewise busy forging ties with other radical groups of various colors, including the Puerto Rican FALN, the Republic of New Africa, and the Communist May 19 organization. They have a special relationship with the exclusively black BLA, the Black Liberation Army, a fiercely aggressive Black Panther splinter group whose members earn their bones by shooting police officers on the street at random.

Eventually the two groups merge, naming themselves the Family. From this union comes a well-organized and avowedly violent political organization with fanatically loyal members and a firmly focused goal: to destroy to its very roots the American government, the American legal system, the American social establishment, and the American way of life.

To further this plan, the Family declares war on the United States, and it is agreed that in the battles to come any tactic may be used, including, if necessary, the killing of innocent people. Such behavior is not only needed for victory but will ultimately work to the common good.

For, once millions of the downtrodden are convinced of the righteousness of the Family's cause and join in the struggle; once the black man and the oppressed of all races rise against the tyranny of the American political leviathan; once the base of the American government is nibbled away in a series of guerrilla campaigns until, like a stone idol, it topples under its own weight, the victors will found a new nation in several Southern states. This country, based now on the *true* principles of freedom, equality, and peace, will be populated by black people.

Those white activists who have helped fight the war of oppression will be welcome to live in this new society, if they so choose, as honored "guests."

THE BATTLE RAGES

Such a long and ambitious war, needless to say, costs a great deal of money, so the Family starts to rob banks.

No one has ever been certain how many financial institutions the Weathermen and BLA actually robbed in the early 1980s, though it is believed that holdups in the Bronx; Mount Vernon, New York; and Paramus, New Jersey, are all their handiwork.

These heists are performed with clockwork efficiency, and the perpetrators' money-grabbing and getaway techniques improve with each job, giving them confidence, finally, to try for a *really* big score: a Brinks armored vehicle, specifically one that pulls up to the Nanuet National Bank at the Nanuet Mall in Rockland County every Tuesday afternoon to pick up the week's deposits.

This truck transports millions of dollars in cash on each run. The transfer of the money from bank to truck, the Family learns from scouting the area, is ordinarily watched over by only two guards. Local police are rarely on the scene.

They decide to strike.

After much planning, then one aborted mission (the Brinks truck arrives late), on the afternoon of Tuesday, October 20, 1985, a group of men from the Family, all in their thirties and forties and all BLA members—Donald Weems, aka Kuwasi Balagoon; Samuel Brown, aka Solomon Bouines; Cecilio "Chui" Ferguson; Samuel Smith, aka Mtayari Sundiata; and several other men who have never been identified—clamber into the back of a red van. With them they carry an arsenal of assault weapons, including high-velocity automatic M-16 rifles, 9mm handguns, and shotguns. Gear at the ready, they drive directly to the mall.

Reaching the strike zone early, the van restlessly circles the parking lot, parks for a while, and cruises again, keeping watch all the while for the truck.

At 3:55 P.M. the armored vehicle arrives. It angles over to the curb, and the guards step out.

The Family's van pulls up quietly behind it.

While the truck's driver sits half-dozing in front, the two Brinks guards, Joe Trombino and his partner, Peter Paige, stroll into the bank. They emerge minutes later, wheeling bags of money.

As Trombino begins loading the truck and Paige stands guard with an automatic rifle, the doors of the red van suddenly burst open, and the armed men, now wearing ski masks and face coverings, leap out, spraying bullets in all directions.

Shots from an M-16 instantly hit Peter Paige from several angles, killing him on the spot.

A sawed-off shotgun is then fired three times at the windshield of the Brinks truck, making holes in its bulletproof glass, and narrowly missing the driver as he dives headfirst to the floor. Another robber, later identified as Donald Weems, has stationed himself at a nearby bus-stop bench before the truck arrives. He now pulls out an automatic weapon and joins the fusillade.

Seeking cover, the other Brinks guard, Joe Trombino, manages to squeeze off a single shot at the attackers before a barrage of bullets tears his shoulder apart, leaving his left arm dangling at his side by a thread of gristle.

"I've got no arm!" Trombino screams, then loses consciousness.

The robbers proceed to remove six bags of money from the Brinks truck, amounting to exactly $1,585,000 (the truck is actually carrying another million dollars, which the holdup crew overlooks). They toss the money sacks into their van and take off in a whirl of tire screech and rubber, narrowly missing clumps of pedestrians who are frozen to the spot watching the carnage.

The entire robbery takes less than four minutes from beginning to end.

WITNESS

A mile away from the Nanuet Mall, a twenty-year-old college student, Sandra Torgerson, is home working on a school assignment.

From her window she can see a boarded-up Korvette's retail store with its football-field-size parking lot. An early version of the gigantic bargain-basement outlet stores that are so much part of the suburban landscape today, this Korvette's has recently gone belly up, and its parking lot is starting to grow weeds.

Glancing out the window as she works, Torgerson notices a red van and a yellowish Honda pull into the deserted lot, and drive up to a U-Haul truck parked inconspicuously to the side. A group of black men with blood on their clothes and rifles in their hands leap from the back of the van and start loading heavy-looking green bags into the U-Haul and Honda. Something really scary is happening, Torgerson can see.

The men work with split-second efficiency.

They finish the job in several minutes and the U-Haul and the Honda speed away.

Torgerson calls the local police.

"It was a little yellow Honda sedan and a U-Haul truck," she tells the authorities. "They went to the right, maybe on [Route] 304. Toward the Mobile Car Wash. A Honda Accord, maybe."

This information is instantly broadcast to police units all over Rockland, and an all-county police alert is sounded. Sandra Torgerson returns to her schoolwork.

Here it is interesting to speculate for a moment on the implications of Torgerson's call and this critical five minutes in American history. For had the young student not reported the suspicious rendezvous in the parking lot, the Brinks robbers hiding in their U-Haul would more than likely have vanished into the mists as they had done so many times before.

History, like forensic medicine and the solving of homicides, is in the smallest of details.

The pantyhose ligature strangling device used in the killing of one of the victims. The same type of ligature was used in the murder of both Susans. The ligature is cut at the loop opposite the knot to remove the strangulation device. In this way the diameter of the opening is preserved and can be measured to determine the degree of compression. If the knot had been opened, we would have had no idea how much compression had been applied to the neck area. *(Photo taken in course of the medical examiner's investigation and submitted into evidence.)*

ABOVE: Portrait of Egil Dag Vesti, the murdered Norwegian fashion model. *(Submitted into evidence for identification purposes.)*

RIGHT: The S&M mask found wrapped around the decedent's head following removal of his body from the smokehouse. His entire body has literally been cooked from jaw to toes, and the flesh has been eaten off his bones by small animals. *(Photo taken in course of the medical examiner's investigation and submitted into evidence.)*

INSET: Detailed photo, front and back, of the S&M mask worn by Egil Vesti. *(Photo taken in course of the medical examiner's investigation and submitted into evidence.)*

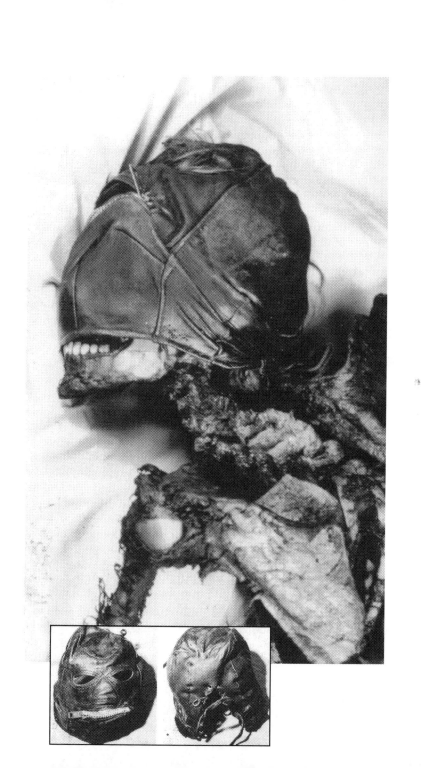

Close-up of the Brink's truck windshield with gunshot holes made by a sawed-off shotgun. Note the thickness of the glass. *(Photo taken in course of the medical examiner's investigation and submitted into evidence.)*

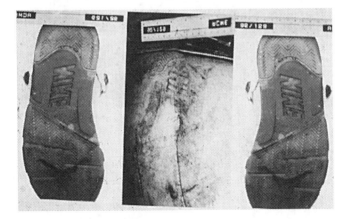

The photo at left, taken from suspect Raymond Navarro, depicts the bottom of the Nike sneaker and clearly displays the Nike letters and treads. The middle photo shows the victim's lower abdominal area with the Nike letters and tread pattern impressed into his skin. The photo at right shows the bottom of Navarro's sneaker with the Nike letters reversed. The size of the Nike sneaker lines up perfectly with the tread mark, and though no blood was discernible on the sneaker under the dissecting microscope, the PCR method (see text) provided thousands of copies of the victim's DNA. *(Photo taken in course of the medical examiner's investigation and submitted into evidence.)*

Photograph of seven-year-old Joan D'Alessandro in her Brownie Scout uniform. *(Courtesy of Rosemarie D'Alessandro)*

Note the yarmulke lying near the hand of the dead burglar. *(Photo taken in course of the medical examiner's investigation and submitted into evidence.)*

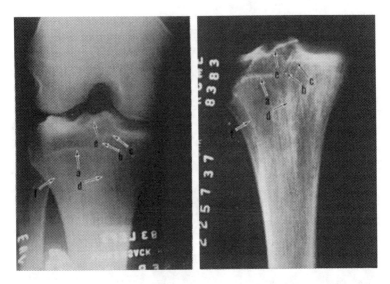

On the left is an X-ray of John Sullivan's knee showing his tibia and fibula. This image was taken at Hackensack Hospital a few years before the journalist's murder. An X-ray of the tibia removed from the coffin is on the right. This bone was properly oriented and X-rayed, corresponding exactly with the X-ray taken at Hackensack Hospital. The numerous features of both bones are identical with one another, showing no incompatible features. *(Photo taken in course of the medical examiner's investigation and submitted into evidence.)*

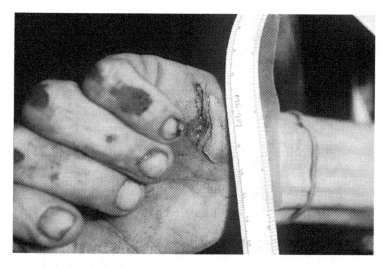

ABOVE: The hand of a hit-and-run victim. A piece of tissue had been avulsed from the victim's hand parallel to the ruler. The piece of tissue is placed adjacent to the avulsed area.

BELOW: The piece of tissue fits like a jigsaw puzzle piece into the avulsed wound.

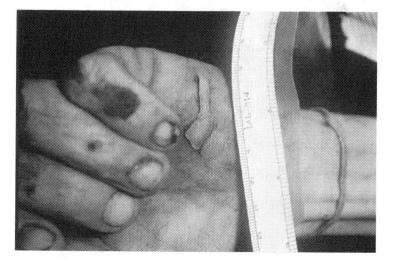

The decedent is turned on his back. Note that he is in full rigor mortis, with both arms suspended rigidly in the air. If he were found in this position, it would indicate that the body had developed rigor mortis prior to being dumped. *(Photo taken in course of the medical examiner's investigation and submitted into evidence.)*

BLOODBATH TWO

At the moment Sandra Torgerson is making her call to the police, both escape vehicles are driving at blend-in speeds down Route 59, a busy suburban highway that leads to an intersection with the New York State Thruway.

Anticipating that the getaway vehicles may be headed in this direction, the police set up a major roadblock at the junction between Route 59 and Mountainview Avenue, near the Thruway's on-ramp. Here four members of the Nyack police force sit in their squad cars waiting for any vehicles that match the radioed descriptions: a U-Haul truck and a yellow Honda (possibly an Accord).

One of the officers, Waverly "Chipper" Brown, is at forty-five a thirteen-year veteran of the Nyack police, and its only African American member. He is much admired by the community for the time he spends mentoring town delinquents and school dropouts. At home he has a wife and two daughters. He plans to retire soon and move to Virginia.

The second policeman, Sergeant Ed O'Grady, thirty-three years old, is an ex-Marine and a Vietnam vet. Currently enrolled in a local college, he is close to accomplishing his lifetime dream of earning a bachelor's degree in criminal justice. He has a wife and three small children.

Also on alert at the intersection are Detective Artie Keenan and Officer Brian Lennon, who sits in the driver's side of the squad car. The police watch carefully as the traffic flashes by; several tense minutes pass before one of the officers spies a U-Haul truck heading in their direction. The red-and-silver vehicle is driven by a young white male. An attractive young white woman sits next to him in the passenger seat.

The police wave them over to the side of the road. The truck stops, and the girl steps out. When she sees guns pointed in her direction she looks frightened and raises her hands, pleading that she and her husband are just minding their own business. "Please, what's wrong?" she shouts. "Can't you put your guns away?"

The driver of the U-Haul has also dismounted by this time, and stands unassumingly by the side of the truck.

Knowing that the robbery at the Nanuet Mall was committed by black men, and disarmed by the young girl's entreaties, the officers relax. "Put the gun back," says Sergeant O'Grady. "I don't think it's them."

But Detective Keenan is not so sure. He wants to check.

"I just wanted to know what was in there," he says in a recent interview. "When I tried to pull the door up, it wouldn't move. I think they were holding it from the inside, because there was a pull-up strap on the back side of the door."

Banging on the door, Keenan still gets no response.

"I called out to O'Grady, who was by the front cab. But before he could answer, before anyone could do anything, the door flew up, and out they came!"

Six men, all heavily armed, leap from the truck in SWAT-team fashion, firing their automatic weapons. In the mêlée the military discipline quickly falls apart, and the fugitives begin shooting off their weapons indiscriminately. (After the gun battle is over dozens of bullet holes are found in a gas pump several hundred yards down the street.)

Officer Waverly Brown is the first to die, strafed by M-16 assault bullets, one of which bursts his aorta, then by a 9mm pistol fired at him point-blank.

Detective Keenan, on the other side of the truck, is shot next, in the leg and the side. He hits the ground, feigning death, then rolls to cover behind a pine tree where he begins to return fire.

From inside the squad car, Sergeant O'Grady cracks off a shot that hits one of the attackers. The struck man reels but does not fall. It is later learned he is wearing a bulletproof vest.

The firefight continues as pedestrians scatter and bullets ricochet off nearby signs and walls; there is screaming, blood, sirens, voices shouting wildly over the radio dispatch, unanswerable now by the three officers still alive but pinned down by fire.

In the midst of the fighting, Officer O'Grady uses up the ammunition from his .357 Magnum and attempts to reload. The next moment he is raked by a line of M-16 bullets that slam him up against the door. He is still alive, but hit in several vital areas and unconscious. Less than two hours later, he will die on the operating table at Nyack Hospital.

The last functioning officer, Patrolman Lennon, is now the target of automatic weapons fire from several sides at once. In the squad car, he is a sitting duck. His escape is blocked by O'Grady's bloody body, now wedged up tight against the passenger-side door. Officer Lennon watches helplessly as the attackers pile back into the U-Haul and drive it directly toward his police car at high acceleration. In desperation Lennon pumps off several shotgun rounds, making the U-Haul swerve, but not enough. The truck collides with the squad car at an angle, splintering glass and metal in all directions, and injuring Officer Lennon.

At this point the scene is a horrific shambles, and the attackers, no doubt aware that police backup units will soon be arriving, scramble to get away.

One of the assailants flags down a BMW, pulls two women out of their seats—one of the women is eighty-one years old—kicks them onto the pavement, and drives off. At this moment, the yellow Honda arrives and stops in front of the U-Haul. Several others pile into the back of the Honda, while still others reassemble and leap into the back of the U-Haul, which races away.

One member of the attack squad is left behind: the white female who was sitting in the front seat of the U-Haul truck, and who tried to dissuade the police from searching the vehicle. Standing on the median strip of Route 59, realizing she has been deserted by her brothers in arms, hearing the sound of sirens drawing closer, she frantically darts across the highway, narrowly dodging several cars. She reaches the other side and dashes toward a clump of woods.

At this very moment an off-duty New York City corrections officer named Michael Koch is driving by the Thruway entrance ramp, and sees the havoc.

He also notices the fleeing woman running across a nearby highway. Realizing that she must be involved in the mayhem, Koch diverts his vehicle to the scene of the crime, jumps out, and begins to chase the fugitive, dodging cars, finally closing in on his target and tackling her.

"He shot him, I didn't shoot him, he shot him!" the woman yells, distraught.

Koch drags her back to the scene kicking and howling. Here Detective Keenan, wounded and half conscious, has managed to call for help.

The young woman, it is soon learned, is none other than Kathy Boudin, survivor of the erupting bomb factory on Eleventh Street, wanted for her violent antics at the Chicago convention, and now an active accomplice in one of the bloodiest criminal assaults in the history of New York State.

The man who was driving the U-Haul, David Gilbert, is a Weather Underground leader, and Kathy Boudin's boyfriend. During a lull in the shootout he hightails it with other fleeing group members, leaving his lover stranded. But soon he is captured as well.

TWO-YEAR FAST-FORWARD

The events that take place in the months following the Brinks robbery—the chase after the shootout; the clever, seemingly endless evasions; the eventual capture of most participants (some get away entirely, unknown to this day)—are another story, not directly related to the forensic inquiry into the robbery itself.

Suffice to say that in January 1982 the FBI locates Donald Weems, aka Kuwasi Balagoon, hiding out in the Bronx. Kathy Boudin is already in custody, and another Weather Underground member, Judith Clark, soon joins her. Other members of the Underground and related radical groups are also apprehended, some of whom eventually stand trial for separate but related crimes.

Meanwhile, at the medical examiner's office, I perform autopsies on the three slain men—two police officers and a security guard—and search for evidence of who among the suspects actually did the killing.

My investigators and I begin those autopsies on the day of the robbery, October 20, 1981. The results are published and given over to the DA and investigative personnel for study. Not until August 1983 does the first trial of several Brinks robbery suspects take place and the forensic evidence from the autopsies become relevant.

EAVESDROPPING INSIDE THE COURT

The long-awaited proceedings are hosted in the courthouse in Goshen, New York, a small town several hours' drive from Manhattan. Judith Clark, Kathy Boudin, Donald Weems, and David Gilbert are the defendants.

Waiving their right to an attorney, and choosing to defend themselves, the three accused members of the Family take every opportunity to reprimand the court, the legal system, and the U.S. government. The defendants chant slogans against imperialism, taunt witnesses, and eventually stomp out of the courtroom, claiming that since the U.S. government is an illegal ruling body the trial is null and void.

"We are at war and have no respect for the laws, the verdict, or the sentence!" one of the defendants shouts. "We will continue to maintain our position as freedom fighters!"

Word of this defiance is meant to be spread near and far over the land, and to rouse the masses to revolution. What the news actually does is deliver an electric jolt to the public, making it aware that the Brinks robbery is the iceberg tip of a grand design involving hundreds of radical conspirators from fanatic groups located across the nation. Sometimes working together, sometimes alone, these organizations aim at nothing less than the violent overthrow of the American government, with intent to kill and destroy those who stand in their way. The robbery of a local bank at a sleepy mall in Small Town USA marks the true beginning of terrorism in the United States.

During the first Brinks trial, I am asked to testify concerning the autopsy findings on the Brinks guard and the two police officers, and to offer forensic opinions concerning the type of weapons used to slay them.

To give you an idea of how the cross-examination of a forensic expert works in a jury trial such as this, and how seemingly small forensic observations can affect a jury's decision, let us enter this courtroom on a day in mid-August 1983, and eavesdrop on the proceedings.

Minus irrelevant sections, here is the actual dialogue that takes place in the Goshen courthouse between the chief district attorney of Rockland County and me:

DA: Doctor, how many autopsies have you performed in your professional career?

DR. ZUGIBE: Well, I have either conducted or assisted in about 10,000.

DA: And you say you are a Board Certified Forensic Pathologist, is that correct?

DR. ZUGIBE: That's correct.

DA: Now I call your attention—did you have an occasion to perform an autopsy on the body of one Peter Paige?

DR. ZUGIBE: Yes, I did.

DA: And when did you first observe the body of the Brinks guard, Peter Paige?

DR. ZUGIBE: I went to the scene at the mall in Nanuet, and I first observed him there.

DA: What condition was he in when you first saw him, doctor?

DR. ZUGIBE: Well, he was lying in a supine position, and he was, of course, he was dead at that particular time, and he was in—he was estimated to have been dead about, oh, about two hours.

DA: Could you please tell us what your autopsy revealed?

DR. ZUGIBE: Yes. The autopsy revealed the following. The wound that we noted at the base of the victim's neck, on the left side, literally destroyed the bottom part of his neck musculature, the platysma muscle and the scalene muscle. The first one-third of the collarbone was gone, was missing. It had literally exploded, leaving a large crater of a hole under the skin that you couldn't see from the outside of the body.

DA: Yes.

DR. ZUGIBE: The subclavian artery, which is the artery that comes off the arch from the heart that goes into the right arm, had a big chunk right out of it, literally missing out of the front of that artery. The carotid artery likewise was transected in half, that is, cut in half, and also had a large piece missing from the front of it.

DA: Sir, what is the carotid artery?

DR. ZUGIBE: The main artery that carries blood from the heart to the brain, right up through the neck. It had a chunk right out of it. In addition to that the trachea, or windpipe—the first two cartilages had a big hole right in the middle. The cartilages of the voice box, the larynx, also were destroyed. The ribs from number one through five were shattered on the right side of that region.

DA: Is there more?

DR. ZUGIBE: [There was an entrance hole] just above the knee of the right leg. But it was very interesting—the bullet hole that went through the pants over that area was only the size of a regular bullet hole. But right under the skin, there we have this big round opening. The bullet, in other words, went through the leg, and it shattered the femur, which is the major bone in the thigh. It exited near the back part of the thigh, and it was a big, big crater exit, about three times the size of the bullet hole going in.

HIGH-VELOCITY FORENSICS

At this point in his questioning, the DA asks me to elaborate on how such an injury is produced—a small, perfectly round hole made where the bullet enters, then a vast, shaftlike cavity carved out directly beneath the skin.

I reply that a high-velocity rifle shooting soft-nosed bullets made the wounds found on the body of the Brinks security guard, Peter Paige.

A high-velocity bullet travels at speeds of 1,200 to 3,000 feet per second. At maximum this means that a high-velocity missile crosses the length of ten football fields in a single second. Examples of such weapons include automatic pistols and service rifles. Bullets shot from low-velocity firearms, on the other hand, such as a revolver, travel from muzzle to target at around 600 feet per second.

High-velocity attack weapons, it is interesting to note, work by means of a spring mechanism that pops cartridges into an empty breech, then ejects the used cartridges after each shot. Forensically, there is an important distinction to be made here, since casings from an automatic firearm are often left at the scene of a crime, either because the shooters do not have the time or presence of mind to gather them up, or because they simply don't care, as in the case of the Brinks robbers.

On the other hand, the casings from cartridges fired out of a revolver

are not ejected, but remain in the drum of the gun until someone empties them by hand. For someone who *intends* to commit a shooting, the
fact that a revolver automatically avoids leaving a trail of casings behind
makes it, in a sense, a lower-risk weapon than an automatic.

As I told the court, the ammunition fired by the high-velocity
weapons used in the Brinks robbery is of a special kind, a type that comes
enclosed in a very soft casing.

The DA asks about the significance of such a casing.

I explain that most bullets are enclosed in a hard copper casing.
When fired into a human being, such bullets pass straight through the
body without causing a great deal of internal shredding or ripping.

A soft-nosed bullet, on the other hand, is not enclosed in a copper
jacket, and when fired by a high-velocity automatic weapon is moving
extraordinarily fast. When such a projectile strikes a thin, soft object,
such as a piece of clothing worn over human skin, it passes through the
material neatly, making a hole no larger than the bullet itself. But once a
soft-nosed projectile enters a person's body and strikes hard tissue or a
piece of bone, it instantly and quite voluminously explodes, producing
what we call a "star burst" pattern, splitting into hundreds of fragments,
ripping out a gaping crater directly under the skin, and often virtually
blowing apart a person's insides.

In a preplanned criminal attack, I add, assailants intending to do
as much damage as possible often use attack weapons that fire such bullets.

The DA asks me to explain further.

I continue: Even if the victim of a soft-nosed bullet is not struck directly in the chest, say, or in the neck, the internal wreckage inflicted by
soft ordnance is so devastating and encompassing that a single high-
velocity missile hitting the thigh can destroy the entire leg.

It is this type of high-velocity, soft, exploding bullet, I tell the DA,
that created the gaping wounds on the undersurfaces of Peter Paige's
body, and that practically tore the left arm off Joe Trombino.

After my testimony on the Paige autopsy, the line of questioning
switches to the autopsy of Police Officer Waverly Brown.

Referring the jury to several blowups of photographs taken of Officer Brown's corpse at his autopsy, the DA asks whether I conducted this examination.

I tell him I did.

DA: Could you please tell us what the results of your autopsy [of Waverly Brown] were, doctor?

DR. ZUGIBE: Yes. First of all, the wounds that were noted were just about at the armpit area. Then they went through the pectoral muscle—that's the major muscle of the chest here [pointing to the photograph]. It went through that area, and it literally exploded at that time, causing a great big hole, and shattering about five ribs in that region. It left a big, big opening. It actually had conducted the kinetic energy of the bullet to about five ribs, leaving a big hole.

DA: There were also other wounds?

DR. ZUGIBE: The other opening in the back of the arm, in the triceps, went through that muscle and entered the chest area. Here it proceeded to destroy the upper and lower lobes of the lung. Then it entered the sac around the heart, and continued on to transect the aorta, which is the largest artery of the body as it comes off the heart and pulmonary artery right next to it. As a result of this massive wound the chest cavity was filled with blood.

DA: And the other?

DR. ZUGIBE: Then we proceeded to dissect the leg area. We noted from the trajectory of the bullet that the individual was shot lying on his belly flat down. Someone stood near his feet and shot him in the direction where the bullet traversed, in the hamstring muscles of the back in an upper angle toward the hip. Here we found the bullet, a .9 mm bullet, at a point just under the crest of the ileum, which is the rounded area of the hip.

DA: Were you able to form an opinion as to what caused these injuries to Officer Brown?

DR. ZUGIBE: Yes. The same type of ammunition as I previously indicated in the case of Mr. Paige.

DA: In the course of your autopsy of Officer Brown did you recover any spent ammunition that did not exit his body?

DR. ZUGIBE: Yes, I did.

DA: What kind of ammunition was it?

DR. ZUGIBE: Well, I had five pieces of—five pieces of part of the ammunition that did strike his chest area which I recovered, and I also discovered or recovered a .9 mm slug from the—from just below the hip area.

DA: In addition to this .9 mm slug that you recovered, were you able to form an opinion as to what caused the other wounds in his body, what type of ammunition caused the other wounds in his body?

DR. ZUGIBE: Other than the .9 mm one that caused the wound to the buttock just below the hip, the other ones, the other wounds that he had—two wounds—well, they were in the region just below the armpit here. They were all from a high-powered, high-velocity rifle.

CONVICTION IS IN THE DETAILS

This testimony may seem scientifically matter-of-fact and not particularly incriminating of any particular defendant. It seems to simply state that the two lawmen died that day because their organs were destroyed by bullets fired from guns. In fact, the jury has much critical forensic information here to mull over, and to found its judgments on.

For example, given the weapons known to have been used by the assailants on the day of the robbery, the prosecution asserts that the soft-nosed bullets that killed Paige and Brown could only have been fired by an M-16 automatic rifle. And witnesses report that only two men were seen firing M-16s during the robbery; one was Donald Weems, a defendant in the Goshen courthouse. The other M-16 shooter was identified by witnesses as Samuel Brown. Brown is not a defendant in the Goshen trial; he will face prosecution soon afterward in a Westchester County court. At his trial, I give the same evidence concerning the ordnance use and the type of injuries sustained during the robbery. Called to the witness stand, Brown limply attempts to rebut this evidence by insisting to the jury that he ended up in the U-Haul by mistake, and that he was sleeping when the gun battle began. But several witnesses identify him as one of the men firing an automatic weapon both at the scene of the robbery and during the shootout near the Thruway ramp.

In short, the seemingly incidental forensic information concerning entry wounds, exit wounds, weapons, and bullet types helps bring to justice the two Brinks robbers who did the actual killing.

Due to ballistic evidence and much incriminating testimony from witnesses, both are convicted, and both receive long sentences that are tantamount to life in prison. Samuel Brown dies in prison in 1986, of AIDS.

IRONIC POSTSCRIPTS

On the same day at the Goshen trial, David Gilbert and Kathy Boudin are also convicted. Before being transported to prison, they are allowed to exchange marriage vows at the Orange County jail.

Gilbert receives a sentence of seventy-five years; he is serving his term in Attica Prison in upstate New York. In a recent essay he contributed to a book on radical movements in America, Gilbert remains faithful to his revolutionary ideals, and unrepentant for the part he played in the killing of three innocent men.

Boudin receives a substantial sentence as well. But, in a flurry of debate and media hysteria, she is granted parole in the summer of 2003, at the age of sixty. To this day protests are held against this decision by police and family members of the murdered Brinks victims.

Perhaps the saddest of all addendums to this tale is that of Joe Trombino, the Brinks guard whose arm was mangled during the robbery in Nanuet.

Forty-seven years old at the time of the shooting, Trombino undergoes three surgeries and a good deal of agonizing therapy to help save his left arm. After two years of rehabilitation he is fit to return to work as a Brinks armed guard. Trombino is delighted at getting a second chance.

"He'd done that for so long," his wife, Jean, is quoted as saying, "it was like he didn't know what else to do."

Then one sparklingly clear, sunny late-summer day in 2001, at the age of sixty-eight, Joe Trombino, still working for Brinks and still going strong, pulls his truck up to the curb of a very tall Manhattan building for an eleventh-floor pickup.

Entering the building around nine A.M., he is not inside very long when the walls begin to vibrate strangely and water pours down from the upper floors. Finding a pay phone, Trombino calls the Brinks operation center, but suddenly the phone goes dead.

A few moments later, the World Trade Center collapses on top of him.

The day is September 11.

CHAPTER 6

Money, Cigarettes, and Telltale Shoes
Solving the Gas Station Killing

> It's disgusting, very bad that money and
> cigarettes are more valuable than being a
> human being.
>
> —AKRAM MOHAMMED, THE VICTIM'S ROOMMATE

THE GAS STATION FROM HELL

IT'S SIX IN THE MORNING ON MARCH 3, 1992.

A passing motorist stops at the Sunoco Skyview Service Center in Pearl River, New York. He pumps his own gas, then looks around for an attendant to pay. The station appears to be deserted.

In the early morning darkness, the motorist walks over to one of the open garage bays. Entering the gloomy premises, he is overwhelmed by the odor of gasoline and chemical fumes. He glances around. Then he freezes.

Near a station wagon parked on a lift, the mangled body of a thirty-nine-year-old attendant is sprawled on the cement floor, face up, in a pool of blood.

The motorist runs to a phone booth and calls 911. The police and photographers are soon on the scene. Several minutes later, I arrive with my crew. We cordon off the crime scene and police start turning away morning motorists. One of them stops at the station, and climbs out of his car fuming. Elbowing his way through the police tape, he starts cursing at a patrolman, hollering that his car is out of gas and that he will be late for work if he can't fill up. The policeman promptly arrests him for crossing a police line and disturbing the peace.

It is now around seven A.M. I enter the building and am overcome by a wave of acrid chemical smells. Bending over the victim, I see he has not yet gone into rigor mortis; since rigor generally begins from three to six hours after death, he can have been dead no longer than about six hours. Parts of his body are still warm, and some of the blood oozing from his wounds has not yet congealed. I estimate he was attacked and killed approximately three hours ago, around four in the morning.

I also see that there are so many injuries covering this poor man's corpse that it is impossible to take account of them all here at the scene. Most obvious is the cavernous wound where some sharp object has been plunged into his chest. Two other gaping stab wounds are also prominent in the chest area. And I see one in his neck.

It likewise appears that the victim has been bludgeoned repeatedly across his torso with a rod or stick. His jaw is fractured in several places, and small puncture wounds pock his face in odd, puzzling patterns. His skull has been shattered, actually pounded in, by what we suspect is the top of a garbage can. His mouth is wide and gaping, showing that several teeth have been knocked out of his head. His face, hair, ears, and neck are smeared with oil and dried and liquid blood. His facial features are almost indistinguishable beneath the bruises, welts, and variety of greasy fluids that cover them. A semidried stream of blood leaks from the holes in his body, tracing a meandering red line that leads into a runoff drain on the cement floor of the garage.

Finally, the murdered man's eyes appear to have been burned and sealed shut by some caustic industrial fluid that has actually melted the flesh along his lids. The skin on his face is red, and blackened with corrosion burns. The origin of the choking chemical smells I encountered when entering the garage is now apparent.

On and on goes the list of wounds—all inflicted, I later learn, for a roll of quarters, two propane lighters, fifty dollars from the dead man's pocket, and four packs of cigarettes. The rest of the station's money is locked up in the office safe. There are no signs it has been tampered with.

So many wounds and welts on a murdered body are unusual. I have the feeling that the killer kept stabbing and beating the victim after he was clinically dead. The whole scene has the look of an amateur robbery performed by bungling sadists.

The next day a reporter who was at the scene of the crime writes that "Rockland County Medical Examiner Dr. Frederick Zugibe remarked today that the 'victim's entire head—it was like taking an egg and dropping it on the floor. The dead man's eyes were sealed, and his corneas burned away by an acid like substance.' According to Dr. Zugibe, 'This is the most brutally beaten corpse I have ever seen. The most brutal killing.' "

A VERY QUIET MAN

It is the most brutal killing I have seen in all my years as medical examiner. Standing in the shadows of the station, gazing down at the leftovers of what once was a man, I have the fleeting thought that perhaps I am in the wrong profession.

Then I remember: There is a need for what we do in forensic pathology. I have a purpose. I can find the person who performed this act, so scornful and belittling of the human spirit. I can help.

After inspecting the body, I take a look around the gas station.

Its condition mirrors the savageness of the attack. Pieces of shattered glass cover the shelves and counters. Blood and grease are spattered on the walls. The victim's bloody jacket and sweater are heaped beneath a wooden workbench. Near the body lies a pneumatic coupling device with a short length of hose attached to it, along with a thick broomstick with a jagged piece broken off. A small white metal drum lies on its side near the victim's head, still leaking occasional drops of fluid and emitting a strong chemical odor. Pieces of teeth and shreds of hair are strewn about the floor, and cans and boxes of automotive merchandise have fallen from the shelves, disgorging their contents over the chairs and tables. The drawer of the cash register has been pried open in a clumsy way, and its read-out window is smashed.

We judge that the struggle and killing took place in the office. Then the dead man's body was dragged twelve feet into the adjoining garage.

It also appears from the mayhem left behind that the station attendant, a short but heavyset man, put up a fight before he was beaten and stabbed. His name, we learn from a co-worker, is Liaquat Ali. He was a Pakistani immigrant who lived with several of his friends in the nearby town of Spring Valley.

Ali came to the United States almost a year ago to escape political persecution in Pakistan, where his wife, sons, and daughter still live. He was working two jobs to support his family back home, the attendant tells us, one during the day, this job at the Skyview station at night.

"He was a very quiet man," Liaquat Ali's cousin tells the press. "Never yelled at anybody. He was thinking to go back to visit his family soon."

THE TWO SUSPECTS

My crew and I set to work immediately, searching the area for clues and collecting evidence. A comprehensive set of photographs is taken of the entire gas station before we remove the body. We also place paper bags over the victim's hands and feet to protect them from contact with external objects (such as other people's hands).

Back to the medical examiner's office with the corpse goes an assortment of possible weapons found nearby, all of which our lab will test for blood, fingerprints, hair, chemicals, and other traces of the victim or the killers or both. These items include the pneumatic coupling and hose, various empty plastic containers, a piece of wire found under the victim's head, and the broom handle with its broken fragment, among other items. Each object is placed in a plastic bag and labeled for study.

As we return to our office and prepare for the autopsy, the DA's office calls to inform me that a large number of possible suspects have been brought to the police station for questioning, and that two of them are being booked on suspicion of murder.

The first suspect, Michael Moore, age twenty-five, breaks down and cries during his arraignment as he is charged with second-degree murder and first-degree robbery. When asked why he is crying he claims he has a bad headache. Moore, it turns out, was charged the previous fall with criminal possession of a weapon. That case is currently pending in the Spring Valley Justice Court.

The second suspect, Raymond Navarro, oddly sporting the same-sounding name as a long-forgotten silent film star, shows no emotion of any sort. Both men have been in trouble with the law before, and both are known drug users. They are also friends. We surmise that the robbery was motivated by the search for drug money.

During the inquiry it is established that seven months ago Navarro worked at the Skyview gas station. He is familiar with the hours the station keeps, and with its physical layout. He and Ali knew each other slightly.

Both Moore and Navarro were seen in the area of the Skyview on the night of the killing. Navarro, we also learn, was convicted a few years earlier of second-degree burglary, and the year before that of harassment.

The two suspects are brought to the Rockland County Correctional Center and held there without bail.

At this early stage of the investigation, there is no hard evidence against either suspect. When they are examined for hair, fingerprints, blood, and other evidence of contact with the slain man, both come up clean. There are no incriminating spots or stains on their clothing.

Both men also have alibis, if thin ones. Neither has an obvious motive to kill Liaquat Ali, especially in such a savage way. When the suspects' apartments are searched, nothing belonging to the murdered man is found. Though Navarro and Ali are acquainted, the relationship seems to be casual at best. Finally, while both suspects are drug users, no drugs are found in their possession. If a case is to be made against Navarro and Moore, it must now be made on a forensic level.

At the arraignment, both men plead not guilty.

PLANNING A FORENSIC STRATEGY

The autopsy of Liaquat Ali is a complex affair that fills our inventory list with descriptions of bruises, cuts, lacerations, abrasions, stab marks, beating marks, fractures, and bone crushings.

The victim's face is badly swollen. Both eyes contain dried blood, and are literally glued shut from a corrosive ammonia-based chemical that is identified in the toxicology lab as carburetor cleaning fluid. The victim's nose is fractured, along with his jaw and skull. There are several stab wounds in his neck that penetrate his thyroid and larynx up to the base of the epiglottis. X rays reveal that two of the gaping stab wounds in his chest extend into the heart. The third is through his lung.

After examining these injuries and the victim's inner organs, we decide that the best way to proceed from here is to take a two-pronged approach.

First, we will analyze the victim's "patterned injuries." Patterned injuries are markings made on a murdered body by a weapon. The study of these markings should help us identify the objects used to attack Ali. Once we identify the weapons, we can then look for incriminating traces or markings on them that will help us link the murderer to the murdered.

Second, we will send out any suspicious items we find for DNA fingerprinting to determine whether these substances or objects can somehow be tied to the killers.

Putting these two techniques—patterned injury examination and DNA testing—together, we have strong expectations of gaining definitive, or at least suggestive knowledge, of

- how Liaquat Ali was killed
- what he was killed with
- who killed him

THE ART OF PATTERNED INJURY FORENSICS

The study of patterned injuries, of matching up wounds or marks on a body with the objects that made them—is one of the most potent tools in the forensic scientist's arsenal. This procedure usually entails searching for a fit between the shape of a killing instrument and the shape of a victim's wound.

But not always.

Revealing patterns may be left behind in a number of ways, and sometimes these patterns are not even located on the victim's body.

In one case, for example, a wad of chewed gum was found several feet away from a murder victim. A forensic odontologist was called in. Two men had been arrested as possible suspects; to find out whether either one was the chewer of the discarded gum, the odontologist made a silicone impression of the chew marks on the wad, then of both men's teeth.

Sure enough, the marks on the chewing gum fit the teeth of one suspect as a handprint in clay fits the hand that made it. Saliva identification tests followed, and these too were a match. Faced with this overwhelming evidence, the man entered a guilty plea.

Many times, of course, tooth markings are made directly on a victim's body by a human bite. In such cases, forensic odontologists compare the bite marks with dental impressions from a suspect.

Biting of the victim is most common in specific kinds of homicides. "Most bite marks," Vernon Geberth tells us in *Practical Homicide Investigation,* "are found in the following types of homicides: (1) the homicide victim involved in sexual activity around the time of death; and (2) the battered-child homicide victim."

Geberth goes on to say that there are two basic bite-mark patterns. The first is inflicted slowly and sadistically, and can be identified by a "suck mark" around the bitten area. There is usually a good deal of tearing and shredding of the skin in such bites, which sometimes makes it difficult for odontologists to take clear dental impressions. The second type of bite displays no suck marks, and usually leaves clear and identifiable teeth imprints behind.

In sex murders of men by men, bite marks are most commonly found on the victim's back, arms, shoulders, armpits, face, and scrotum. On battered children they scar the abdomen, scrotum, and buttocks, and are often done in a rapid and enraged manner, ripping skin and lacerating tissue. In sex murders of women by men, bites most commonly take place during rape and tend to be inflicted on the breasts, the inner thighs, and the vulva.

Although in most cases bite marks appear on the body of the victim, the tables can sometimes be turned, with the victim biting the assailant in self-defense. In one well-known case, a young woman was kidnapped and raped by her abductor inside his customized van. During her ordeal, she had the presence of mind to bite down hard on the rubber casing that ringed the frame of the van window, leaving a permanent imprint.

The man who was accused of committing this rape was eventually convicted by the woman's tooth marks, found in his van on the window rubber where she had left them two years earlier.

THE COOKIE CUTTER

In my own career, I recall one case in particular where injury pattern matching alone solved a homicide.

The case was known as the Cookie Cutter Case, and for good reason. Three individuals lured a thirty-six-year-old machinist from a local bar to their apartment with the promise of a big cocaine sell. The dealers planned to substitute a worthless powder for the cocaine, but when they discovered that the intended scam victim had no money they became enraged. They dragged him downstairs to the back of their apartment, beat him up, stuffed him in the trunk of his own car, and drove him to a secluded area along the Hudson River that is used as a local dump. Here they beat the machinist across the face until he died; then they jammed his body under a discarded sofa.

Several days passed. The man's body was discovered, brought to our office, and autopsied. There were no suspects so far, and the instruments used in the murder were nowhere in evidence.

Then an acquaintance of the victim spotted his friend's automobile parked in the driveway of one of the killers. Knowing that his friend was murdered, he called the police, who found a bumper jack and other automotive tools in the trunk. The three cocaine sellers were arrested.

During the autopsy, I had noticed that one of the wounds on the victim's face had a peculiar U shape, with a deep indentation in the bottom of the U. The wound was so crisply carved out it looked as if it had been made by a cookie cutter.

On a hunch, I took another look at the tools from the back of the victim's car. Sure enough, the shaft on the automobile's bumper jack was

U-shaped at either end. Examining the jack for traces of body tissue, I found coagulated blood mixed with a greasy substance identified as keratin, a tough outer layer of the skin. Using a specialized histochemical test, we established that the keratin was human in origin.

Next, using dental casting material that sets with almost no shrinkage, I made a negative cast of the U-shaped end of the jack. Then I used a low-melting-point metal to make a positive cast from the first impression.

Finally, I surgically removed a swatch of skin from the victim's face where the U-shaped wounds were located.

I placed the patch of skin with the U-shaped wound over the cast of the jack shaft.

It was a perfect fit.

Since the jack was found in the trunk of the murdered man's car; since it contained tissue cells and human keratin; and since the car, in turn, was found in the driveway of one of the suspected drug dealers, all three men were charged with murder—and, eventually, convicted.

INSTRUMENTS OF DOOM

Still another kind of injury pattern matching helps me to close the net on the suspects in the gas station murders.

From the autopsy, I determine that the cause of Liaquat Ali's death is brain trauma and hemorrhaging due to beating and stabbing.

But what objects have caused these wounds?

During the autopsy, several sets of abrasions are found on the upper portion of Liaquat Ali's torso. One set forms a ladderlike line of deep, evenly spaced cuts. Two other abrasions beneath and to either side of these cuts are shaped like rectangles. Below and between these rectangles is the imprint of a perfect circle. These shapes recall the pneumatic coupling device I found next to the victim's body at the scene of the crime.

I take this device and place it over this series of indentations. The superimposition is uncannily precise. The upper part of the coupling, with its nozzle, coupling device, and screw shaft, slips easily into the ladder of cuts. The two rectangular marks under these wounds fit the corners of the coupling's base. A round knob at the base of the coupling superimposes itself on the circular mark.

Here, for certain, is one of the weapons the killers used to beat Ali.

Next, I examine a series of concave contusions on the victim's body. These appear to have been inflicted with a long blunt instrument. Embedded in the wounds are tiny fragments of wood. From similar cases I know that injuries inflicted by wooden dowels or heavy industrial broomsticks appear on a body as long parallel lines. And the contusions on the victim are indeed consistent with the shape of the industrial broomstick found near his body. So that is Weapon Number 2.

Next, I investigate the stab wounds on the victim's chest. Wooden splinters are dug out of these wounds, and the broken end of the broomstick (Weapon Number 2), which is covered with blood, fits perfectly into the stab wounds.

Weapon Number 3 is the broomstick, which was used for stabbing as well as beating.

Then I examine the stab holes in the victim's neck.

These narrow slits with their slightly abraded edges are the work of a blade; there is no doubt about it. Since no cutlery was found at the scene of the crime, I record these marks as "probable" knife wounds, hoping that the actual weapon will be discovered in the course of the investigation. (Indeed, a few days later a knife is found in the back of Michael Moore's car. Precision measurements indicate that this knife is consistent with the size of the slit marks on the victim's neck. The knife also tests positive for blood, but there is not enough blood on the blade to determine its type.)

Finally, where is the garbage can lid that was used to smash in Liaquat Ali's skull? It is nowhere to be seen on the garage premises, and despite much searching is simply never found.

Still, we have four out of five murder weapons. Enough to make a quorum.

FORENSIC LIGHT TECHNIQUES

Up to this point in the autopsy we have determined the cause of death and identified the murder weapons. Because the knife in Michael

Moore's car has not yet been found, we still have no links between this evidence and suspects.

Then, a breakthrough.

After matching up the injuries to the instruments, I place the naked body of the victim on a table and perform a routine procedure, examining his corpse under various types of light, moving down his body quadrant by quadrant, searching for suspicious markings.

In general, normal incandescent light reveals the obvious marks that can be seen in the light of day or under a floodlight. Under a strong normal light, Ali's body reveals nothing unusual.

I try indirect lighting, hoping that in the shadows and strange shapes that an angled dim light makes an evidentiary surprise will appear; but there is nothing significant here either.

The third lighting alternative, fluorescence, is more high-tech, involving a special high-wave blue light. When fluorescent light strikes human skin, some of the light is reflected off while some travels into deeper layers of the skin. The atoms in these deeper layers absorb the light and enter a state of atomic excitement, vibrating more quickly than usual.

When this excitation period ends, residual electric energy is released from the skin cells stimulated by all the movement. This energy makes the cadaver literally glow. It is an eerie effect. In the process, latent patterned injuries that might go unnoticed in ordinary light can be seen quite clearly. Using fluorescence, for instance, fibers invisible to the naked eye, tiny bits of debris, a single hair, a microscopically small dot of semen, even fingerprints reveal themselves.

I fluoresce the corpse of Liaquat Ali; disappointingly, no unusual marks or stains appear, even though I study his body for some minutes.

Finally, I decide to employ a light-detection method known as narrow-band imaging (NBI), which uses ultraviolet light as its source.

Ultraviolet light—or, more accurately, ultraviolet radiation—is a wavelength or vibration level that on the electromagnetic scale occupies a wave band situated one band above ordinary daylight. Produced naturally by the sun (it wreaks havoc on unprotected sunbathers' skin), ultraviolet light can be generated in the lab by artificial sources such as mercury vapor lamps and black tubes.

Using this technique, a number of organic compounds such as semen, urine, and saliva absorb light in the ultraviolet spectrum, becoming visible to the examiner. Blood itself does not fluoresce. But it does appear darker under ultraviolet light examination, and so may be identified by this test as well.

Besides revealing human fluids, old scars, and ligature marks, plus tangible leftovers such as paper fibers and dried ink on old documents, NBI does something even more pertinent to my goals: it shows handprints, footprints, and shoe prints made on a body.

HIDDEN LETTERS

I beam the ultraviolet light directly on the abdomen, and this time, yes, definitely, a patterned impression appears that is consistent with the sole and heel of a shoe. A faint outline on the right edge of the sole containing dirt or greaselike markings is noted.

Most meaningfully, beginning at 1.5 centimeters below the dead man's navel, a series of letters running in a vertical line can plainly be seen.

Using a reticule—a magnifying loop with calibrated markings on the lens for taking exact measurements—I can see that the lower letter in this sequence is an "N," and that it measures 3 centimeters by 1.4 centimeters.

Above it is a letter "I" of the same size, and above this an incomplete "K," also of the same dimensions. The last letter is indistinguishable.

Finally, on the heel of the shoeprint I find the patterned impression of a shoe tread.

It is all here before me.

Despite the missing last letter, the math is easy to do.

First, I have the imprint of the sole of a shoe. I know its size and its partial outline.

Second, the sole of this shoe has treads on it, the kind you see on sporting-type footwear.

Finally, I can see that the three letters clearly spell out N-I-K.

Adding an imaginary "E" to this series, I derive the magic name NIKE, one of the most popular and high-profile brands of sneakers in the world.

I inform the police detectives working on the case of this evidence, and ask them to bring to the lab any sneakers they can find that are owned by the suspects.

Less than an hour later, while the autopsy is still in progress, two detectives arrive carrying a bag with a pair of sneakers belonging to Raymond Navarro. I turn over one of the shoes, and to my delight find the conspicuous Nike mark imprinted on its sole. Further visual and microscopic examination of the shoe quickly establishes that it has the same length and style as the sneaker impression found on the murdered man's abdomen, though no visible blood is discovered.

We set a thin layer of plastic sandwich wrap over the sneaker impression on the corpse's abdomen, to prevent contamination. The sole of Navarro's sneaker is then placed directly over the shoe impression on the dead man's abdomen. The letters N-I-K seen under the ultraviolet light match perfectly, as do the heel and the visible part of the sole outline. Finally, we examine and measure the letters on the sneakers with the reticule. They are of the same dimensions as the letters impressed on the body.

Later on, after the area is measured and photographed, a gentle washing of the body reveals that most of the letters and tread patterns are permanently contused, not just stamped with dirt and blood.

Poor Liaquat Ali. He was not simply walked on in the course of his beating and torture; he was stomped on with enormous force on the softest and most vulnerable part of his body, almost definitely by Navarro, who owns the sneakers. I theorize that this stomping was a kind of grand finale, done on a physical level to make sure the victim was dead, and on a figurative level to seal the deed, just as a judge brings down the gavel at the end of a trial.

What Navarro did not know was that by taking this last brutal swipe at his mauled victim he was leaving a signature that could be read, deciphered, and used to bring him down.

DNA TELLS ALL

Although no blood cells are observed on the shoe soles under the dissecting microscope, I know that if this sneaker belongs to the perpetrator, blood cells must nevertheless be present. The testing methods I normally employ are designed to demonstrate that a blood sample does not belong to a given person. The only way to prove that blood does belong to a given individual is DNA fingerprinting.

Before I approach this fascinating and somewhat complex subject, I should note that when even the tiniest amount of blood is left at the scene of a crime (or anywhere else, for that matter) it is extremely difficult to remove entirely. It does not matter what kind of surface the blood is on—glass, plastic, linoleum, paper. Wipe it, wash it, disinfect it, douse it with acid or lye, sandpaper it, sandblast it—no matter. A few cells can usually be found.

Even more remarkably, dried vestiges can remain on certain surfaces for extremely long periods of time. By the reckoning of a generation or even of a lifetime, they never disappear at all. Forensic anthropologists are often able to find and analyze dried blood traces found on bodies that date back to the Bronze Age.

Blood is indeed thicker than water, and more viscous—it sticks, a tremendous boon for forensic pathologists, especially in a killing like this one.

I send the telltale sneakers up to a DNA laboratory I frequently use, which is associated with Harvard University. Along with them go the broken broom handle, the hose and coupler, and a sample of Liaquat Ali's blood.

Explicit instructions are provided: Search for the victim's DNA on these items using the Polymerase Chain Reaction (PCR) technique.

THE ANATOMY OF DNA FINGERPRINTING

DNA "fingerprinting" has nothing to do with actual fingerprints; the term simply means profiling or identifying. It is, of course, a relatively new scientific tool, and is still sometimes controversial. Though it became a byword among the public during the O. J. Simpson trial in 1995, it was first developed a decade earlier, in England.

The basic principle of DNA testing is that every human being who is now alive, or who has ever lived throughout all time, owns a unique set of genes. Every cell of every human being contains a code unique to that individual, like the bar codes on supermarket products.

This DNA—deoxyribonucleic acid—is the principal carrier of ge-netic data in human beings and in almost all other living organisms (with the exception of certain viruses). When studied through an elec-tron microscope, its shape is that of a spiraling rope ladder, scientifically known as a double helix.

Because each person's DNA is unique, when samples are taken from blood, semen, or other bodily fluids at a crime scene or during an au-topsy, and are then compared with the DNA of either the victim or the victim's suspected killer, a match is either made, or not. If it *is* made, then the degree of certainty that this DNA belongs to this person is au-thoritative. By that I mean that the standard for most DNA testing is that there be no more than one in a million chances that the test is in error. In practical terms, this means there is little or no chance for error at all.

This one-in-a-million standard, moreover, is conservative.

In DNA tests, possible error is ranked at one in 5 million, or some-times one in 10 million, reassuring numbers for forensic pathologists.

How does DNA fingerprinting work?

Two types of procedure are currently used in crime laboratories. The first, known as restriction fragment length polymorphism or RFLP, was the first DNA test developed. To conduct this test, the technician ex-tracts a sample of DNA from the blood, semen, or other parts of the vic-tim or suspect. Enzymes are used to slice the sample into fragments, which are then suspended in a gel. Next, the fragments are put through a kind of electronic strainer to sort them by size. Then they are sucked up by a blotting process onto a membrane.

This membrane is placed over an X-ray film. A radiation process ex-poses the film and produces images of the DNA fragments. A match is made when the patterns taken from the DNA sample found at the crime scene fit those of the victim or suspect.

Though RFLP was a miracle in its time, it has its limits. A large sample is needed to get reasonable readings. The wait is long, taking up to six weeks or longer to produce results, and in the process, the techni-cians who run the tests are exposed to various amounts of radiation.

A quicker and in some ways more efficient method of DNA testing, polymerase chain reaction (PCR), is also used today, especially when a sample is too small for RFLP, or when a blood sample has become degraded.

The PCR method of DNA fingerprinting makes use of the self-replicating nature of DNA, which allows one strand of DNA to copy itself. In the first step of PCR, a machine called a thermocycler heats a single double helix of DNA until its two intertwining strands separate.

Next, an enzyme (originally extracted from scummy pond water) constructs two new strands of DNA, using the original strands as templates.

Finally, single strands of identical DNA known as primers are produced that assemble themselves into longer molecule chains. This process results in the duplication of the original DNA. From this point on, the procedure can be repeated many times, with each DNA strand creating two new copies, and so on and so forth, until the numbers of strands reach the billions in a matter of hours.

These extracted DNA strands are then compared with samples from the subject in question, and a match either is made, or is not.

In the DNA lab, the materials taken from the garage crime scene are tested and a DNA match is made. The blood on the sneakers and weapons definitely belongs to Liaquat Ali.

We have caught one of our men, at least. He is the owner of the sneakers.

THE LONGEST SENTENCE

From now on, the story is simply one of crime and punishment.

During preliminary questioning and at the separate trials of Moore and Navarro, the sequence of events that night at the Skyview gas station is slowly pieced together from the suspects' lies, pleas, admissions, and mutual accusations.

Navarro admits to the police that the robbery was his idea. (He later retracts this admission.)

The plan, he tells questioners, was for him to walk casually into the gas station and to engage his "friend" Ali in conversation.

Moore was to follow a moment or two later and order the attendant to fall to the floor while Navarro pretended to be an innocent bystander. Moore was to grab the cash from the register and take off. But the plans quickly went awry when Ali, instead of hitting the floor as ordered, took a swing at Moore. Reading the situation too well, he also went after Navarro.

Enraged, Navarro tossed commercial carburetor cleaner into Ali's eyes, blinding him on the spot.

Moore beat Ali with his fists, then with the broom and garage tools, while Navarro attempted to jimmy open the cash register. In the struggle, one of the assailants knifed Ali in the neck.

Who actually did the stabbing is never learned. At his trial, Moore claims that the knife found in his automobile was a plant. Navarro counters that Moore used the knife, then hid it in his car. Navarro claims he struck Ali only when he thought the attendant intended to injure Moore. Moore tells police he was prying open the cash register while Navarro was busy mauling Ali and killing him.

Each man claims to be the dupe of the other, a reluctant puppet of a sadistic and determined mastermind. Each claims to have tried to stop the other from hurting the victim so badly. Each accuses the other of killing Ali, of hatching the plot, and of inflicting most of the physical damage.

After some deliberation, the jury decides that Moore was the murderer and ringleader. Chief DA Kenneth Gribetz, observing that the accused "has shown no remorse whatsoever," asks the presiding judge, Judge Meehan, to impose the maximum sentence for both men.

Little persuasion is needed. Moore gets twenty-five years to life.

A few months later, at his trial, Navarro receives the same sentence.

It is the harshest sentence ever handed down in the state of New York for a murder that does not involve the killing of a police officer. DA Gribetz has the last word, spoken over the blood and bones of this senseless killing: "My only regret in the outcome of this case," he tells several journalists, "is that the State of New York does not have the death penalty."

CHAPTER 7

Joan

Whoso shall offend one of these little
ones . . . it were better for him that a
millstone were hanged about his neck, and
he were drowned in the depth of the sea.
—MATTHEW 18:6

A LEAFY SPACE BETWEEN TWO BOULDERS

IT IS A SUNDAY IN APRIL 1998.

Rosemarie D'Alessandro is making a pilgrimage to Harriman State Park in upper Rockland County, accompanied by her husband, Michael, and their two sons.

The family has never had the heart to visit the scene of the crime before. They are not even sure exactly where it is. Two police sergeants and a journalist volunteer to escort them.

Making their way down a wooded slope, the sergeants come to an abrupt halt after several minutes and point to a leaf-covered belt of earth in a cleft between two boulders.

"So this is where he put her," Rosemarie says quietly.

She studies the narrow strip of ground for a long time without speaking, then gazes up at the thin stand of trees surrounding the area.

"Well, we'll make sure he stays in jail forever," she says. "He purposefully put her here. This is hidden from the road. This was well thought out."

The two boys tie a green ribbon to a tree next to one of the boulders while Rosemarie and Michael pick up the rusted beer cans and pieces of broken glass that litter the area. Then they clear a small plot of earth in the cleft between the boulders and plant an Easter lily to mark the spot. It was on this same day twenty-five years ago that the body of their seven-year-old daughter, Joan, was found. She had been raped and murdered, and dumped between these two rocks.

"She was just all smiles, very spunky, very bright," Rosemarie reminisces in a quiet voice. "She was for social justice. She was pure love, and I got to know what love was all about because of her."

The family sits quietly together in the warm spring sun for some time. Finally, Rosemarie turns to the journalist. "I get my stamina from never feeling alone," she says. "I get my strength from my daughter. What I go through is nothing compared to what she went through."

A few more minutes pass; then the family stands up in unison.

As they walk slowly away from the site, they can hear the music of running water from nearby Minisceongo Creek. Rosemarie D'Alessandro turns for a last look. The buds on the wild mountain laurel that surround the rocky outcropping where her daughter's body was abandoned twenty-five years ago—and that flower but once every two years—are just beginning to bloom.

This is as it should be. Today is Easter Sunday.

EATEN WHOLE

Who can truly understand the mind of a child killer? Who can fathom the power of berserk instinct unleashed on the innocent?

Psychological theories abound, we know. Scholarly studies on the subject are filled with terms like "irresistible compulsion" and "exploding pent-up rage." Therapists probe deeply into psychopathic childhoods and deviant minds. They study the structure of aberrant sexuality. Yet finally experts and laymen alike stand mute and emptyhanded before the dark landscape of human wickedness; they are left wondering, wondering.

And there is a related mystery too, whose by-product shows up with shocking consistency on the medical examiner's autopsy table. This is the "nice guy" mystery; the "ordinary" man, the "ordinary" woman mystery. The enigma of the cheerful student who works behind the 7-Eleven counter; the grandfatherly retiree you chat with now and then at the Laundromat; the wry nurse at your pediatrician's office; your child's science teacher. All are pleasant people—conventional, normal. They laugh and frown, complain and dream along with the rest of us. Until the day one of these "normal" people lets slip the monstrous inner thing, a creature suddenly, not human, and eats you whole.

"He was always smiling, always willing to help you out," his neighbors in the building tell the police after the ordinary man stalks and kills five teenage girls. "Everyone at the office looked up to her so much," say several co-workers after the ordinary woman drowns her two children. "He is the last person in the world I would suspect of a crime such as he is charged with," says a bystander about the ordinary man who lives on the quiet suburban street near the D'Alessandros.

HAS ANYONE SEEN JOAN?

It is April 19, 1973. Seven-year-old Joan D'Alessandro lives in Hillsdale, a suburban New Jersey village located on the commuter train line to New York City. It has hilly parks and duck ponds; there is a picture-postcard Victorian train station in the center of town.

Joan's story begins on this Thursday before Easter, a holy day for practicing Catholics. Students at the local parish school are given the day off, while students at the public school have to attend classes. Joan is one of the lucky ones.

That afternoon, after a lunch of ricotta cheese and apples, Joan and her older sister, Marie, decide they will spend the next few hours delivering Girl Scout cookies to people who have ordered them on the block. Joan is a member of a local Brownie troop. Marie has graduated to Girl Scout status.

Running from door to door, the sisters drop their cookies off at every neighborhood residence but one, a brown-and-white ranch house three doors away from their own. The occupant, a young man named Joseph McGowan, has not yet returned from Tappan Zee High School in Rockland County where he teaches eleventh-grade chemistry. This delivery will have to wait till later.

After the sisters finish their rounds, Marie heads off to softball practice, while Joan goes home to play in her front yard.

An hour or so passes and then, around 2:45 P.M., Mr. McGowan pulls into his driveway in his imported red sports car.

Joan runs into the kitchen, grabs two boxes of Girl Scout cookies, and shouts, "There's the man who's going to buy my cookies!" to her mother. "I'll be right back," she adds, then runs out the front door and skips down the street to make the final delivery.

When Joan does not come right back, her mother is unconcerned. Joan has many friends on the block, and Hillsdale is known to be one of the safest communities in northern New Jersey.

Then dinnertime rolls around, and Joan is still not home.

Mrs. D'Alessandro starts to worry; soon her worry turns to real anxiety. It is not like Joan to be this late. She and one of Joan's brothers walk over to the McGowan house. They ask Mr. McGowan if he knows where Joan went after dropping the cookies off that afternoon.

Mr. McGowan stands in the doorway, his wavy hair neatly combed, his long sideburns carefully trimmed. He is a large man, six feet two and 200 pounds, but his mild manner and pleasant face give no hint of intimidation.

No, he has not seen Joan at all today, he tells Mrs. D'Alessandro. Right after returning from work he walked to the supermarket, shopped, and did not return home for an hour or so.

"Sorry," he adds, lighting up a slim cigar. "Hope you find her soon. She's a good kid."

At the high school where Joseph McGowan teaches, he meets and talks to young people every day, and is generally well regarded. The twenty-six-year-old bachelor receives positive comments from most of the children on his block, too. When questioned, several local kids describe him as "nice" and "okay." A few are on a first-name basis with him, calling him Joey. Still, a paperboy later tells a journalist that the McGowans—Joseph lives with his mother and elderly grandmother—"are the type of people you waved to and they never waved back."

So he gets mixed reviews—like any ordinary man.

Mrs. D'Alessandro returns home, realizing now that something has definitely happened to Joan en route between her house and the McGowans'. Alarmed, the entire D'Alessandro family now undertakes a house-to-house search of the area. None of the neighbors within a radius of several blocks has seen her that day. It is beginning to get dark.

The family calls the police, who begin their own search of the neighborhood. After midnight, bloodhounds are brought in from a police barracks in Hawthorne, New York, across the Hudson River. The dogs find nothing.

A thirteen-state alarm is now sent out with Joan's description. The alarm reports that at the time of Joan's disappearance she was wearing a turquoise short-sleeved blouse, maroon slacks, and red sneakers with blue and white stripes.

By the next day, Good Friday, fifteen New Jersey police departments, several fire departments, a large group of Veterans of Foreign Wars, and hundreds of civilian volunteers working in teams are launched on a frantic mission to find the vanished child.

The search parties knock on doors, make phone calls, check backyard swimming pools and tennis courts, comb the woods, and rummage through garbage cans. Television crews; priests; reporters; schoolchildren with their parents; the D'Alessandros' cousins, uncles, and aunts who live in the area—all visit the family, offering their support. After several days of such good intentions, so many people have tramped through the house that Mrs. D'Alessandro is prompted to tell a friend that "our carpet changed from tan to dark gray."

HOPES

Then on Friday afternoon a promising lead turns up.

A quarter mile from Joan's house a police detective searching a bus in a school parking lot finds a box of Girl Scout cookies behind a seat, along with a small girl's sneaker.

There is excited buzz for a few hours while the shoe is checked out. But the lead fizzles. It belongs to a little boy who rides the bus every day, and the box of Girl Scout cookies is many months old. The search goes on.

By Saturday morning Detective David Kramer of the Hillsdale police tells the press in a tired voice, "There is nothing to indicate anything right now except that she's gone."

As a last resort, Joan's parents go public: "I am willing to make any arrangements with the people who kidnapped my daughter," Mr. D'Alessandro says on radio and TV. "I'll go anywhere to meet them, and do anything they say. I just want my little girl back."

The parents then sit by the phone, waiting for *the* call.

"I plead with the people who took her either to give her back to us," Joan's mother tells a reporter. "Let us know where we can find her, or just let her go anywhere so somebody can spot her."

During the search period, two mysterious calls come in, one at 8 P.M. Friday, another the following day. In both cases the caller says nothing for several moments, then hangs up. A certain desperate hope arises in the family. If a kidnapper is out there somewhere demanding ransom, Joan is probably alive.

But investigators are dubious. Most ransom kidnappers know exactly what they are doing and what they want. In the investigators' experience, they tell the D'Alessandros, few make calls to the kidnapped person's family, then get cold feet and hang up. It is just not part of the pattern. "Probably a weirdo," says one detective. "You'd be amazed at the number of cruel nuts there are in this world!"

In the end, the attempt to find seven-year-old Joan D'Alessandro turns out to be one of the largest manhunts ever to take place in New Jersey. Thousands of people are involved, many of them top-flight professionals. Yet all the selfless efforts are to no avail. Even the Hillsdale chief of police, Philip Varisco, who has cut short his Florida vacation to join the search team, is pessimistic. "We have no recourse," Varisco tells a group of reporters, "but to believe that the child was abducted. She was not one of those wandering types."

By now it is Saturday night, and the manhunt for Joan has reached stalemate.

Truth be told, there really is no need for hundreds of well-intentioned citizens to hunt for Joan any longer. No need to look under porches and send teams of dogs into the woods. The key to the girl's disappearance lies a good deal closer at hand.

DEATH IN THE DEAD OF NIGHT

At one o'clock in the morning on Easter Sunday, April 22, the desk officer on duty at a Rockland County police headquarters receives a call from the Bergen County Prosecutor's Office. The body of a little girl believed to be Joan D'Alessandro may be situated near an outcropping of rocks, he is told, just off Gate Hill Road in Harriman State Park.

Rockland police are promptly dispatched.

Officer John Forbes, the first to reach the location, discovers the body of a female child lying in a wedge-shaped crevice between two boulders.

Richard Collier, a New York City FBI agent who is a neighbor of the D'Alessandros and a longtime friend of Joan, is sent to Harriman to make an identification. Agent Collier stares at the body for a moment, then nods, expressionless. "Yes, that's right—this is Joan. That's right."

Soon thereafter, I receive a call from the Rockland Medical Examiner's Office, reporting that Joan D'Alessandro's body has been found in an area under my jurisdiction. I quickly get out of bed, dress, and drive to the site, getting there around two A.M.

By this time, the area is cordoned off. Joan D'Alessandro's small body, I can see, lies between two rounded rocks: it is this leafy slope that her family will visit a quarter of a century later. Photographs have been made by the BCI, diagrams drawn, measurements taken, and notations jotted down. However—I suppose because the search for Joan has generated such passion among the public—the crime scene is overpopulated with a variety of detectives, photographers, reporters, police, FBI, gawkers, all milling round and all elephanting over the delicate flora and fauna surrounding the site. At this point I bellow as loudly as I have ever bellowed before: *"I want every unauthorized person out of this area now!"*

After most of the herd scurries away I investigate the immediate area where Joan's little body lies, finding that indeed, irreparable damage has been done to the site. Fortunately, though, from what I can see, Joan's body has not been tampered with or moved. This is the most important thing. I begin my exam.

Now at any setting where a murdered body is found, negative feelings are always common among investigative professionals—including disgust and anger. But dejection and tears are out of place in such a situation. If a medical examiner, or for that matter anyone on a law enforcement team, follows the path of sentiment, professional objectivity is compromised.

Tonight in Harriman, though, the situation is different.

A seven-year-old girl has been murdered, mutilated, and dumped in the woods. She could be my daughter, or your daughter, or a daughter of the police officers who go about their business tonight staring blankly ahead, avoiding each other's eyes, cursing under their breath; few attempt to make conversation of any kind and several wipe away tears. "I almost broke down," Patrolman Forbes is quoted as saying. "I have four children of my own, and this was the saddest sight I've ever seen."

Squatting next to the body and looking it over, I see that Joan is naked and is lying in a partly supine position, with her head twisted hard to the left. Numerous lacerations and bruises cover her skin, especially in the head and neck area. She rests on the incline between two rocks, with her head facing downhill.

The first critical clue I find is inconsistent lividity. Rather than pooling in her back, as we would expect from her position, the blood has congealed in her abdomen, purpling the skin there.

So we know already that Joan was murdered in another location, left in that spot for more than six hours while the blood settled and congealed, then dumped here in Rockland.

Also, Joan is naked and her body temperature more or less matches the air temperature. This tells me she has been dead for at least thirty-six hours, the maximum time it takes for all heat to drain out of a corpse so that it assumes the ambient temperature.

This slow surrender of heat, interestingly, does not follow a consistent pattern. During the three to five hours immediately after a person dies, the body seems almost reluctant to surrender the precious warmth generated by its internal combustion system. Once these initial hours pass, cooling begins in earnest, the rate of heat dissipation depending on several variables.

For example, is the body covered or naked? Is it lying on snow, or in a rain forest? Emaciated people cool more quickly than the obese. And, of special relevance in this situation, the bodies of infants, young children, and elderly persons lose heat more quickly than those of teenagers and adults.

Another important guidepost for determining Joan's time of death is the fact that when her body is found it is entirely out of rigor mortis.

Rigor mortis, the stiffening of muscles after death, is due to a chemical reaction directly dependent on the temperature surrounding a body (the colder the temperature, the more slowly rigor develops). Beginning several hours after all vital signs cease, it is noted first in the facial area, then proceeds to the upper and lower extremities. After twelve hours it is usually complete. Finally, after twenty-four to thirty-six hours, the body passes out of rigor, this time in the reverse sequence, from the bottom of the body to the top.

Generally speaking, the more physical exertion or struggle that takes place before death, the sooner rigor begins. Moreover, the sooner rigor begins, the sooner it passes. In Joan's case, conditions such as outside temperature, body weight, nudity, and wind currents, and the fact that she probably struggled to some extent before her death lead me to estimate that approximately fifty hours have passed since her murder and the body's abandonment.

This time line is pushed up by some hours during the autopsy by the eye potassium degradation test. (See chapter four, "The Slashed-Face

Murder," for an explanation of this test.) Ultimately, I estimate that Joan has been dead for at least seventy hours and probably a bit longer, which means she died on the day she disappeared.

It seems highly likely to me that Joan was murdered an hour or so after she left her house to deliver that last batch of Girl Scout cookies to her neighbor three doors down the block. The enormous search effort made by so many concerned neighbors and law enforcement personnel was futile from the start.

NEATLY FOLDED CLOTHES

After Joan's body has been examined where it lies, we make a thorough search of the nearby area. The most suspicious item is a gray plastic shopping bag lying near her corpse. The word "Mobil" is printed on it in large letters.

The bag contains a sadly familiar inventory of belongings, neatly packed: a pair of red-and-white sneakers, a turquoise-blue shirt, maroon slacks, a set of white socks, rolled up, and a pair of white panties, stained with blood. Joan's slacks are folded so methodically they look as if they have been ironed.

The only other evidence found near the body is a bottle of Cold Duck wine with a label on it from a liquor store in the nearby town of Bardonia. The bottle is open but only a small amount of wine is gone. Nothing indicates that the bottle has been exposed to the weather for more than a day or two. It is sent to the lab for fingerprinting.

My final impression of the scene is that Joan D'Alessandro was abducted, beaten, sexually molested, then strangled. We will know more of the details at the autopsy.

Finished with our on-site examination, the forensic team packs up, and we prepare to drive Joan's body to the lab. First, though, a priest is called to the scene from a local Roman Catholic church. With police detectives, patrolmen, photographers, and FBI agents looking on in the harsh glow of police lights, thinking their private thoughts, the priest quietly gives Joan last rites.

Before we leave, I make the formal declaration, pronouncing her officially dead.

WHEN IS DEATH DEATH?

To persons unfamiliar with forensic protocol, going through the motions of proclaiming a cold, lifeless body officially deceased may seem a needless and pompous redundancy. The fact that criminal inquiry cannot proceed until this declaration is made, no matter how urgent the need for rapid investigation (as in Joan's case), might also seem a matter of red tape run wild.

Until the early 1960s, such criticisms would have been valid. Up to that time, the famous forensic description in *Black's Law Directory* was the standard definition of death, used by just about everyone in the field of criminal investigation. *Black's* described death as "a total stoppage of the circulation of the blood, and a cessation of the animal and vital functions consequent thereupon, such as respiration, pulsation, etc." People were dead, in other words, when their heart stopped beating and their lungs stopped breathing. This definition stood for more than a century, making the determination of death at the scene of a crime a cut-and-dried affair that rarely caused problems for coroners, for the families of the deceased, or for the police.

The 1960s, however, saw the development of heroic technological measures to sustain the heart, lungs, and other organs after all spontaneous electrical activity in the brain had ceased. The first organ transplants were performed, seemingly bringing the dead "back to life." Now the definition of death started to become a less certain affair, and the issue of "When is dead dead?" often became an ethical question as well as a biological one.

From the medical examiner's viewpoint, moreover, when first examining a violated body, certain complications can at times make it difficult to say precisely when and even *if* death has taken place at all. At the scene of the crime, the obvious is once again not always the true.

Suspended animation, for example, sometimes follows on traumatic shock, especially in incidents involving electrocution. All vital signs appear to be shut down, and the victim gives every indication of being quite thoroughly extinguished. Yet far below, in the deepest arteries and channels of the human viscera, a faint pulse continues. The same is true when barbiturates are used in poisonings or attempted suicides. All the classic sights and sounds of life cease; but deep inside the beat goes on, undetectable by all but the most sensitive medical instruments.

Sometimes a person who has apparently drowned, and who shows no signs of physiological activity, is revived minutes later with respiratory aids. Persons submerged in freezing cold water often survive remarkably long periods of oxygen deprivation. In one episode, reported in a 1963 issue of the *British Medical Journal*, a five-year-old boy fell into an icy river and remained under the surface for twenty-two minutes. Pulled to shore and worked on by paramedics, he was fully revived and never developed a single physical deficit from his ordeal.

Given all these possibilities, from a medical examiner's point of view, and from that of the police and other investigative agencies as well, a formal pronouncement of death is a watershed moment and must be backed up with a good deal of hard biological evidence. This includes

- The absence of all nervous or muscular reflexes throughout the body
  - Pallor and loss of elasticity of the skin
  - Complete cessation of heartbeat and cardiac activity of any kind
  - Complete cessation of respiration for more than five minutes
  - A body temperature at or below atmospheric temperature
  - Stillness, fixation, and bilateral dilation of the pupils of the eyes
  - An absence of any reflex in the eyes when a light is shined in them
  - A clouding of the cornea
  - Flaccidity of the muscles and a flattening of the body areas in contact with the surface where the body rests

AUTOPSY

After the on-site examination is completed in the park that night, and all the criteria for formal death are met, Joan D'Alessandro's body is transported to the medical examiner's office in Pomona and autopsy begins.

From the start, we can see that the wounds and injuries on her body are dreadful. The fact that they were inflicted on a seven-year-old suggests an assassin harboring anger and cruelty of unfathomable depths. These injuries include

- Fracture of the neck
- Strangulation
- Dislocated right shoulder
- Deep bruising
- Laceration under the chin and inside the upper lip
- Fracture of both sinuses
- Rupture of the hymen
- Frontal fracture of the skull
- Swelling of the face, with both eyes blackened and swollen shut
- Contusion and hemorrhage of the brain

Assessing this complex assortment of wounds, our goal now is to assemble the parts of the picture into a coherent narrative that tells us what really happened to Joan D'Alessandro on the day she went out to deliver Girl Scout cookies and never came home.

To begin, among the most obvious pieces of anatomical evidence is that Joan has been raped. This is a sex killing.

The massive injuries to the victim's upper body next disclose that after the rape she was severely beaten: her skull and neck were fractured, her teeth loosened, her upper lip and chin cut, and her lungs and liver bruised.

Finally, fractures of the thyroid cartilage on one part of Joan's neck, along with massive accumulations of blood beneath it, make it clear that after the beating she was manually choked. However, neither the brutal beating nor the choking immediately ended her life.

The reconstruction that tells us this is rather complicated; here it is in a nutshell.

Joan's face and body are significantly swollen. If she had died immediately after the assault, the body functions that stimulate swelling would have shut down at once, and no swelling would appear. Such swelling, moreover, takes approximately half an hour to reach its maximum, which this swelling has done; therefore, Joan lived for at least thirty to forty-five minutes after the rape and beating, though she was almost certainly unconscious at the time.

Further examination of the victim's neck then turns up a surprising discovery. Upon close study of the laryngeal cartilages, the hyoid bone, and the amount of blood seen in two different areas of the neck, it appears that Joan was choked not once but twice.

A picture of what happened that Holy Thursday now begins to emerge, like the image on a photographic plate.

First, Joan was raped. Then she was beaten, choked, and left lying somewhere for at least half an hour. Finally, perhaps because he was uncertain whether his victim was totally silenced, the killer returned and strangled her again.

Ironically, the autopsy results suggest, though they do not prove, that Joan's life functions had more or less ceased by the time the assailant wrapped his hands around her neck this second time. If Joan did indeed show vital signs at this moment, they would have been mere reflexes, most certainly her last.

The killer, a novice, had, in essence, tried to murder a little girl who was already clinically dead.

SUSPECTS

Even as Joan's autopsy is taking place at the medical examiner's office in Pomona, police and FBI investigators in New Jersey are trying to ferret out her killer.

No known sex offenders live in the Hillsdale area, but a lead turns up that looks as if it will quickly break the case. Several homeowners in the D'Alessandros' neighborhood describe seeing a man in a dark-colored automobile cruising Joan's street at the time she disappeared. The man slowed down in front of several residences, these witnesses report, craning his neck to get a better look at each house. Noticing this suspicious behavior, an on-the-ball neighbor jotted down the car's New York license plate.

The car belongs to a resident of Monsey, in Rockland County. He is quickly taken to the police station and questioned. Yes, he admits, he was cruising around Hillsdale that day. And yes, he was studying the houses on certain streets.

Why? Because he is interested in buying a house in this part of New Jersey, and is canvassing the area for a suitable piece of real estate. He even stopped to talk with several local people about the neighborhood.

The suspect insists that he left Hillsdale around two o'clock in the afternoon—Joan dropped out of sight a little before three—and was back in a Monsey bar within the hour, having his regular afternoon cocktail. The bartender and the other regulars confirm his story. The suspect quickly falls off the radar screen.

Several other men are also under suspicion. One of them, a man from the neighboring town of Cresskill, was seen wandering around Joan's block at the time of her disappearance. Despite hours of grueling questioning, the suspect stands his ground, insisting he had simply lost his way that afternoon and offering no other alibi.

It turns out that he was visiting a lady friend in the area. The lady friend was definitely not his wife. Another dropped lead.

THE ORDINARY MAN

While the investigators are following up various leads and going down dead ends, the prosecutor's office in Hackensack has its eye glued to one man in particular: neighbor Joseph McGowan.

The young science teacher is called to the station several times for questioning. In the beginning his story appears to be airtight; he repeats it smoothly and amiably each time. The day of Joan's disappearance, he tells police, he comes home from school, parks his sports car in the driveway, strolls to the supermarket, shops in a leisurely way, then walks home carrying three bags of groceries.

McGowan is an attractive young man, a graduate of Montclair College, a local school, where he was an honors student. He's a high school teacher with no criminal record. A solid citizen.

As the police dig, however, inconsistencies begin to pepper the young man's alibi.

If McGowan went to the supermarket that Thursday, the interrogators want to know, where are the grocery bags?

He doesn't know. He probably tossed them. He's not sure.

Where is the supermarket receipt?

He probably threw that away, too.

Where?

In the garbage can, in the kitchen.

Can he find the slip now and show it to them?

No, he took the garbage out the following day.

Did he take the garbage out at night or during the day?

During the day.

Did anyone see him do it?

He doesn't think so.

What days does the sanitation truck normally pick up on his street?

He's not sure.

How can he not remember what days they pick up the garbage on his own street?

Monday and Thursday, he thinks.

Thinks?

Knows.

Okay, but he said he took the garbage out the next day, Friday. That means the garbage sat stinking on the street for three days straight before the truck came by for a Monday pickup. Does he always put garbage out so many days in advance?

Sometimes.

Why?

He just does.

Now, at the supermarket: At what counter did he check out his groceries?

The first counter near the door. Maybe the third. He's not certain.

Did anyone see him at the supermarket that afternoon? A particular checkout person? A neighbor? A friend?

Not that he can remember.

What food did he buy at the market?

McGowan's a bit fuzzy on that. Some apples, maybe. Bananas. Breakfast cereal. Ah, a couple of steaks.

Did he freeze the steaks?

No, he and his mother ate them the next day.

Can he show them some of the other items he bought that day? Like the bananas or apples?

Well, yes, maybe. He can't be sure. They may all have been eaten by now.

More vague replies follow to questions that should have quick, easy answers; more loose ends appear. McGowan may be a respected high school teacher, but his house was the last stop Joan made before vanishing. Lieutenant Fallon, who leads the interrogation, is troubled. "There are a lot of little discrepancies in his story," he tells other investigators.

The police decide to administer a lie detector test.

McGowan fails.

Exhausted, confused, perhaps even conscience-stricken for a moment, McGowan breaks down.

Yes, he killed Joan. He greeted her at the door of his house, lured her into the basement, sexually assaulted her, beat her up, slammed her head against the concrete floor of the basement, and strangled her. All the while he was doing this, his hard-of-hearing eighty-seven-year-old grandmother was sitting on the sofa upstairs, watching a soap opera on TV.

Thinking Joan dead, McGowan then went upstairs, leaving her sprawled on the cellar floor for some minutes. He came back a while later and saw her twitch—or at least thought he saw her twitch. So he choked her again, just to make sure. One member of the police department is particularly graphic about this part of the story, telling reporters that the killer "picked her up by the throat, and shook her like a rag doll."

Several hours later, McGowan picked Joan's body up off the floor and wrapped it in a sofa cover; he packed her clothes neatly in a plastic bag, drove across the state line to Rockland County, and deposited her remains a few hundred feet off Gate Hill Road in Harriman State Park.

In a cleft between two boulders.

JUSTICE SERVED—SORT OF

The prosecutor's office charges Joseph McGowan with the murder of Joan D'Alessandro. Bail is set at $50,000, and the suspect is transported to the Bergen County Jail in Hackensack, New Jersey.

Word of McGowan's confession soon spreads to the public, and to the state prison system, which is often the first to learn that a particular suspect is being charged with a specific crime.

In any prison, status is normally measured by the barbarity of an inmate's crimes. There is, however, one felony that is never tolerated: molesting or killing a child. Such offenders are universally despised, and to assassinate one of them gains the killer enormous praise and respect from other inmates. With his fancy college education and wealthy suburban upbringing, McGowan quickly becomes a prime target. He must be locked up in a separate cell with guards posted at the door to ward off all self-appointed enforcers.

Concurrently, anger is mounting on the outside among the public when it learns what low bail has been set for a confessed child rapist and killer. As a Hillsdale resident tells a local reporter, "Where before our streets were ringing with the sounds of play and laughter of children, now all we see are empty streets. Parents are deathly afraid to even let their kids play on the front lawn cause they're scared they will be abducted in the way Joan was abducted." One father offers an especially comprehensive solution: "Kill this one and every other one like him, and the number of these killings will stop damn quick!"

Superior Court Judge Morris Pashman orders McGowan's bail revoked. He does this both to quiet the public outcry, and to protect the suspect from harm. To the delight of many, McGowan will now remain in jail until he comes to trial.

Still, at Tappan Zee High School, where McGowan teaches, the science department supervisor calls him "a fine and conscientious teacher." And at Montclair State College, a small but prestigious institution, the mood is grave. McGowan was a member of the Model UN, a dormitory counselor, a skilled intramural softball player and bowler. He had also belonged to a popular fraternity noted for the intelligence of its members. To even his smartest college chums, he was known as "the brain."

On April 24, 1973, McGowan is charged with the murder of Joan D'Alessandro in one of the fastest indictments ever recorded in New Jersey history. He is found guilty on all counts and is sentenced to life imprisonment.

Justice is done—except that McGowan is eligible for parole in fourteen years.

Now begins another chapter in the Joan D'Alessandro story. It has little to do with forensic pathology; rather, it is the remarkable saga of one woman's campaign to ensure the safety of children, not only in New Jersey but everywhere in the United States.

AGAINST ALL ODDS

While serving his "life" sentence, Joseph McGowan, predictably perhaps, is a model prisoner, accumulating large numbers of work and good-time credits. Prison personnel describe him as "gentle, cooperative, hardworking, and unassuming." In 1987, after fourteen years of picture perfect behavior, his first hearing for parole comes up.

Parole is promptly denied.

But to Rosemarie D'Alessandro, the good news is also the bad. The fact that McGowan's appeal is turned down today means there is a chance that it will be granted at a future hearing. His next opportunity for parole comes up in six years, in 1993.

Knowing that the man who tortured and killed her seven-year-old daughter might be released from prison in the not so distant future, freed to dine at restaurants, to date, perhaps even to find a job teaching young people in another part of the country, not only angers Rosemarie D'Alessandro but rings an alarm bell deep inside her: What risks will be unleashed on other children if such a man goes free?

By now, Rosemarie D'Alessandro knows child rapists have one of the highest rates of recidivism—of repeating their criminal behavior. Child rapists are also known to be among the most difficult of all personality types to rehabilitate. A majority of those who prey on children, studies show, live normal, unobtrusive lives. Until one day, overpowered by relentlessly gnawing sexual needs, they can no longer resist the inner demons, and a child suffers and sometimes dies. Such assaults are often spontaneous and unplanned. The murder of Joan is a case in point. If killer rapists get away with their first offense, criminal studies show, they quickly develop a bloodlust, raping and killing children with increased frequency. Such men, Rosemarie D'Alessandro knows well, are a disease without a cure.

The years pass quickly, and 1993 soon approaches. Criminals who have killed more frequently and brutally than McGowan have been granted parole in the past, Rosemarie knows. She also learns from the legal grapevine that because McGowan is a model prisoner, certain members of the parole board may be disposed toward granting him a second chance.

To make certain this does not happen, Rosemarie decides to take matters into her own hands, and to launch a campaign for better child protection laws. These laws, she insists, must mandate that anyone who kills a child during a sexual assault be sentenced to life imprisonment *without any possibility of parole.*

A lofty goal, surely, and a valuable one.

But most likely a quixotic one as well. How does one person set such an enormous plan into motion? How does a single untrained and unempowered citizen go about convincing the entire U.S. government that a new group of laws is needed?

Rosemarie decides to launch her campaign at the level where political change usually begins—at the grassroots. First, she forms the Joan Angela D'Alessandro Memorial Foundation. Next, she starts calling friends, explaining that McGowan will soon be eligible for parole and that unless something is done to stop his release the killer of a seven-year-old girl may roam the neighborhoods of Hillsdale soon again.

Rosemarie sends out fliers. She networks. She puts up posters and signs on local bulletin boards. She and other volunteers go door to door with petitions, asking people to write their state assemblyman, begging him to support new state and national legislation against sex offenders. She visits newspaper offices and radio stations. She gives interviews. She holds a candlelight vigil. She uses memorial foundation funds to legally fight McGowan's parole efforts, and to bring what is rapidly becoming known as "Joan's laws" to the doors of the White House itself.

For nine straight months, Rosemarie D'Alessandro dedicates her life to letting people know that the law does not protect their children as fully as it could, and that all it takes to ensure that any man who rapes and kills a child will never, ever be free to do so again is a presidential signature.

When McGowan's second parole hearing date arrives, thanks to Rosemarie's efforts, thousands of people now know that a convicted child murderer may go free. Public opinion strongly opposes the release. Parole is again denied.

But McGowan will not be put off so easily this time. He quickly appeals, on the grounds that he is being imprisoned for unfair reasons. A hearing is scheduled in appellate court. Meanwhile, the parole board insists that McGowan show solid evidence that he will never commit a crime again. Part of this proof is to be provided by his interviews with therapists who specialize in criminal psychology. John Douglas, the inventor of criminal personality profiling and a world expert on predicting criminal behavior, is called in on the case.

With notebooks full of data obtained during interviews, Douglas and his colleagues soon reach a unanimous conclusion: the prisoner, Joseph McGowan, possesses all the personality traits found in a serial killer.

They strongly recommend that the appeal be denied. Which it is.

JUSTICE DONE—FOR MOST OF US

Rosemarie D'Alessandro continues her efforts to pass the Joan Laws. Several more years of tireless campaigning pass, until what began as a one-woman crusade in a suburban New Jersey town ends up grabbing the attention of politicians in the most powerful circles of American government.

On April 3, 1997, Joan's Law is signed into state law by New Jersey governor Christine Whitman. The law declares that any person who murders a child under the age of fourteen in conjunction with a sexual offense will never be eligible for parole.

The next year, a federal version of the same law is signed by President Clinton, mandating life imprisonment without chance of parole for child killers.

But Rosemarie D'Alessandro is still on a roll.

In the fall of 1999, she proposes a Justice for Victims Law that eliminates the statute of limitations for wrongful death actions brought in cases of child murder, manslaughter, and aggravated manslaughter. This law permits victimized families to sue criminals right away if the criminals acquire an inheritance or other assets while in jail.

The law is quickly passed, and on April 19, 2001, Joan's mother is the first to put it into action.

During the course of his term in prison, McGowan's mother dies, leaving her son a legacy of more than a million dollars. McGowan secretly uses this money to buy influence and to hire high-priced lawyers to spearhead his campaign for future release.

Learning of McGowan's windfall, Rosemarie uses the convicted killer's own weapon to her advantage, accomplishing this bit of jujitsu by winning a $750,000 wrongful death civil judgment against the convicted killer.

Thanks to the new law, McGowan does not contest. The money goes to Joan's foundation.

Eventually the Joan Laws exert a profound effect on the criminal justice system of the United States, especially in California, where the Megan Laws are soon passed, providing similar protection to families and children.

Finally, in April 2004 Rosemarie D'Alessandro is honored with a Special Courage Award by U.S. Attorney General John Ashcroft. At the ceremony, Ashcroft announces a Department of Justice grant of $542 million for victim assistance to families that suffer the sexual abuse and murder of a child. The money to support this grant comes from the Crime Victims Fund, established in 1984 by the Victims of Crime Act, landmark legislation that significantly improved support to crime victims nationwide—and that was inspired by Rosemarie D'Alessandro's dogged crusade. The same year, Governor George Pataki also signs a bill that eliminates parole for predators who molest and kill children in New York State.

The governor signs this version of Joan's Law during a ceremony held several feet from the boulders where Joan D'Alessandro's body was discovered in 1973. "A sex predator who would kill one of our children should not see the light of day again in this state," the governor proclaims.

And so it would seem that Rosemarie D'Alessandro and her family can claim victory on all fields of battle. But reality never quite fits our fullest expectations: the protection of the Joan Laws is not retroactive.

For the D'Alessandro family this means that, despite his conviction, his evident guilt, his parole turndown, his lost appeal, his futile civil suit, and the amount of public opinion in his disfavor, the killer of Joan D'Alessandro can theoretically still go free.

Joseph McGowan's next parole hearing comes up in less than five years.

CHAPTER 8

One . . . Two? . . . Three!
The Child Minder Autopsies

Now rumors spread the town—strange
   happenings in that place
of children if they cried, of hands tied, of
   towels bound round the face,
of talk of cancer, of pumpkins in the night,
   of acts of God, of fate, of fright.
—DR. JOHN EMERY, PROFESSOR OF PEDIATRIC PATHOLOGY,
      AND EXPERT WITNESS FOR THE PROSECUTION

WE COMMAND you to appear before Branch No. 1 of Circuit
Court at the Court House in the City of Appleton, in the State of
Wisconsin, the week of June 16th through June 27th, 1986, at 8:30
o'clock in the afternoon of said day.

Then and there to give evidence in a certain cause to be tried between the STATE OF WISCONSIN

And SANDRA PANKOW.

JURY TRIAL—You will be notified of the exact date and the exact
time in the near future.

HEREOF FAIL NOT TO COMPLY, on pain of the penalty that
will fall thereon . . .

ORDINARY PEOPLE

ON THE PREVIOUS PAGE YOU WILL FIND A PAGE OF A SUBPOENA ISSUED ME by the state of Wisconsin. It was delivered to my desk some time ago, during a busy week at the Rockland County Medical Examiner's Office.

My first thought when I read this official document was that the State of Wisconsin in general, and the Wisconsin city of Appleton in particular, had lost their minds—or, at least, were skating on the thinnest of legal ice. To my knowledge, there is no law anywhere in the United States mandating that a forensic expert *must* testify at any type of trial, murder or otherwise. This task is always paid discretionary work, especially when the expert witness in question does not reside in the state where the crime has been committed and/or where the trial is taking place. True, at the time I received the subpoena I had been involved in this sinister case for several months, but only as an adviser and long-distance pathology consultant.

More to the point, I was hereby being summoned to provide expert testimony in a trial that would once again drive home to me a definitive rule of forensic psychology: When unspeakably wicked events happen in quiet, wholesome places—or, to put it another way, when ordinary people are confronted with the horror of naked evil—their tendency is to deny the evidence of their reason and senses; sometimes—often, perhaps—to an irrational degree.

LOVING CARE

The story of these fearsome events begins in Appleton, a small Norman Rockwell–ish city near the northern shores of Lake Winnebago.

Town chronicles inform you that Appleton boasts the second-oldest coed college in the country, and the first electric cable car. It was the childhood home of John Bradley, one of the flag raisers at Iwo Jima. The greatest of modern magicians, Harry Houdini, came to Appleton from Hungary with his family while still an infant. The writer Edna Ferber graduated from the local high school that now bears her name. According to a recent report from Farmers Insurance Group, Appleton is one of the ten safest places to live in the United States. With farming, a large paper industry, low taxes, and an enviably high rate of employment, the town is populated with neighborly, hardworking people who have long been accustomed to a safe, pleasant life.

One of these hardworking people is a thirty-five-year-old housewife named Sandra Pankow.

Sandra Pankow is married, apparently happily, and the mother of two sons, one from a previous marriage. Her husband works nights and sleeps at home during the day. She is a tall woman and somewhat overweight, always, she tells friends, "fighting the battle of the bulge."

Pankow is also a onetime nurse's aide who now supplements her family's income by running a small babysitting operation from her home. She offers three bedrooms, each with a crib; a playroom with TV; and a basement filled with infant toys. Friends and acquaintances visiting the Pankow nursery are invariably impressed by its tidy, serene atmosphere. "It was amazing," a friend once remarked. "Even when she had a full house you would never hear any of the children crying."

Specializing in children between the age of one and two, Pankow has been, as she calls herself, a "child minder" for over a decade. Her self-described specialty consists of "caring, attentive, and loving one-on-one attention provided to special boys and girls of a tender age."

ONE

One bright, cold December day in 1980 a thirteen-month-old named Kristin Michelle Hamilton is dropped off at the Pankow nursery a few minutes before noon. Kristin's mother, Cindy, has been bringing Kristin (and occasionally Kristin's older sister, Lisa) to the Pankow nursery for several months. Today she informs Pankow that her daughter has a cold, and that she will be returning to pick her up early.

At three-thirty that afternoon Mrs. Hamilton receives a telephone call from the Pankow house. Several minutes earlier, Pankow announces to Mrs. Hamilton, she entered the nursery to check on Kristin, who had been napping since one.

"I could tell something was wrong the moment I entered the room!"

Pankow almost shouts. "I could sense it. I looked at Kristin closely, then I realized what was going on. She wasn't breathing!"

According to Pankow's report, the child had no pulse and all her vital signs had ceased. Being a former nurse's aide and knowing resuscitation methods, she reports, she carried Kristin to the couch in the living room where she patted Kristin, shook her, and finally administered mouth-to-mouth resuscitation and CPR, all to no avail.

An ambulance is called and rushes to the scene. Kristin is transported to St. Elizabeth Hospital in Appleton, and in the emergency room several more attempts are made to bring her back, all unsuccessful. At around 4:30 in the afternoon an attending physician officially pronounces Kristin Hamilton dead. Her parents arrive soon after and make a formal identification.

These events happened in 1980. As you will remember from chapter one, before the advent of the medical examiner system, when an unexplained fatality occurred doctors and police investigative agencies relied on the town coroner to determine if the cause of death was natural, accidental, suicide, or murder.

Coroners, you will also recall, were not always pathologists by training. Though these officials often had a background in medicine, until the mid-1980s a majority of town and even major city coroners had no more knowledge of forensics than an ordinary doctor.

So the body of the Hamilton baby is not taken for study to a separate medical examiner's facility—there are none—but is autopsied by a pathologist coroner at the St. Elizabeth Hospital emergency room.

From interviews with Kristin's parents, it is learned that two months before her death Kristin suffered an ear infection, and that twelve days before she died she took a tumble down a flight of stairs. Three days before her death she vomited twice and developed a cold, but her stools were normal. Apart from these minor problems, she was in excellent health.

Autopsy findings also show that Kristin is well-nourished, with no bruises or external abnormalities. During dissection, her organs are described as unremarkable. All her abdominal organs appear to be normal, and there are, according to the coroner's report, no signs of foul play anywhere on the child's body.

"The cut surfaces of the lung exude no significant fluid," the coroner writes in his report, "and there is no apparent consolidation or hemorrhage. No petechiae [pin-size hemorrhages] are evident on the pleural surfaces. The central bronchial mucosa [lung coating] is covered by a slightly bloody fluid, and there are no lesions."

In short, there are no physical signs or anomalies to show how and why Kristin Hamilton died. In such cases, by default, the cause of death is attributed to SIDS—sudden infant death syndrome.

BUT STILL . . .

But still, several doctors in Appleton are surprised by these findings. SIDS is a relatively rare event, they maintain. What's more, the diagnosis was not made by a forensic pathologist. One doctor presses to investigate the incident further; another wants to bring in experts from the state university for a second and third opinion.

But the police are resolute. A thorough investigation of the Pankow household shows no irregularities or signs of violence. Everything in the house is up to code, and the official coroner's report clearly states that no external object (such as a pillow or hand) has interfered with Kristin Hamilton's respiration. The child, for medical reasons unknown, simply stopped breathing. Why push the matter further? A wide-scale investigation will only upset the parents further, police insist, and turn up nothing in the process.

And anyway, Sandra Pankow has run a reputable nursery service for years, as everyone knows, and her clients rave about the care she lavishes on her little ones. Pankow is a bright, soft-spoken, quietly religious woman, and is generally looked on with affection and respect by the community. Her friends and family are appropriately supportive in her hour of need.

"Sandra's been through a big trauma," one neighbor tells the Appleton newspaper. "She's wrung dry by this terrible ordeal. I feel so badly for her. Why is it the good ones always have such bad luck?"

And so, despite a few muted rumblings from the medical and legal communities in Appleton, most people are entirely satisfied that Kristin Hamilton's strange demise is pure accident. Sometimes these things happen.

Case closed.

THE MYSTERIOUS SIDS

Sudden infant death syndrome, often called crib death, is a frightening disorder that for unknown reasons causes healthy infants to die suddenly in their sleep. Statistically speaking, 2 out of every 1,000 babies born in the United States die of SIDS every year. This comes to approximately 8,000 such deaths annually. Infant boys are more likely than girls to succumb to the malady. The younger a mother is, the more prone her child is to SIDS. The disease is common in winter and rare in summer, and it frequently strikes infants who are born prematurely. Oddly, infants with a twin brother or sister are far more vulnerable to crib death than singletons are.

J. B. Beckwith, a pediatric expert, defines sudden infant death syndrome in the following way: "The sudden death of any infant or young child which is unexpected by its [medical] history, and in which a thorough post-mortem examination fails to reveal a cause."

A second widely published definition, by Dr. L. Adelson, a forensic pathologist, tells us that SIDS is "the death of a child who was thought to have been in good health or whose terminal illness appeared to be so mild that the possibility of a fatal outcome was not anticipated."

A forensic diagnosis of SIDS is a diagnosis of exclusion. That is, during an autopsy all known causes of rapid infant death—suffocation, infection, choking on vomit, overexposure to heat or cold, food stuck in the throat, poison, fever, foul play, and so forth—must be counted out. When no pathology, accident, violence, or other underlying cause of death can be detected, a diagnosis of SIDS is listed on the death certificate.

Yet, as with cancer, a confounding feature of this ailment is that although its medical origins are unknown, a number of external factors appear to contribute to it. The American Academy of Pediatrics tells us that healthy infants who habitually lie on their stomachs have a greater chance of dying suddenly in their sleep than do infants who sleep on their sides or backs. Babies who bed down on polystyrene-filled cushions have a slightly higher incidence of SIDS than those who sleep on down-stuffed pillows. Whether this phenomenon is due to suffocation or to chemicals in the stuffing is unclear. Mattresses, beds, bedclothes, and bedding have all been considered as suspects in SIDS deaths, along with bleach in diaper wash, secondhand smoke, air pollution, bottle feeding, radiation, environmental bacterial infection, and a number of other seemingly unrelated influences.

SIDS, in short, is an enigmatic killer caused by unknown forces. It is especially difficult to identify; and during an autopsy is often misdiagnosed—or, worse, overdiagnosed.

TWO?

After the disturbance surrounding Kristin Hamilton's death subsides, Sandra Pankow continues to provide baby care for the busy working mothers of Appleton. The fact that a child has died in her care causes little concern.

Meanwhile, perhaps oddly, perhaps understandably, Pankow starts to develop a passionate interest in SIDS. She reads widely on the subject, keeps up with the latest research, and talks to experts at SIDS organizations. Before long, she is something of an expert on sudden infant death syndrome, and Appleton's doctors begin to consult her on technical issues of crib death. This attempt to turn a liability into an asset ups Pankow's stock even more among the citizens of Appleton. For a while, she is something of a hero.

Then, two years later, in August 1982, a nine-month-old boy named Shawn Bloomer dies at the Pankow nursery.

Pankow says that several minutes after Shawn was dropped off that morning she fed him milk and cereal, then laid him on a blanket to watch television. A few minutes later, he was rubbing his eyes, so she put him to bed, on his tummy, his face turned to one side. At nine o'clock she checked and found him quietly asleep. Three and a half hours later she went to pick him up and found him dead.

Again, resuscitation efforts are applied with no success, and the infant is transported to the hospital by ambulance, where he is immediately declared dead. The autopsy, carried out five hours later, finds a well-nourished baby with rigor mortis already setting into his arms and jaw. While there is no evidence of trauma to his body, petechiae are found in the lungs and pleura, a possible sign of asphyxiation. But the coroner seems unconcerned. The child's body shows no bruises or blood spots, and all the internal organs are unremarkable and fully intact.

Once again, because the child shows no specific symptoms of illness or accident, the coroner cites SIDS as the cause of death.

At this point, common sense tells us that the police, the hospital, attending physicians, the town DA, friends, neighbors, relatives, *someone* would begin to sound an alarm over the fact that two infants have died in two years at the same babysitting establishment for no apparent reason.

But no.

Once again sympathy rings out for the poor child minder, the victim now of two tragic fates. After the official autopsy and police reports are filed, after Pankow is found innocent of any misdeed, and after the drama dies down, town authorities see no reason to press the matter any further, and the parents of Shawn Bloomer make no move to litigate. Some people, it is true, are now uneasy about Pankow's ability to provide adequate care at her center. Others hear rumors about strange abuses in the Pankow basement—rumors that the police investigate but determine are nothing more than spiteful gossip. By and large, most people in Appleton consider that Sandra Pankow is simply a sad victim of circumstances.

THREE!

Three years later, just before Halloween 1985, a third child dies in the care of the Pankow child-minding service.

The story is a chilling replay of the first two tragedies. Six-month-old Tyler Kloes is delivered to the Pankow house by his mother early in the morning. He is restless, Pankow reports, and is put down to sleep right away. Twenty minutes later she finds him dead in his crib. Resuscitation is attempted, without success. Tyler is taken away by ambulance, and pronounced dead at the Appleton hospital.

There is a saying in police work: "One is a random accident, two a suspicious coincidence, three a definite murder." With the death of Tyler

Kloes, the Appleton police, the Appleton medical establishment, the Appleton legal agencies, even friends and neighbors of the Pankow family begin to draw dreadful conclusions. This time, instead of undergoing a cursory autopsy at the hospital, the child's body is transferred to the department of pathology at the University of Wisconsin–Madison, where an extensive dissection and forensic exam is carried out.

This study reveals evidence of attempted resuscitation but no external trauma. Pankow is not telling a lie on this count. There is, however, extensive congestion in the child's lungs, as well as deep hemorrhages in the lungs and thymus gland, both classic signs of suffocation.

"This was apparently a normal boy with no evidence of a terminal illness," a university examiner writes, "but with the stigma compatible with an asphyxial death. The situation presenting therefore, was that of a dead 6-month-old child in whom the autopsy findings were negative from the viewpoint of a terminal disease, but in whom findings, while compatible with those described in SIDS, were also those of asphyxia."

INTO THE DARKNESS

A supply of previously unreported tales concerning Pankow's strange behavior and peculiar mental condition are now turned up by the fleet of detectives giving serious attention to this case.

It is discovered, for example, that from 1980 to 1985 nine calls were made from the Pankow residence to the fire department requesting an ambulance and rescue unit.

Three of these calls were for the "SIDS" deaths. Several others were of a quite different nature. One concerned a domestic dispute: Pankow complained that her husband was physically abusing her. In another call, Pankow declared she had taken an overdose of medication. A third was made because Pankow was suffering from acute mental distress accompanied by seizures—the product, she tells an investigator, of a nerve condition in her spine.

Detectives also learn that Pankow has been telling friends she has inoperable brain cancer, with less than a year to live. She has confided to a social worker, Greg Otto, that she is suffering from late-stage cancer caused by stress over the two infant deaths in her home. Pankow also tells the National Foundation for Sudden Infant Death that she is terminally ill and that she intends to include the Foundation in her will.

Yet despite all these tragic claims, investigation shows that none of the medicines Pankow is currently taking—Tigan (prevents vomiting), Compazine (a tranquilizer), Lomotil (for diarrhea), and Bellergal (sedative)—is for cancer. What's more, no medical record exists in the state of Wisconsin showing that Pankow has ever received a diagnosis of cancer.

"It should be noted," reads a supplemental remark in the police report of Sergeant R. J. Soper, "that a medical release form as obtained from Sandra Pankow on the 29th day of October, 1985, and various medical records were obtained from various medical facilities, and all medical records to date indicate there is no apparent reason why Sandra Pankow should be telling anyone that she has a cancerous tumor."

Meanwhile, Pankow's neighbors are concerned and confused. Up to this point, they have given the child minder the full benefit of the doubt. Now troubling reservations and then blatant accusations bubble to the surface.

One friend is distressed because Pankow is known to be a victim of epilepsy-like seizures. Under state law, no one who suffers from seizures of any kind may be licensed to run a day care center. Another neighbor, a nurse, reports seeing Pankow give sleep-inducing drugs to several of her client children. Tyler Kloes's mother reports the especially disturbing fact that after her son's death Pankow informed her that if Tyler had not died from SIDS he would have died soon anyway.

"Why?" Mrs. Kloes asked.

"Because his body was riddled with cancer," Sandra replied.

One set of parents, referred to Pankow by an employment agency, tell police that before they started taking their one-year-old son to the Pankow nursery he never napped during the day, and actually suffered from a mild form of childhood insomnia. At the Pankow nursery he was immediately put down to nap every day and would stay asleep for hours.

"I don't know how you do it," the boy's mother repeatedly told Pankow, never guessing that her son might have been drugged. "You must have a magic spell."

"Just an old-fashioned Christian potion—love," Pankow replied.

More seamy information surfaces. It is revealed that Kristin Hamilton's mother sent her older daughter, Lisa, to the Pankow nursery for several months before Kristin's death. One day Lisa came home crying and told her mother that when Sandra got angry at the babies for making too much noise, she put tape over their mouths or tied their hands behind their backs.

At the time, Mrs. Hamilton discounted this as a child's fantasy. But two boys, ages six and nine, later confirm the account, stating that when they were cared for at the Pankows' house three years earlier Sandy would tie them to the bed and gag them when they cried.

Yet another mother tells of arriving at the Pankow house earlier than usual and finding her infant son in a cage in the basement. A heavy piece of wood covered the wire prison, apparently to keep the child from escaping. The mother grabbed her son, ran out of the house, and never returned. Her reasons for not filing a complaint are never explained.

At one point in the inquiry a member of the investigative squad, Detective Carroll, asks Pankow whether a particular room in her house was used as a napping place for the children. Pankow's response, according to the detective, is that "they have christened all of my bedrooms."

"I felt that this was an unusual response," Carroll writes in his report, "and I asked her again to explain where the deaths had taken place. She stated that there had been a death in every one of the bedrooms in the home."

The inappropriately evangelical wording of Pankow's reply is soon mirrored by an especially creepy episode that takes place around Halloween, shortly after the death of the third child, Tyler Kloes.

Several days after Tyler's funeral, his grandfather shows up at the Appleton police department carrying a small pumpkin. The pumpkin was found on Tyler's grave early that morning by Tyler's mother, the grandfather explains. She showed it to him, and he promptly brought it to the police. The pumpkin is uncut, the police note, but has the word "angel" written on it, and a strange jack-o-lantern face drawn on one side in magic marker. Printed on the other side are the words "Happy Halloween to you up in heaven."

The pumpkin is photographed and preserved. When interviewed, a groundskeeper at the Appleton cemetery reports that two or three days after Tyler's funeral he was accosted while at work by a tall, heavyset woman in her early thirties.

The woman wanted to know where the Kloes grave was.

The groundskeeper pointed it out and went back to his business. The woman strolled over to the freshly dug grave and gazed at it for some minutes.

The next day she came again; and the day after that.

On the fourth day, according to the groundskeeper, the woman arrived early in the morning and assumed her place at the grave site, remaining for an unusually long period of time. She did not seem to be carrying anything when she arrived, but shortly after she left he noticed a small pumpkin sitting on the burial site.

Sandra Pankow's husband, Doug, is immediately interviewed concerning the pumpkin incident. The police report of the interview reads in part, as follows: "Around Halloween each year his children and Sandy decorate pumpkins. He [Doug] stated that Sandy likes to decorate the pumpkins with faces using a magic marker, and that she does not like to cut into them."

THE BABY KILLERS

Enid Gilbert, M.D., is director of surgical and pediatric pathology at the University of Wisconsin. Internationally known in pediatric pathology, and the author of the two-volume definitive work on the subject, *Potter's Pathology of the Fetus and Infant,* she is also an expert in determining whether a SIDS-like fatality is, in fact, due to SIDS or to suffocation—accidental or intentional. After the third unexplained death takes place at the Pankow baby center, Appleton police call in Dr. Gilbert to help them get to the bottom of things.

Working with statistical tables and a massive number of SIDS death reports, then carefully doing her math, Dr. Gilbert determines that, statistically speaking, the chances of three SIDS deaths occurring in the same house under the same person's care within a five-year period are in the range of *one trillion to one*. Though estimates by other pediatric specialists are more conservative, registering in the mid-billions, mathematicians will tell you that on the scale of human affairs, any number over 500 billion is tantamount to infinity. As the nationally known medical examiner Vincent Di Maio tells a reporter from *Time,* "Two SIDS deaths [in the same family or nursery] is improbable. But three is impossible."

Dr. Gilbert is also aware that while common medical wisdom insists that deaths from SIDS and deaths from suffocation are extremely difficult to tell apart, in many cases the two can be distinguished. To accomplish this, a medical examiner must be expert at knowing which symptoms to look for, and where.

Finally, Dr. Gilbert knows that as many as 20 percent of the 8,000 babies who supposedly die of SIDS in the United States each year actually succumb to other causes, murder by suffocation being among the most common. The number one culprit in such killings, studies show, is the mother herself.

Why would a mother slay her own child? Generally, for reasons that are either utilitarian or psychotic. A common motivation is insurance money. Another is frenzied frustration elicited when a child cries too long or too loud. In rare instances, the motive is sheer sadism.

Some mothers kill their offspring simply to receive loving attention from friends and well-wishers. Such "sympathy junkies," Dr. Di Maio remarks, "usually keep killing until they're caught—or run out of children."

Finally, a few mothers suffer from a rare mental disorder known as Munchausen's syndrome by proxy. In "ordinary" Munchausen's syndrome, victims fake or even induce sickness in order to receive pity and attention from medical authorities. In Munchausen's by proxy, a mother injures or kills her children rather than herself. She acts in this way for the same reason Munchausen's syndrome sufferers do—to bask in the sympathy of others.

It is, of course, difficult for most of us to imagine that a father or mother would kill their own child; and mercifully, the investigative searchlight in such crimes does not fall on parents alone. Statistically speaking, the second most likely perpetrator of infanticide, as Dr. Gilbert explains to Appleton investigative authorities, is the professional day care nanny. She, too, often murders out of a pathological need for attention and sympathy from the community, as in Munchausen's by proxy; or from a desire to appear sick and needy owing to all the woes that beset her from the death.

Dr. Gilbert begins a thorough study of all three infant deaths at the Pankow establishment.

FOOTSTEPS BACK TO THE GRAVE

Even a quick review of official reports in the Pankow deaths shows that significant mistakes, both of omission and of commission, have been made in the autopsies of the three Appleton infants.

Troubled and alerted by these findings, Dr. Gilbert contacts a colleague in Britain, Dr. John Emery, professor of pediatric pathology at the University of Sheffield. Like Dr. Gilbert, Dr. Emery is a world authority on distinguishing between crib death and intentional suffocation.

Dr. Gilbert also calls me to ask if I will lend my expertise to the case. Knowing that I have worked on infant murders disguised as SIDS deaths, and that I have made a long-term study of the pathology of suffocation, she is optimistic that the three of us, working as a team by mail and telephone, and conferring on a regular basis, can solve the mystery of the trillion-to-one infant deaths.

We start by reviewing the coroner's reports of the first two.

The findings in both resemble those in the case of the third deceased child. There is no sign of terminal infection, but markings are present on the neck tissue that are consistent with asphyxiation. In the first death, that of Kristin Hamilton, hemorrhages in the neck tissue were noted, along with tiny hemorrhages in the eye. Both of these signs are usually the result of suffocation, but at the time no one flagged the findings for further study.

Taking this information into consideration, the three of us conclude that there is enough suspicious evidence in this case to order an exhumation of the first two children. It is agreed that Dr. Gilbert will perform the autopsies, and that she will specifically search for suspicious signs that were overlooked, unrecognized, or ignored during the original autopsies.

FACES OF ASPHYXIA

In forensic pathology, death by oxygen deprivation, or more formally, asphyxia, is an area of specialization unto itself.

Medically speaking, asphyxia occurs when an outside "mechanical" object—a hand, inhaled fluids, a crushing weight—either cuts off the airways that deliver oxygen to the lungs, or interferes with blood flow to the brain. The associated term "hypoxia" refers to conditions in which insufficient amounts of oxygen reach body tissue. Hypoxia, in turn, generates cyanosis, a dull blue discoloration of the skin, lips, and fingernail beds that spreads and deepens as the oxygen level drops in a victim's blood.

Hanging, drowning, strangulation, suffocation, inhalation of poison gas, and throat-clogging substances like sand or clay are the most common causes of mechanical asphyxia. Fortunately, each of these leaves a unique forensic signature, enabling medical examiners to pinpoint the means and cause of an asphyxial death. These signs and patterns can be subtle, and usually require laboratory knowledge to identify.

When victims are hanged, the type of death depends on where the noose is on the neck and the position of the body. If the noose is high on the neck, with both sides of the noose extending in an upward direction, meeting at the back of the head, the hanged person's face will become extremely flushed because the heart is pumping blood through the carotid arteries. But the blood cannot return to the heart because only the veins are compressed. Strangulation is the result. If, on the other hand, the noose is low on the neck, with both ends tied tightly behind the neck, both the arteries and veins are compressed and the face assumes a grayish, pale color. Death is imminent.

Or another scenario: Meter readers must frequently take readings in confined spaces such as underground pits. In such places there is often garbage spillage, due to rain. The bacteria present in these pits may then use up all the oxygen, leaving behind only deadly carbon dioxide. When the meter readers descend into these pits they immediately become unconscious, and death promptly follows. I have described this condition, known as confined space syndrome, in the *Journal of Forensic Sciences.*

The type of asphyxia central to the Pankow case is suffocation. During suffocation, the reduced supply of oxygen to body tissue stresses respiratory capacity to the limit, causing victims to gasp for air. In the thrashing about that follows, cyanosis develops, the anxiety reflex burns up oxygen reserves, and thick congestion develops in the lungs, all making it increasingly difficult for the victim to breathe. During this struggle for air, the victim's veins swell, the facial skin becomes puffy, the pupils dilate, and the eyes bulge. Often a person's tongue protrudes in gruesome ways, and foam or blood-stained saliva may drip from the mouth and nose. (In rare cases of suffocation, a person may develop a so-called vasovagal reflex from stimulation of the vagus nerve in the neck, causing cardiac arrest.)

Most significantly from a forensic point of view, when victims are in the advanced throes of suffocation petechiae begin to appear. These, you will recall, are pinpoint-size capillary hemorrhages, and a signature marking of suffocation. Sometimes forming in large colonies that resemble heat rash or a cluster of measles, in other instances they are so small or few that magnification is needed to see them at all.

Though petechiae normally appear in predictable physical locations such as the lungs, the whites of the eyes, and in the membranes surrounding the eyes and eyelids, if oxygen levels become especially low, and if engorged capillaries have enough room to burst open, showers of petechial hemorrhages can appear on practically any part of a suffocating person's body. While there are a few other clinical situations besides suffocation that can promote petechiae, these causes are usually evident and easily identifiable.

THE SECOND ROUND

Kristin Hamilton is the first child to be exhumed. Kristin was buried five years ago; her body was embalmed at the time of death, and her viscera, removed during autopsy and well preserved in embalming fluid, are neatly packed in a plastic bag inside her coffin.

Carefully examining her remains, Dr. Gilbert notes a number of significant features.

• There is darkening, caused by hemorrhaging, of the upper gums around the incisor teeth and along the upper ridge of the gums. These markings are strongly suggestive of suffocation. Dr. Gilbert also finds a linear bruise on the gums, a mark that can only have been made by a large object, such as a hand, pressed tightly against the face and mouth.

Surprisingly, the original coroner's report includes no reference to any of these vividly suspicious bruises. The reason for this omission, the three of us decide, cannot fairly be called incompetence: pathologists are not trained to recognize important forensic findings. Moreover, bruises often take up to twenty-four hours to appear on a body after death. The pressure marks in Kristin's mouth may not have been visible until after the child was dissected, embalmed, and buried.

• A significant number of petechiae and frank hemorrhages are found in the child's lungs. These markings also went unnoticed in the 1980 autopsy, which suggests that the lungs received a very cursory examination. On appropriate inspection, such hemorrhages are readily visible. Lung hemorrhages of all types must be studied under the microscope to confirm the gross findings, and to establish whether the hemorrhages are due to any cause other than asphyxia. In the repeat autopsy, tiny lung pieces are taken for microscopic examination, and the rest of the lung is placed in formalin for further examination in a day or two. The formalin, a solution of formaldehyde in water, will turn hemorrhagic areas shades of black, white, or gray, showing me their full size and extent.

At the original autopsy, no microscopic samples or studies of any kind were made. Today it is basic procedure first to study the body tissue of a suffocated person with the naked eye, but not to cut into the organs immediately. One or two days later the tissue will, as it were, ripen, making it easier to see many of the gross lesions that were unrecognizable in a fresh sampling. At this point, the lung tissue is cut into thin slices, made into slides, and studied under the microscope.

Still another reason to wait a day or two before making microscopic lung studies in asphyxial deaths is that hemorrhages that are allowed to develop for several days after death turn shades of black, white, or gray, becoming easier to identify and analyze under magnification than the reddish hues found in fresh cellular tissue. In the Kristin Hamilton autopsy, the suspicious hemorrhages in her lungs are more clearly visible five years after her death than they would have been the day she died.

• Groupings of petechiae are found on the whites of the child's eyes and eyelids, in the conjunctiva of her eye, and in the membranes surrounding her eyes. Such clusters are significant indicators of suffocation. These blood spots are *never* found in the eyes of a SIDS child without some other obvious cause. Indeed, hemorrhaging of any kind in the eyes is highly atypical of SIDS.

• Further gross and microscopic study confirms significant signs of bleeding in the lungs, plus the presence of foreign material in the air sacs. SIDS deaths rarely show such symptoms. Internal bleeding is also noted in the neck, an unusual symptom in SIDS cases, but common in victims who have been strangled or suffocated.

Shawn Bloomer. The exhumation and autopsy of Shawn Bloomer, the second child to die at the Pankow establishment, is less revealing than the first.

Shawn is not embalmed in the same way as Kristin Hamilton. His viscera are not present in the coffin, and his body was stuffed with sawdust to make it appear full and intact at his funeral viewing. The skin and tissues on his body are largely autolyzed, which literally means "self-digested."

Still, we find hemorrhaging and petechiae visible in his remains. Both are compatible with asphyxiation. No other conventional cause of death can be found.

What are we to make of the evidence from these two disinterments?

In our final autopsy report, Dr. Gilbert, Dr. Emery, and I conclude: "The first child showed *incontrovertible evidence* of death due to *external asphyxia.* The other two had no direct evidence of a mechanism of external asphyxia. Still, *evidence compatible with asphyxia was present in both, making a similar diagnosis of asphyxia the most likely diagnosis.*"

And then we have the surrounding facts and circumstances: the mathematical improbability of three SIDS deaths occurring in the same household, under the same nursing care; the testimonies of neighbors and visitors concerning Pankow's negligence; the claims of clients and parents that Pankow abused, drugged, and even caged and tied the children in her care; and the fact that Sandra Pankow exhibits behaviors suggesting she is emotionally unstable.

Taking all this into consideration, and combining scientific fact with circumstantial evidence, our conclusion, made with a reasonable degree of medical probability, is that all three Appleton infants *have been murdered.*

And also, that Sandra Pankow is almost certainly the one who did it.

END GAME

The trial of Sandra Pankow lasts only eight days.

Her defense consists of well-known forensic pathologists maintaining that each of the three infants died of SIDS. As if to give the lie to her own defense, the defendant sits motionless and wide-eyed throughout the proceedings with her hands covering her nose and mouth in the position one assumes when hearing of or witnessing a dreadful event. Occasionally she cries. One member of the jury later remarks that during the trial he rarely saw the defendant's face full-on.

A forensic pathologist from the University of Wisconsin, Dr. Robert Huntington III, tells the court: "I must, alas, conclude to a reasonable medical certainty that Kristin Hamilton died an asphyxial death. Her airway was blocked." A medical statistician demonstrates to the jury how small the probability is that three SIDS deaths could occur at the same house in a five-year period.

The prosecution's case builds with a seemingly inexorable momentum. Then, suddenly, in the middle of this incriminating barrage, Christopher Pankow, Sandra Pankow's fourteen-year-old son, causes a collective dropping of jaws by claiming that he has tied up and covered the mouths of many babies under his mother's care.

Previously granted immunity from prosecution, Christopher is called to the stand by the defense and asked whether he was jealous of the attention his mother paid to Kristin Hamilton and Shawn Bloomer. Christopher says he was.

The defense then asks whether he ever tied babies up and gagged them in his mother's house.

After a long pause, Christopher quietly nods. Though he then claims he had nothing to do with the deaths at his mother's nursery, it nonetheless looks as if the shadow of blame is now shifting from mother to son.

This shift is short-lived. Testimony given the next day establishes that Christopher was not at the Pankow house the day Shawn Bloomer died, and was probably not at home on the days the other two children died, either.

Had Pankow's son really abused the day care babies, as he claimed? Was he copycatting Mom? Or was he simply making a pathetically noble attempt to take the blame on himself? These questions were never answered, not during the trial and not in the years that followed.

Meanwhile, the damning testimony against Sandra Pankow continues.

Witness David Janssen, fourteen, describes going to the basement of the Pankow home with Christopher to get a Popsicle from the freezer. Janssen claims that Christopher led him to a crib and showed him a baby "with his hands tied behind his back and a cloth tied around his mouth." The baby was still alive, Janssen reports.

A nine-year-old boy likewise testifies that he saw Pankow tie a towel over the mouth of a crying baby. Another young witness saw a similar event take place, while two adults testify to seeing Kristin Hamilton in the Pankow basement the day she died. (Pankow told some investigators that Kristin died on the living room couch, others that she died in a crib in one of the bedrooms.)

Judy Olsen testifies that she left work early one day to pick up her fourteen-month-old son from the Pankows, only to find him "in a corner of a cold, dark, musty basement in a playpen with a heavy wooden cover over the top." Sandra Pankow, she tells the jury, was not with the children and was, in fact, taking a shower at the time. Similarly incriminating testimony is given by neighbors, townspeople, and parents.

Yet, as one newspaper reporter asks in the middle of the trial, "Why is it that all these people waited so long to tell the horror stories they are telling now?" Hints of an answer may be found, I believe, in a statement made by one of the jurors several months after the trial. "It's never nice to think that the people in your town are monsters," she said. "We all prefer, I think, to think the best of others, and to turn away from the possibility of evil until someone comes along and shakes us, and says, 'Look, look—here's the bloody truth!' "

Finally Enid Gilbert, John Emery, and I are called to the witness stand.

Dr. Gilbert tells the court that in her expert opinion all three deaths were caused by asphyxiation, not SIDS or other natural causes. Although she characterizes the defense attorney's questions as "silly," and insists that he not query her many impressive credentials, Dr. Gilbert stops short of calling the deaths homicides.

Dr. Emery follows Dr. Gilbert to the witness stand. Here he volleys out at the defense attorney: "The evidence of asphyxia is as clear-cut as anyone is ever likely to get in dealing with deaths of this type!"

Asked whether a towel tied around her mouth could have caused the bruising on Kristin Hamilton's gums, Dr. Emery replies, "Yes, I think so." He too, however, falls short of calling the death a homicide.

Finally, it is my turn on the stand. Weighing the evidence as I understand it, and deciding that the guilt in this case screams out from the four directions, and from the graves of three innocent children, I decide to break the invisible taboo that so far—and for such a long time—has shielded the Appleton child minder from the reprisals she richly deserves.

To begin, the defense attorney brings up the bruises on Kristin Hamilton's gums. These, he insists, were clearly produced by the efforts of Pankow and the rescue squad to resuscitate Kristin, not by the pressure of a pillow or hand.

I reply that since by all reports, including Pankow's, the child was already dead when resuscitation attempts started, these efforts could not have caused the bruises. A bruise is an injury to tissue caused by breaks in the walls of small blood vessels. These breaks cause bleeding within the tissues without disrupting the surface of the tissue. In order for a bruise to occur, the heart must be pumping blood to the broken blood vessels, driving the blood into the tissues under pressure.

The defense attorney then posits that the petechiae found in Kristin Hamilton's autopsy are not necessarily proof of suffocation; petechiae, he asserts, can result from many other types of deaths as well.

I reply that SIDS, by definition, is a death that has no discernible causes, so the argument is meaningless.

More to the point, what the defense says may be true with respect to petechiae in the lungs, though even so the extraordinarily large amount of lung hemorrhaging is strongly suggestive of a violent death. The important argument here, however, is that petechiae are *never* found above the neck and around the eyes in SIDS deaths. In the absence of alternative medical explanations such as certain types of heart disease, such petechiae are a forensic scientist's direct route to a diagnosis of suffocation.

Finally, Kristen Hamilton was thirteen months old when she died. SIDS is most common in infants between two and seven months old; it is rare after nine months. What's more, an important aspect of SIDS investigations is to examine the scene, particularly the crib, and how the baby is lying when found. None of this was done.

"All these things taken into consideration," the court records report my summation, "I would cluster all the deaths together as asphyxial deaths due to external asphyxia."

Two days later, after less than seven hours' deliberation, the jury agrees. Pankow is found guilty of two counts of second-degree murder.

Each charge carries a maximum sentence of twenty years.

CHAPTER 9

The .38-Caliber Yarmulke

Key words: Self-defense. Reconstruction.
Distance wound. Yarmulke. Police brutality.
—ABSTRACT OF ARTICLE ON THE "YARMULKE KILLING,"
JOURNAL OF THE FORENSIC SCIENCE SOCIETY, 1989

EXCEPTIONS TO THE RULE

I WAS ONCE INFORMED BY A HASIDIC COLLEAGUE OF MINE THAT THERE are more Hasidic Jews living in Rockland County than in Tel Aviv. Whether this is so or not, a large and thriving Hasidic population certainly does live in Rockland, especially in the midcounty towns of Monsey and New City.

Here these inheritors of ancient Jewish tradition are justifiably proud of their reputation as peace-loving, pious, and most of all law-abiding citizens whose communities carry on their affairs, somewhat miraculously, with a minimum of the disturbances that bedevil our modern culture such as drunkenness, drugs, juvenile delinquency, and family violence.

One could, of course, say that characterizing Hasids—or any other cultural group for that matter—in this way is ethnic bias. Indeed, any time someone makes a broad generalization about a specific culture or race, be the observation positive or negative, somewhere a pricked-up ear takes notice and trots out accusations of stereotyping.

Perhaps it is stereotypical to call the Hasids quiet, nonviolent people. But though some might argue the point, others would agree that a majority of stereotypes have a grain of truth.

More to our purposes, however, every truth has its exceptions.

A NOT SO STEREOTYPICAL BURGLAR

Twenty-three-year-old Neil Bernstein is a case in point.

This quiet young man wears the dark suit and hat of the traditional Hasidic man. He attends shul on a regular basis, has a long beard, and says his prayers. Every day he industriously practices his profession at a jewelry firm in New York City. Then he returns home in the evening to be with family and friends, blending in unobtrusively with the busy Hasidic community where he was born and raised. Neighbors describe him as a "mensch," an upright and concerned young man who is close to his family and generous in giving to charity. He has spent his past two summers working in a camp for retarded children in the Catskill Mountains.

But as is so often the case, appearances cover up as much as they reveal. Beneath his well-mannered conventional surface, Neil Bernstein is a complex and tormented young man who leads a secret life: he is deeply addicted to heroin.

He keeps this alarming fact concealed from all but family and close friends, but the cost of his ever-escalating addiction has driven him to housebreaking and back-alley theft. By the time we meet our protagonist, he is already a practiced second-story man. Several days before our story begins, he is arrested carrying a suitcase filled with jewelry, and the goods are quickly traced back to a house in his neighborhood.

Freed on $2,500 bail, he awaits a trial that could send him to the penitentiary for as long as four years. The Bernstein family, quite understandably, is keeping these matters a secret; but even the looming threat of prison and family disgrace is rarely enough to make an addict break the habit; nor does it stop him from chasing after the money to feed that habit. Any way he can.

SHOOT FIRST

On the afternoon of May 15, 1981, Neil Bernstein is busy casing out a burglary job. The house he intends to enter is located on Forshay Street in an affluent neighborhood in Monsey. Bernstein knows the area intimately: his home is two doors down on the same street.

As he stands on the sidewalk, surveying the target and looking up and down the quiet road, the signs are encouraging: no one around; easy access through several ground-floor windows; a large, empty house with inhabitants who do not return from work until seven o'clock each night, and who own many choice, salable goodies.

But from the start of this caper, the young man's behavior is erratic.

Instead of sneaking into the well-treed backyard of the house to reconnoiter, Bernstein boldly approaches the main entrance. In front of the entire neighborhood, he uses his bare fist to smash in a small glass window adjacent to the front door. The sound of shattering glass echoes up and down Forshay Street. In the process he slices one of his fingers.

After making several futile efforts to reach through the broken pane and unlock the door, Bernstein runs to his car, which is parked nearby, and rummages through the trunk to find a rag to wipe the blood off his hand. Then he trots around to the backyard, looking for an easier point of entry. Finding none, he returns to the front, this time kicking in a large bay window with a resounding crash, and entering through the gaping hole.

Predictably, a neighbor across the street hears the clamor, looks out her window, spies a burglar at work, and phones the authorities. Within minutes a squad car arrives, and Patrolman David Lamond, a nine-year veteran of the Ramapo Police Department, jumps out and dashes to the house of the neighbor who made the call.

She tells Officer Lamond that a black man with short kinky hair, dressed in a black suit and black hat, is in the process of burglarizing the house across the street.

After radioing for a backup unit, Lamond approaches the house, checks the back patio to make sure no accomplices are waiting there for the burglar to toss articles out a window, then enters the house through the broken bay window. Ironically, this same house has been robbed several times already in the past year, and it is now equipped with a state-of-the-art alarm system. Why the buzzers and sirens go off when the patrolman enters and not when the thief bangs his way in remains a mystery.

Inside, Officer Lamond finds the house in disarray, with furniture overturned and drawers ransacked all over the living room, dining room, and den. Scuffling sounds come from the floor above. Climbing the stairs, he catches sight of a young man standing in the second-floor hallway, carrying a large amorphous bag.

For a brief moment, the two men stare into each other's eyes.

The housebreaker, Officer Lamond sees, is white, not black; his suit is blue, not black; his black hair and beard are by no means short and kinky. He is not wearing a black hat. He is wearing a black yarmulke.

The patrolman quickly draws his Colt .38 revolver and orders the intruder to surrender.

The man at the top of the stairs is frightened and desperate. He drops what turns out to be a leather bag full of pilfered household articles, and races down the hall, into a nearby bedroom. Here he breaks a window overlooking the back of the house, climbs onto the ledge, and squats for a moment, gazing down, no doubt with some misgivings, at the stone patio below.

Then he takes the leap.

All the time our protagonist is making his escape, Patrolman Lamond is close behind, dashing up the stairs to the blaring whine of the alarm, running down the hall, and making his way into the bedroom. He arrives at the broken window just moments after the burglar has made his jump.

Looking down at the patio, Patrolman Lamond sees the perpetrator sprawled out on the stone patio below, obviously dazed. He again commands him to cease and desist.

Instead, the man staggers to his feet, turns in a clockwise direction, and looks up at the window where the cop is standing. He turns back, takes a step as if to make his getaway, then stops and whirls again, so that the upper half of his body is facing the officer.

With this movement, Neil Bernstein seals his fate.

Staring down from the second-story window, Patrolman Lamond sees what appears to be a black revolver with a four-inch barrel clutched in the burglar's left hand. The officer is in a highly exposed and cramped position, leaning far out a window rimmed with shards of broken glass. His .38 is clenched in his right hand.

Hanging here out to his waist with the alarm sounding in his ear, sensing the closeness of the knife-like glass fragments around him, believing that the intruder is aiming a pistol at his very visible and partially immobilized hulk, fearing for his life, he fires his .38 pistol in what he believes is self-defense. His shot hits the burglar directly in the head.

Spinning in a half-circle, the struck man crumples to the cement floor, facedown. As he collapses a small dark object flutters out of his left hand and lands on the patio close by.

The officer dashes downstairs, runs into the backyard, approaches the downed intruder, who is now lying very still, and looks for the gun.

But the man is unarmed. What the patrolman took for a snub-nosed pistol in the confused blur of the moment is, he now realizes, a yarmulke that the young man was clutching in his left hand as he made his turn.

As any law enforcement professional will tell you, two major terrors haunt the dreams of every police officer.

The first is being killed or maimed in the line of duty.

The second is killing an unarmed or innocent person by mistake.

Patrolman Lamond may have shot the Hasidic burglar in imagined self-defense. But he will soon have to make his case and prove his innocence before a grand jury, an angry press shouting police brutality, and the entire Hasidic community.

Patrolman Lamond knows he has a serious problem.

AT THE SCENE

Squatting next to the young man's inert body and hoping for a miracle, Lamond takes Bernstein's pulse.

Something, perhaps? He calls for an ambulance, runs for oxygen and first-aid equipment from his patrol car, rolls the victim on his back, and starts to perform cardiopulmonary resuscitation. But a deadly .38 caliber slug has drilled its way through the intruder's skull, cutting a channel deep into his brain. First aid is useless.

In minutes, the backup units arrive with sirens bellowing. Several patrolmen clamber out of the car and run to the back of the house, where they find Patrolman Lamond still trying to revive the fallen thief. The arriving officers take one look at the body in its pool of blood and gently urge Lamond to call it quits. Then they cordon off the area and call my office.

Arriving at the scene a few minutes later, I briefly examine the body, check for vital signs, and formally pronounce the bearded youth in the conservative dark blue suit dead. It is precisely four o'clock in the afternoon.

That same evening the police officer is placed on administrative leave. A hearing before a grand jury is scheduled to take place when he returns.

Five hours after the shooting, Lamond's chief of police gives a brief press conference; he refuses to speculate on the details of the shooting, saying only that Patrolman Lamond is "a seasoned veteran officer" and that his rights will be well protected.

"I'm certain it was justifiable," Lamond's lawyer tells a group of journalists. "Certainly it was his belief he was dealing with somebody who was armed. There was a burglary in process, and he was in jeopardy. I'm confident he'll be vindicated. He's a good cop."

Which is true. Patrolman Lamond boasts an exemplary nine-year career. His fellow officers describe him as friendly, introspective, independent, and always careful on the job.

His record has only one tiny flaw: he and another officer were once put on temporary suspension for refusing to get a haircut. The case was never brought before the police review board, and both officers were quickly reinstated. As one member of the force tells the press, "David's a really, really, really good cop."

THE .38-CALIBER YARMULKE

Such are the circumstances of the strange, awkward, and, I think, unique homicide I am called to oversee that May afternoon.

Standing in the backyard of this upscale suburban house, I gaze down on the young intruder who lies twisted where he has fallen, covered in his uselessly shed blood. His body is in a supine position a short distance to the left of the upstairs window from which he made his foolhardy jump. The yarmulke in question is three inches from his hand and appears to have several small bloodstains on it.

As I stand here I cannot help wondering what really happened, and why Patrolman Lamond would shoot an unarmed, callow youth who was trying to run for his life. Among the police detectives who work this case, and among the many journalists who report its ins and outs through the coming months, this disturbing episode will soon be dubbed, not without black humor, the ".38-caliber yarmulke case."

An hour later the young man's body is transported to the medical examiner's office.

His father is notified, but his mother is in the hospital convalescing from a severe heart attack, and her family is afraid to break the news. As the case goes public and controversy begins to swirl, she remains blissfully ignorant of her son's demise.

CLOSE-UP AND FAR AWAY

The next morning we begin the autopsy.

We remove and examine the deceased's clothes. He is dressed in characteristic Hasidic garb with black shoes and blue socks, dark blue pants, white shirt, black belt, and dark blue jacket. He wears an upscale watch on his wrist, a 10-karat-gold Tissot; a professional emblem, no doubt, of his work in the jewelry market. There are no bullet holes in his clothes. A single shot to the head has done the trick.

At the time of the break-in the young man was wearing a yarmulke, the same one he clutched in his hand as he floundered on the patio.

The yarmulke, of course, is the cloth skullcap worn by observant Jewish men. They wear it at home and at work as well as in the synagogue. Its purpose is to remind the wearer that he stands before God at every moment, "both in the shadows," as one Hebrew scholar phrases it, "and in the light."

We examine the yarmulke, take notes on its dimensions and condition, photograph it from a number of angles, enclose it in a plastic bag, and set it aside with the other evidence.

Then we open up the victim's torso with a scalpel. All vital organs are intact and unremarkable. When Bernstein's blood is examined in the lab, however, toxicological studies reveal significant findings. Using a system known as thin-layer chromatography (TLC), we detect large amounts of morphine in his blood and urine.

It now becomes clear why Bernstein acted in such a bungling and foolhardy way throughout. While he was attempting to break into a house in the middle of the day in a neighborhood where everyone knew his face, and then while he tried, with unimaginable idiocy, to outrun a trained officer of the law who was in hot pursuit with a loaded revolver—he was sleepwalking through the whole misadventure, made dumb by heroin. As a family friend later told a journalist, "It wasn't the gun or the cop that killed Neil. It was a needle."

We next turn to Neil Bernstein's head. His face, mustache, and beard are covered with blood. Its source is a bullet hole in the back of his head, 0.9 centimeters in diameter. It is located 5 centimeters to the right of the skull's midline, and 6 centimeters below its crown. This bullet hole and the damage it did now become the primary focus of our examination.

BULLET-HOLE LANGUAGE

The first thing to determine is whether Patrolman Lamond fired at Bernstein from close-up or at a distance, and hence whether his bullet produced a contact wound (from a gun pressed directly against the victim's skin), a near-contact wound (from a gun fired about an inch away), an intermediate wound (from a gun fired at a distance of several inches or more), or a long-distance wound (from a gun more than a few feet away). Any indication that the bullet was discharged from close-up will mean that Bernstein was not shot from the window above the patio, indeed that he was perhaps killed execution style; any such finding will quickly turn what appears to be a police arrest gone awry into a brutal murder.

I start by washing the victim's head wound and shaving the skin surrounding it. Close examination of the area is made under a strong light with a high-power magnifying glass. Using the methodology developed by Dr. Vincent Di Maio in his authoritative text, *Gunshot Wounds*, I now search for evidence of the gun's distance from the skin when fired.

Hard-contact wounds. In hard-contact bullet wounds, the gun's muzzle is pressed tight against the victim's body. This pressure leaves an after-impression of the gun's barrel on the skin. The edges of such wounds are burned and deeply embedded with soot that cannot be washed off. Soot and shavings are also deposited inside the wound.

Loose-contact wound. The gun barrel is pressed lightly against the victim's body and fired, leaving a slight but identifiable indentation on the skin. A small ring of soot is left around the hole but can be wiped away.

Near-contact wound. The gun is held an inch or so away from the victim and fired. In this case, powder grains from released gases produce a dotted mass of pinpoint hemorrhages known as tattooing in the area circling the wound. A relatively wide zone of soot and grease is also baked onto the skin from this type of discharge, and only some of this debris can be scrubbed off.

Intermediate-range wound. The muzzle of the gun is held several inches away from the victim and fired. The shot produces a zone of powder tattooing consisting of individual tattoo marks that cannot be wiped off. These tattoo marks are stained with blood elements from struck capillaries, and are reddish brown to orange red in color. Medically these bloodstained marks can be used to show that a victim is alive and his heart pumping blood at the moment he is shot.

Distant-range wounds. Distant-range bullet wounds, made by a gun held two feet or more from the victim, are relatively clean, showing a minimum of blood and smudging. These wounds produce no tattooing, no soot rings, and no smoke burns, and there is no grease circling the wound.

As a point of forensic interest, distant bullet wounds and intermediate bullet wounds to the head tend to be small and round at the point of entry, with a circular perforation known as an abrasion collar around the edges and minimal signs of bleeding. Contact and near-contact wounds, especially to the head, are often stellate—star-shaped—because of the violent blowback of materials and gases slamming against the scalp from the explosion.

Even bullets that enter their target from long distances and that contain no smoke particles, metal fragments, or other debris may produce a dark edge around the wound. This discoloration is due to surface grime on the bullet proper, which wipes itself clean on the skin as it enters, forming a "soiling ring" around the hole.

Contact wounds are characteristic of suicides as well as murders. Sometimes it is difficult to tell the two apart, although the vast majority of self-inflicted wounds appear in classic spots on the head such as the temple, the forehead, and the roof of the mouth. An entry wound found at an atypical location such as the heart, or especially on the cheek, is usually a sign of foul play. Suicides almost never shoot themselves directly in that most sacred of all body areas, the face. Medical examiners also suspect that a wound is nonsuicidal if it was inflicted from a distance greater than an arm's length. Though a few people determined to kill themselves without foul-up build elaborate self-killing devices complete with springs, pulleys, and trip wires, most suicides simply hold a gun to their temple and pull the trigger.

The wound that killed Bernstein has the characteristics of a distant-range wound: it is clean of tattooing, soot, smoke, or grease. It was clearly *not* inflicted at close quarters. The general outline of Patrolman Lamond's story holds up so far.

THE FATAL SLUG

I cut more deeply into the midforehead region and probe for the bullet. I find it—a copper-jacketed bullet in relatively good condition—and use plastic forceps to remove it.

It corresponds in shape and type to a bullet found nearby. This slug has passed through the back of the cranium and up into a frontal lobe, where it came to rest. For this reason there is no exit wound in the front of the victim's head.

The slug also lacerated enormous amounts of tissue as it passed through the brain, and its explosive force produced massive hemorrhaging. These traumas are the direct cause of the man's instantaneous death.

Finally, both nasal cavities inside the head are filled with semi-clotted blood. Small hemorrhage spots can be seen over both eyes: these markings are typical in a person who has been shot in the brain. A small contusion darkens the eyebrow. There are others on the chin, hand, and right kneecap, all produced, we agree, by Bernstein's landing hard on the patio.

Finally, we send the fatal bullet out to the ballistics lab, where ballistics experts use a comparison microscope to verify that the bullet removed from the victim's brain was, after all, fired from Patrolman Lamond's gun.

A comparison microscope is a large ocular instrument with two separate eyepieces that provide a three-dimensional view. Prisms are mounted over the tubes in such a way that two objects can be studied either separately or simultaneously. These separate images can also be projected onto a single split screen for side-by-side comparison.

Using this extraordinary instrument, the lab worker can see that the bullet that killed young Bernstein and a test bullet fired from Patrolman Lamond's gun have the same scratches and striation marks ("lands" and "grooves") on their flanks. Only bullets fired from the same gun will match in this way. Even a bullet fired from a different gun of exactly the same caliber, make, and model will be scratched and striated in a different way from the comparison bullet.

Does proving what seems obvious, that the bullet that killed Neil Bernstein was fired from Patrolman Lamond's revolver, seem a waste of lab time and the taxpayer's dollar? It's not. Keep in mind that there were no witnesses to this crime, no hidden cameras, nothing to record the event, no one to report objectively what took place. All the medical examiner's office and the law have to go on is the testimony of the patrolman who did the shooting. And not only are Lamond's job and reputation on the line, but also, if police malfeasance is proven in court, he may go to jail.

There are many possible questions concerning Patrolman Lamond's testimony: Might one or two other people be involved in this house-breaking? Might their names have gone unmentioned in Lamond's report? Could Lamond and the burglar have been working together?

Could the shooting have arisen from a dispute between partners in crime? Was it an accident that happened as both men simulated a rob-bery and chase? Or, from another perspective, could the killing have been motivated by anti-Semitism? Highly unlikely though all these pos-sibilities are, sometimes bizarre twists do occur.

Finally, even after our office and other investigators are convinced that the bullet that killed Neil Bernstein came from the patrolman's gun, that the gun was fired from a distance, and that the sequence of events described by Lamond is plausible, one deeply troubling question hangs over the investigation.

After making his leap from the window and landing on the patio, did Neil Bernstein really stand up and turn to face the patrolman with yar-mulke in hand, leading the officer to shoot in what he thought was self-defense?

And if he did, why is Lamond's bullet lodged in the *back* of Bern-stein's head, not in the front?

THE MINITHEATER OF MURDER

Although the physical reconstruction of a crime is one of the most common procedures used by forensic pathologists to determine the mechanism, manner, and cause of a victim's death, it does not get much play in the press and is conspicuously absent from television documentaries that profile forensic tales. Why this is so, I am not sure; reconstruction in its many forms is one of the most valuable tools we have in establishing what actually took place at the scene of a homi-cide.

You will remember that in the case of the slashed-face murder, de-scribed in chapter four, the DA asked witnesses from the Holiday Inn to stand on a ladder overlooking the suspect's Lincoln Continental, a sim-ulation of their vantage point the day of the killing.

In another high-profile homicide I was involved in, reconstruction was largely responsible for solving the crime. The victim was a man named Kenneth Hiep, a garbage carter in Congers, New York.

In a business largely controlled by the Mafia, Hiep made the mistake of attempting to operate independently, and of not forfeiting a slice of his earnings to the men in dark suits who periodically paid him a visit. For many months, he refused to be intimidated by the Mob or to make the demanded payoffs; finally, two hit men were put on the case. Cornering Hiep in an empty lot, they stabbed him to death. When his body was discovered in a garbage dump, it bore more than eighty knife wounds.

Two primary suspects were apprehended. Both had numerous cuts and slices on their hands. Investigators believed these cuts were acquired both during the stabbing and afterward, when the two suspects allegedly dragged Hiep's body over piles of jutting rock and debris and down a steep precipice to its final dumping place.

The suspects protested.

They had sustained these cuts, they explained, from the window of an automobile that both of them drove at work. The front window on the driver's side of this vehicle, they insisted, continually came off its track in the doorframe. Every time they gripped the plate of glass and tried to fit it back on its runner, its sharp edges would nick their hands.

To investigate this claim, we first interviewed workers at the nail salon that both suspects visited the day before Hiep disappeared. According to the manicurists on duty that afternoon, there were no cuts or bruises on either man's hands during their treatment.

Next, we impounded the suspects' car and set up a reconstruction, performing a series of tests on the front window to see how sharp its edges really were, and how likely someone gripping it would be to slice up his hands.

Examining the front doorframe we found that, just as the suspects had claimed, the front window was loose in its track and easily slid into the window well.

Our staff next established the window's weight, how it fit in a person's hands, and how much strength was needed to lift it and refit it on its track.

The first thing we found was that the window was relatively light, and that it could be hoisted up and moved around with little effort. An eight-year-old child could have done it with ease.

More important, we found that the top and side edges of the glass were entirely smooth. Then, to test the matter in a practical way, my assistants and I repeatedly lifted the window from its setting, moving it this way and that, then replacing it on the track. During these tests none of us sustained a single cut to our gloves, or, as we grew bolder, to our bare hands.

I also found that if I wrapped my hand over the top edge of the glass and then pressed the hydraulic button to raise the window, with my hand resting between the top of the glass and the doorframe, the pressure was negligible: it barely creased my palm.

So our reconstruction established that the suspects' alibi for their cut hands was a lie.

STOP-ACTION RECONSTRUCTION

If the burglar on the patio was facing Patrolman Lamond with what seemed to be a weapon in hand, why did the patrolman's bullet strike him in the back of the head? The worst-case answer is that the patrolman shot and killed an unarmed fleeing man, a practice that will bring down the wrath of just about everyone.

The fact that the patrolman perjured himself when claiming he mistook a yarmulke for a weapon would discredit his case even more. After all, if we place a yarmulke next to a police revolver it is difficult to see a great deal of resemblance between the two.

In the next few days, Patrolman Lamond is interviewed several more times and is asked to explain in detail why his bullet struck the back of the fugitive's head.

Confused concerning the details of those few whirlwind moments, Lamond focuses his wits and memory, finally telling interrogators the following:

First, Bernstein faced him with the seeming weapon. A black yarmulke jutting out of an intruder's fist in a certain way, and seen from a distance, the patrolman insists, can and in this case did resemble a pistol.

In the next one or two seconds Bernstein began to turn for the second time, presumably to run away. (This fact is indeed in the patrolman's original report.)

But by this time Patrolman Lamond was an arrow in flight, reacting to the weapon he thought was pointed at him, and firing by reflex just as Bernstein started to make his second turn. At this point, the burglar has revolved just enough so that the bullet strikes the back of his head.

The scenario Lamond proposes is logical and even believable, but is it physically possible? We decide to reenact the event from beginning to end, and to perform time-lapse studies of the process to see if the action fits the claims.

We start by positioning a member of my staff on the patio of the burglarized house, in the precise spot where the burglar turned to face the police officer on the day of the shooting. He is holding a black yarmulke in his left hand, just as the victim did that day. Another investigator stands at the second-story window and, holding a camera, assumes the same position as the officer.

At this point, the man on the patio re-creates the precise movements Lamond describes Bernstein as having made. He falls to the patio as if jumping from the second story of the house. He then stands up, turns to run, turns back again to face the officer with yarmulke in hand, and in a microsecond's time turns yet again as if to escape. All these activities are carefully timed, photographed, and documented.

Our conclusions from this walk-through, and from the sequence of photos that result, appear as follows in the case report:

> Our findings indicate that there was ample time for the deceased to have turned so that the back of his head faced the police officer during the time it took to extend his arm and pull the trigger. Moreover, the trajectory from the window to the back of the alleged burglar's head was determined to be consistent with the bullet track found in the autopsy. It was thus the opinion of the medical examiner that the testimony

given by the police officer was consistent with autopsy findings and scene reconstruction.

It is also established from the photographs that the black yarmulke held by the medical examiner appears as a menacing dark object when seen from the vantage point of the upstairs window. When squeezed tightly in several tests, an inch or two of the cap projects from the clenched fist, taking on the pointed shape of what can easily be construed as a gun barrel or snub-nosed pistol.

With the test results completed, the case is brought before the grand jury. No indictment is brought against Officer Lamond. His actions are deemed reasonable under the circumstances, and he is cleared of misconduct. The officer is reinstated on the force, where he continues to perform his duties in an exemplary way. Until . . .

LAST JUDGMENT

Several years after Lamond's exoneration, Neil Bernstein's family files a suit in federal court against him and against the town of Monsey. They hire Dr. Louis Roh, a deputy medical examiner and forensic pathologist from the Westchester Medical Examiner's Office. Dr. Roh maintains that his studies show that the yarmulke was on Bernstein's head at the moment he was shot. He also claims that a photograph of the yarmulke plainly shows a bullet hole.

If this is true, the family claims, it proves that the yarmulke was not in the victim's hand but on his head, where it belonged. And why, the lawyer for the family asks, would Bernstein have taken his yarmulke off in the heat of the chase, anyway? He certainly had more important things to do while running for his life than to reach up and remove an article of clothing that he normally never took off in public.

In theory, this accusation is easy to rebut. Just find the intact yarmulke in the DA's evidence archives and present it as evidence. Unfortunately, the DA's office has lost the yarmulke. Without it, the family's case has at least a chance of succeeding, and the too neat coincidence that the yarmulke has been misplaced just when it is needed as evidence also casts a shadow on the original police investigation.

However, both at the scene of the crime and at the autopsy my staff and I studied the yarmulke and photographed it a number of times. At the inquiry we display these pictures, proving conclusively that there is no bullet hole in the cap. The hole the Westchester forensic pathologist identified on the yarmulke is actually a drop of the victim's blood (blood spatter was also photographed on the ground near the dropped yarmulke at the scene). I testify that when I inspected the yarmulke at the scene of the crime it was intact. Several other police investigators and forensic agents who studied the yarmulke at that time agree.

Finally, I present our reconstruction studies to support the photographs. I also bring in Dr. Yong Myun, a deputy medical examiner and forensic pathologist from the Brooklyn Medical Examiner's Office who is also an expert in time-lapse reconstruction, and who testifies that our time sequence and reconstruction are consistent with Officer Lamond's story.

The judge rules in favor of Lamond, and dismisses the case.

CAD: A POSTSCRIPT

Before ending this chapter I should mention that if Neil Bernstein's killing occurred today, another method of reconstruction would be put to use along with physical re-creation: computer-aided design (CAD).

The use of CAD in forensic reconstruction is becoming increasingly popular with lawyers and law enforcement agencies today in direct ratio to the controversy it spawns. The graphics in these minifilms are usually an amalgam of animation, film, and computer-aided design, with the predominant mode depending on the computer programmer and the art personnel designing the clip.

In an alleged hit-and-run auto accident, let us say, the computer programmer may create an animated view of the road as seen by the driver as she rounds a steep curve. We then witness the same accident, this time seen from the victim's point of view as the car swerves in his direction and knocks him off the side of the road.

Even more sophisticated forms of CAD are virtual reality renderings that give viewers the illusion of walking through the scene of a crime and that allow them to make a range of choices and decisions along the way. In such films viewers can, for example, turn right into this living room or turn left into that kitchen. They can walk to the top of the stairs if they choose. Or they can walk halfway up the stairs, turn around, descend, and open the door to the basement instead, all the while observing the virtual surroundings constructed by programmers on the basis of available evidence, eyewitness testimony, and perhaps—and herein lies the controversy—a bit of extrapolation on the part of the programmer.

In the case of the yarmulke killing, a computer reconstruction might walk the viewer through the burglarized residence, observing what both the intruder and the patrolman saw the day of the crime. Viewers would be brought to the window ledge in the upstairs bedroom, where they could view the patio below, just as the intruder probably saw it the moment before he jumped. Viewers would also witness the event from Patrolman Lamond's perspective, looking down at the intruder holding a pistol-shaped yarmulke in his hand.

The ultimate value of such reconstructions is that they re-create crimes "on film" that can then be shown in court, bringing evidence to the jury in visual form. Many lawyers who use CAD reconstructions give a running commentary on their clips, explaining details to the jury and, if they are forthright, pointing out portions of the sequence that are based on supposition or partial evidence.

The problem, of course, is that programmers, being neither witnesses to the event nor God, do not really know what happened at the scene of a crime and to some extent must wing it. The resulting danger is obvious: a forensic computer animation ends up creating reality rather than reporting it.

Though CAD technology is clearly a promising tool in forensics, it is also in its infancy and is used today both with reservations as to its accuracy and with the knowledge that what viewers see are not the facts but interpretations of the facts.

CHAPTER 10

Finding Out Who
The Case of the Missing Reporter

Have no illusions. Your brother is not a
priority. Hire a private investigator.
—A U.S. STATE DEPARTMENT STAFF MEMBER,
SPEAKING TO DONNA IGOE,
SISTER OF THE MISSING REPORTER JOHN SULLIVAN

NOTE ON MY DESK

He didn't want to interrupt your meeting, but the State Department
guy would like to talk to you at length about the John Sullivan case. The
Salvadorans have not been very cooperative, he says, like a stone wall.
Wants to know if he could call you tomorrow morning at eight. Says to
tell you that at this point in the search he's not optimistic about ever
finding the reporter's body, or even if it was found, making any kind of
positive identification.

Like you, perhaps, I keep a message pad near my phone at home. The
above was recorded by my wife.

I am not surprised by the fatalistic tone of the diplomat's message.

Several years ago, I know, a twenty-six-year-old American freelance reporter named John Sullivan flew to the revolution-torn nation of El Salvador on a risky assignment for (perhaps surprisingly) *Hustler* magazine. Sullivan was to interview Salvadoran peasants who had survived mass executions reputedly engineered by their own government.

The ruling regime at this time, as journalists were just beginning to reveal to the world, had long denied farmers and peasants their basic rights of protection, land ownership, and freedom of employment. These indignities had gone on so long that many poor laborers were now turning a friendly ear to guerrilla revolutionaries who defied the government and offered them the promise of social change and a more prosperous life.

Not anxious to be deposed, or even to make small concessions, the government dealt with villages that sympathized with the guerrillas by sending in—to my knowledge this was the first time in history the term was ever used—"death squads" that systematically tortured and killed segments of the town's population.

Schoolchildren, priests, doctors, dying hospital patients, nuns, the very elderly—no one was immune to the slash of the death squads' machetes. In one famous incident, a heap of more than eight hundred slaughtered Salvadoran men, women, and children was found in a deserted village, many of them hacked to bits, with their genitals mutilated and strewn along the streets.

Based on this information, and on reports from other journalists and human rights activists, it was Sullivan's job to look into the massacre rumors, speak with peasants who had witnessed them (or escaped from them), and to write a 4,500-word article that would make world governments take notice, and perhaps initiate diplomatic steps to help prevent yet another twentieth-century mass slaughter.

THE DISAPPEARED

John Sullivan would no doubt have been pleased to hear his colleagues speak of him as a rising star. Though relatively new in his profession, he had already been on the scene at several Central American hot spots, and he was particularly enthusiastic about this assignment to El Salvador, telling his mother before he left that this article might make his international reputation.

On December 28, 1980, Sullivan arrives in the capital, San Salvador. He is driven to the Sheraton Hotel, where he checks into his room.

Several hours later he disappears. He is never seen or heard from again.

Nine days later, a reporter from the Associated Press contacts Sullivan's parents and sisters, informing them that John Sullivan is now officially regarded as missing.

After waiting several more weeks for word from their son and making standard inquiries to the U.S. government, to no avail, the Sullivans take matters into their own hands, querying everyone they can find in American and Salvadoran diplomatic circles concerning the whereabouts—and the fate—of their son and brother. Despite endless entreaties to the State Department and attempts to contact government officials in El Salvador, no useful information is forthcoming. Desperate, the family places an advertisement in several Salvadoran newspapers every week for fifteen straight months, offering a reward for any information regarding the whereabouts of the missing man.

After almost a year and a half of waiting and hoping, the family receives a letter. It is from a Salvadoran man who grimly identifies himself as a member of the death squad that killed their son. The writer claims that Sullivan was mistaken for a leftist Belgian priest, Rogelio Punceele, who after receiving death threats had gone into hiding from the Salvadoran government several days before Sullivan's arrival, and that as a result of this mistake Sullivan was kidnapped, tortured, and killed the day of his abduction.

The young reporter, the writer says, establishing his bona fides, was carrying the sum of $500 on his person the day he was kidnapped. He adds that Sullivan begged for his life in broken Spanish as he was being tortured.

A few days later a second letter arrives. A handwriting expert confirms that it is in the same hand as the first. Again eager to prove that he is the real thing, the writer provides detailed information concerning Sullivan's attempts to inscribe a message on the wall of his cell, plus descriptions of the length and appearance of a scar on his left leg.

A third letter then announces that the murdered man's body is buried in the tiny town of Nuevo Cuscatlan, about twenty miles south of San Salvador, and that the burial was witnessed by several town officials.

A final letter provides additional details about the killing, along with a crudely drawn map showing the precise location of the grave.

Denying the veracity of the letters but mercilessly egged on now by the press, the American and Salvadoran governments are forced to respond—and to dig.

SPLINTERS

In July 1982, following the instructions on the informant's map, a body is exhumed from a shallow ditch in Nuevo Cuscatlan, not far from a heavily guarded government electric facility. Though Nuevo Cuscatlan officials formerly denied any knowledge of this burial, the day the remains are removed U.S. government officials in El Salvador find local records stating that an unidentified and mutilated body was buried in this grave on December 29, 1980, the day after Sullivan's disappearance.

A year and a half has now passed since the Sullivan family first began seeking word of their son. They have no illusions that the corpse, settled into its shallow bed of lime and clay, will be well preserved and easy to identify.

What they did not bargain for is that when the digging is complete no body at all is brought out of the ground, only a small pile of crushed and splintered bone fragments. So many parts of the skeleton are missing, including much of the upper torso, the skull, and both arms, that a preliminary examination of the pieces by Salvadoran experts indicates that the victim either died from being blown up, or was blown up after he died.

Local authorities transport these melancholy remains to a Salvadoran forensic lab for analysis. Judging from X rays, the lab reports that these bones belonged to a man approximately forty to forty-five years old. John Sullivan was twenty-six.

According to their anthropological measurements, the man's approximate height was five feet eight inches. John Sullivan was six feet tall. The Salvadoran lab also declares that the X rays of a right knee bone sifted out of the fragments do not resemble microfiche X rays sent them of John Sullivan's right knee, made at Hackensack Hospital in New Jersey in 1972, following a knee injury. Indeed, they find little relation between the exhumed body parts and John Sullivan's anatomical records. In their opinion, therefore, the skeletal pieces unearthed in the ditch outside Nuevo Cuscatlan do not belong to the missing American reporter. These remains are so few and so mutilated, the Salvadorans go on to say, that their identity can never be established no matter what forensic means are used to test them.

The Sullivan family is unconvinced.

THE RIGHT TO RECLAIM OUR DEAD

During the numerous homicides I have participated in since my first days as medical examiner, I have noted that their investigation is focused with a kind of monomaniacal intensity on a single goal: *Analyze the evidence to catch the killer.* This aim is the Holy Grail of all forensic pathology.

But not invariably.

Occasionally the use of forensic methodology, along with police investigation, computer detection, and every other known means of tracking down a killer, proves useless. The murderer simply cannot be caught—ever.

In the case of John Sullivan, locating his death squad assassin and bringing the felon to justice is clearly such an impossibility. Given the circumstances of Sullivan's death, it simply cannot be done. The young man's eradicator is thousands of miles away, protected by distance, time, walls of jungle, and fear of reprisals, his executioner's face well hidden behind the mask of his government's guilt and paranoia.

And yet in such cases, despite the fact that the killer is uncatchable, there is still a need, sometimes a pressing one, for forensic investigation. This need now frames itself as a mercy for those left behind—relatives, friends, loved ones. It is at this point less a matter of criminal justice, more of humanitarian dignity.

For the fact is that in certain homicides the questions of who did the killing, where, and when, and how, eventually prove irrelevant. What matters, finally, is the need to be sure that a recovered body, or even the fragments of a body, belong to the person we loved. The search through the debris of the World Trade Center for the smallest personal token or traceable DNA sample is a gripping example of this very human longing.

Thus, though the doctors in El Salvador insist that the remains in Nuevo Cuscatlan are untraceable, the Sullivan family maintains that, since their informant's letters have been so accurate on so many details, there is no reason to doubt what he tells them now concerning the burial site. Perhaps, the family argues, the Salvadoran scientists have made a mistake. Or perhaps more sinister political motives lurk in the lab's findings, orchestrated by a government with no wish to be caught bankrolling jungle death squads that kill American reporters.

Gradually, other people begin to reach the same conclusions. The Sullivans, persistent and persuasive, win over doctors, lawyers, media personnel, and politicians to their cause. The case of the missing New Jersey reporter gains ever wider public notice and, as the Salvadoran government continues to buck the investigation, national notoriety.

Finally, in the first months of 1983, pathologists at the Smithsonian Institution, studying the Salvadoran X rays, declare that these bones belong to a man in his twenties, contrary to what the Salvadoran forensic pathologists claimed.

At this point the family consults New York City police detectives, who recommend that they contact my office for help because of my reputation for solving thorny forensic cases. The media quickly get wind of their request, and a great deal of fuss is made over my participation. Local reporters long ago took to calling me the Rockland Quincy; now one New York City newspaper article lards it on especially thick: "The Sullivan mystery might seem like a perfect case for Sherlock Holmes or Philip Marlowe—or for Dr. Frederick Zugibe, Rockland's own version of the legendary sleuths."

Despite the hoopla and the apparent impossibility of finding a solution, I agree to work on the case, pro bono. No family, I and many other forensic pathologists believe, should have to pay for the right to reclaim its own dead.

After studying the Hackensack X rays of Sullivan's knee, I speak with a number of Rockland County officials and ask to use our forensic facilities at no charge. Most of the officials already know of the Sullivan family's desperate quest; they quickly agree.

And so, while 98 percent of forensic homicide investigations look for a method, a means, and a murderer, this case will be an exception, an exercise in pure forensics, with no payoff other than emotional closure.

We go to work.

POLITICS AS USUAL

First, we ask the Salvadoran forensic lab to send us X rays of the left knee bone and leg of the exhumed remains.

After some hedging, they agree.

Once the pictures arrive, they are compared to the microfiche radiographs of Sullivan's left knee from Hackensack Hospital. It is difficult to match the American microfiche and the Salvadoran X rays in a precise way, because the latter were taken at different angles from the former, perhaps intentionally so. Still, there is a striking similarity in the bone formation of the tibia, the shinbone, in both images. It encourages me to press the issue.

Now it should be pointed out that for almost two years before I was brought in on this case, the Sullivan family, along with their many political allies, had repeatedly asked the Salvadoran government to ship the body parts unearthed in Nuevo Cuscatlan to the United States for further anthropomorphic studies and X-ray work.

Among medical establishments of neighboring countries, such a request is common. But oddly, Salvadoran officials refuse, citing an obscure law prohibiting the shipment or transfer of any unidentified human remains out of their country.

Fair enough.

Or unfair enough, depending on your perspective. Meanwhile, the American embassy in San Salvador is asked by several congresspersons to exert pressure on the Salvadoran government.

But again, no.

Despite repeated entreaties by U.S. Congresswoman Marge Roukema of New Jersey and other government officials, American Embassy personnel in El Salvador drag their heels at a tortoise-like pace. Inquiries go unanswered. Requests are unfulfilled. Evidence turned up is ignored. It is, after all, American embassy officials insist, El Salvador's sovereign right to maintain possession of the contested bone fragments if they so choose.

What possible reason, people start to ask, could the American Embassy in El Salvador have for blocking the Sullivan investigation?

The best theory anyone can come up with is politics as usual.

If the body of John Sullivan is positively identified, the American government will be forced to acknowledge the existence of Salvadoran death squads, something the Reagan administration staunchly refuses to do. A similar political deadlock is unfolding one Central American country over, in Nicaragua.

When and if this slur on human rights is made public, our government will be obliged to cut back its annual funding to El Salvador. Because the guerrillas in this country have strong Communist leanings, a cut in aid to the Salvadoran ruling elite means a reduction in its military strength as well, and thus a helping hand for Communist encroachment.

This, at least, is the theory. All we know for sure is that the powers that be in both governments have a vested interest in keeping the body bag of unidentified bones at home in Central America, and that they are ready to go to the mat with anyone who tries to change that.

"Have no illusions," Sullivan's sister is told by an American diplomat. "Your brother is not a priority. Hire a professional investigator." A similar slice of cold comfort is offered by a former U.S. secretary of state, Edmund Muskie. "Do you think your son is the only one this has happened to?" he asks Sullivan family members when they ask for his help.

In some ways, the Sullivan situation resembles the script of a 1982 film, *Missing*, based on the true story of a young American freelance writer named Charles Horman, who was executed by soldiers during the 1973 military coup in Chile for knowing too much about America's involvement in the overthrow of the president, Salvador Allende. In this remarkable film, a series of heartless U.S. diplomats and bureaucrats work hard to foil every attempt made by Horman's wife and father to locate him; and then, once they learn for certain he is dead, to find his body; and then, once they find his body, to have it shipped back to the United States.

As to my own role in the Sullivan quest, the prospects for success seem minimal. Without the actual body parts from El Salvador to study, definitive identification will be impossible. Despite the amazing energy and persistence of the Sullivan family, at this point it seems that the case of the missing reporter may never be resolved.

Then, as in a fairy tale, a champion steps forward.

THE CHAMPION

He is Congressman Robert Torricelli of New Jersey, recently elected to his first term in Congress, and a member of the House Foreign Affairs Committee. Torricelli makes the Sullivan family's cause his own, going so far as to travel to El Salvador and meet with several of the country's leaders, including President Alvaro Magana and Foreign Minister Fidel Chavez Mena. His trip is sponsored by the Commission on United States–Central American Relations, a private human rights organization that over the past several years has taken a personal interest in the Sullivan family cause.

No one knows exactly what is said at Torricelli's meetings with Salvadoran officials, but on his return the congressman announces that the Salvadoran government has done an unanticipated 180-degree turnabout on international body shipping policies and has graciously agreed to ship the possible remains of John Sullivan to the United States at once.

Torricelli remarks to the press that when the Sullivan family repeatedly asked for help during the two-year search for their son, American officials in El Salvador were "not helpful to these people."

"You can look at it two ways," Torricelli warns. "It was either calculation or neglect. I fear that worse is involved here than neglect."

COFFINS WITHIN COFFINS

The first item of business is to assemble a team of forensic investigators. The team includes myself as director; Drs. James Taylor and Robert DiBennerdo, professor and associate professor of anthropology at Lehman College, who are consultants in forensic anthropology to my office; Dr. Noah Weg, a forensic radiologist who is consultant in forensic radiology to my office; my senior medical investigator, James Costello;

and Dr. Peter DeForest, professor of criminalistics at the John Jay College of Criminal Justice in New York City.

Finally on February 20, 1983, a parcel marked "Human Remains" is removed from the freight hold of a plane at a Newark International Airport cargo depot and placed on a dolly. Present at the unloading are the sisters and brothers-in-law of John Sullivan. In attendance also are two representatives from Congressman Torricelli's office.

After a few words are said, a staff member from the Rockland County Medical Examiner's Office picks the parcel up, loads it into a van, and drives it to our office. Here the parcel is placed on an examination table in my lab, and I begin to take stock. The remains, we can see, are housed in a dark royal blue canvas bag sewn on both sides with a blue mattress stitch. The bag is addressed to Dr. Fred Zugibe at the Rockland County Medical Examiner's Office in large yellow letters that for some reason glow in the dark.

The package is photographed; then the blue mattress stitch is cut at one end and the contents are removed, a tiny brown metal box. We later learn that this container is the type of coffin used in El Salvador to bury infant children. Opening it, we find a smaller metal box inside that is soldered shut along its four edges.

A propane torch is used to melt the seal.

Inside the box are two heavy-duty orange plastic bags, one packed tightly inside the other. The inner bag plus its contents weighs twenty-two pounds. The contents are dark brown soil that contains wood particles, stones, roots, pieces of cloth, and several skeletal parts, some of which appear to be fractured. Of the twenty-two pounds of material, only fourteen pounds are from the body itself—not a great deal to go on when attempting to identify a human being.

MATCHING X RAYS

Sifting through the roots and earth, we carefully remove the skeletal parts and lay them out on an X-ray stretcher. They are photographed and radiographed.

Pieces of fabric found in the dirt packing are likewise arranged on the stretcher, and more pictures are taken. While sorting through the dirt, we find a number of individual metallic teeth that have been stripped off a zipper. Several of these are stuck to one of the vertebrae.

Examining the remains available to us, and realizing how few pieces of the person we have to work with—the Salvadoran pathologists were quite truthful on this score—we begin to realize that the job before us is a daunting and, I must say, somewhat intimidating one. The usual means of identifying a dead body—dental plates, possessions, finger-prints, DNA studies, eyewitness reports, facial reconstruction, tissue samples, scars, tattoos—are all useless. As for the skeletal frame, we have only some ribs, the sacrum, parts of the pelvis, a few vertebrae from the lower spine, and a majority of both legs. The skull, upper extremities, upper spine, and most other important structural parts of the body are all missing. No traces of soft tissue remain on the bones; no identifying grease, animal marks, or odors are present.

Looking over these remnants, I have little doubt that they are from a body that has not only decomposed in the earth for several years, but has at some point been intentionally torn apart and broken to bits, no doubt to make identification impossible. It is as if some canny killer had anticipated that at a future date a team of forensic scientists would be doing just what we are doing here today, and had taken extreme measures to thwart us.

But even bare bone fragments tell a tale, sometimes a comprehensive tale, and our forensic department fortunately has access to state-of-the-art bone-testing methods that will help us establish critical circumstantial facts. With this information, plus comparative radiological studies, plus a bit of luck . . . who knows?

We begin by making full-size X rays of the bones of the left leg. These pictures are taken to verify that the Salvadoran government has, in fact, sent us the remains shown in the previous X rays. Happily, the major features of our X rays agree with the images from San Salvador. Scattered zipper teeth are noted in both films, further evidence of the remains' authenticity.

Satisfied that we are working with the right body, we now compare our recently taken X rays of the leg and knee joint with the films made of John Sullivan's leg at Hackensack Hospital. Comparisons of density patterns and other morphological features are made by our forensic radiologist consultant, Dr. Noah Weg, and they provide gratifying results: we conclude that the Hackensack X rays and those of the leg from El Salvador show the same bone.

Dr. Weg meticulously radiographs the victim's lower knee and leg bone more thoroughly using numerous projections, angulations, and rotations until he is able to precisely match the angles used in the Hackensack X rays. These comparisons match perfectly.

DETERMINING AGE

The Salvadoran forensic team, you will recall, asserted that the body exhumed outside of Nuevo Cuscatlan was forty to forty-five years old.

My consulting forensic anthropologists, Dr. James Taylor and Dr. Robert DiBennerdo, and I agree to use a dating method developed in 1957 by T. W. McKern and T. D. Stewart. This technique is accurate to plus or minus three years, and is particularly effective when skeletonized remains are the only parts available for study.

We analyze the various ridges and valleys that have formed along the surfaces of the victim's pubic bone, where both sides are joined at the pubic symphysis. These markings, called ramparts, are especially prominent in young people. As age progresses, and as the ramparts wear thin, the ridges become more difficult to analyze, making this test most dependable for men and women under the age of thirty.

Calculating the depth and shape of the ramparts, then matching up the measurements with representative charts for different ages, our lab estimates that the pubic bone under scrutiny belongs to an individual in the second half of the third decade of life—a person between the ages of twenty-six and twenty-nine years old.

John Sullivan was twenty-six years old when he died.

For further confirmation, we make a study of the recovered joints, searching for lip-shaped ridges. Such lipping is carved out along the joints by arthritis, and usually begins in males after the age of thirty-five.

No evidence of lipping is found anywhere else on the body.

Clearly, we are in the right ballpark as far as age is concerned. We are dealing here with the remains of a person not yet out of their twenties.

DETERMINING RACE

The conformation of human skulls differs considerably from race to race, and forensically speaking, the best way to establish racial identity is to examine the markings and formations on a deceased person's skull.

For example, the orbit—the frontal part of the skull that houses the eye—has a triangular shape in Caucasians, like aviator glasses. In blacks, the orbit is almost rectangular. Among East Asians it is somewhat elliptical. Computer measurements of facial angles, dental patterns, jaw protrusion, size, and other structural features of the skull produce further evidence of race in today's forensic lab. This evidence is almost always accurate.

Unfortunately, our current remains are minus a skull. Distinguishing this person's race will be problematic.

Still, there are ways.

The Caucasian pelvis, for example, is broader than the Negroid or East Asian pelvis. The pelvis we are studying is especially broad. Our body's thighbone is bowed, and the ileum bone is long relative to the thighbone. Both features are signatures of Caucasian bone structure.

Studied, too, are several hairs found in the earth surrounding the remains. These hairs are straight and light in color, characteristic of fair skin and a light complexion.

Finally, the victim's right thighbone is so much longer than the average among men of the Nahua-Pipil, the indigenous people who live in the Nuevo Cuscatlan area and make up most of the population, that the body is unlikely to be that of a local.

The person we are autopsying is Caucasian.

DETERMINING SEX

When a forensic examiner has only fragments of a skeleton to work with, the bones in the pelvis provide the most reliable markers of sex. In females the sacrum, the triangular bone that connects the two sides of the hips, is designed by nature to serve as a birth canal. The female sacrum is therefore short, wide, and flat. In men it is narrow and long. The sacrum we have in this case is relatively well preserved, and its characteristics are those of the male anatomy.

There is an indentation in the pelvic bone, the "sciatic notch," which is wide in females and narrow in males. The notch on the pelvic bone under study is narrow. The socket of the thighbone in men is larger than it is in women; our specimen's socket is large.

Highly accurate measurements are next made of certain areas along the victim's hips; the results match the established measurements for males.

Finally, women who have been pregnant show indentations, known as parturition pits, along their pubic bones. No such markings are found on our sample.

The person we are studying is a man.

DETERMINING SIZE

The best gauge of a person's stature, when one has only a partial skeleton, is the length of the thighbone. Using ratio formulas established for white American males, we estimate that the person whose thighbone we are examining stood at least five feet ten inches tall and at most six feet tall.

John Sullivan was six feet tall.

The size of his skeleton, observation also shows, is adapted to large muscle attachments consistent with a male body. Its general massiveness indicates that it carried a substantial weight.

John Sullivan weighed approximately 185 to 190 pounds.

ANALYZING THE FABRIC REMAINS

Pieces of fabric found in the earth surrounding the body are examined and photographed before and after being washed in a mild chemical solution.

Of particular interest is a patch of corduroy, light brown to tan in color, with several pockets attached to it. The surface of this material has an eight-wale-to-the-inch weave, typical of American corduroy manufacture; a label reading "Made in USA" is sewn into a seam. Under the microscope, the corduroy can be seen to consist of flat, translucent twisted fibers characteristic of cotton.

Found, too, are three pieces of tightly woven grayish-white canvas. Microscopic examination shows that these are primarily composed of cotton, but with polyester fibers added in, a mix typical of American-made canvas overgarments.

Along with the above, remnants of tan-colored bikini-style cotton shorts turn up, plus a scrap of blue polyester mesh with a seam along one edge.

Last, two decayed but intact tan polyester socks are discovered in the earth surrounding the remains, both displaying the same ribbed pattern from ankle to toe.

From the Sullivan family, I learn that before leaving the United States John Sullivan packed a pair of tan corduroy trousers, and that he was fond of wearing bikini-style underwear. He also owned a poplin jacket with a canvas weave similar to the weave on the grayish-white fabric sample. The piece of blue material matches the family's description of an Adidas-type jogging undershirt owned and often worn by Sullivan. The tan socks are consistent with Sullivan's shoe size. This finding is further supported by a reconstruction of the body's foot bones that Investigator Costello and I perform. We obtain a pair of the deceased's shoes from his family, then place our reconstructed foot in a shoe-measuring device obtained from a shoe store. The size is totally consistent with John Sullivan's.

FINAL FORENSIC OBSERVATIONS AND CONCLUSIONS

We conclude the autopsy by evaluating the overall condition of these remains in an attempt to explain their fragmented state. In my view, only one conclusion is possible: so much damage has been done to the upper parts of the body that they must have been exploded away.

This observation is supported by the Inspection Report of Armand Augusto Palma, justice of the peace in Nuevo Cuscatlan, who examined the body on the day it was buried. The Inspection Report states that the pectoral parts of the corpse were shattered, and that most of the upper sections were blown apart by what was most likely an explosive material: "Death appears to have been caused by the explosion of some sort of device because there are no bullet or stab wounds." To this observation Palma adds, "The cranium and face, pectoral and visceral part and fleshy front part of the thighs were destroyed."

During my research on this case I learn that the region of El Salvador where the remains were exhumed is forested with large trees, and that a good deal of logging is done. One of the preferred means of felling these massive trees is to wrap a flexible coil of plastic explosive around the trunk and detonate it. The explosion blows the trunk apart, and the tree topples. Salvadoran death squads use this type of explosive from time to time to eliminate their victims.

Therefore, in assessing the blown-apart condition of the body, noticing evidence of burns to the bones on the upper part of the skeleton, and knowing that no radiopaque fragments of any sort showed up in the X rays—that is, no bits of metal or shot consistent with *non*dynamitelike explosives are present—I conclude that the damage done to this body is consistent with a plastic or dynamite charge. Whether this explosion occurred before or after death, I cannot tell.

What I *can* tell for certain, taking the long list of forensic evidence into consideration, is that the bones before me on the autopsy table belong to the reporter John Sullivan.

"It's final," says Sullivan's mother to the press after we gently present our evidence to the family. "There's nothing else we can do for Johnny but keep him in our prayers."

The search for news of their son's fate, they also tell media questioners, has cost them three years of their lives and $20,000 in expenses, plus their faith in the U.S. government's foreign policy.

GATHERING OF THE CLAN

> John T. Sullivan III, free-lance writer who was slain in El Salvador while on assignment, will be eulogized by a New York television reporter at a memorial Mass today.

Above is the lead to a March 1983 newspaper article describing a memorial Mass held for John Sullivan three years after his disappearance.

Sponsored by the Committee to Protect Journalists, and chaired by Walter Cronkite, the event is attended by 400 friends, fellow journalists, and Sullivan family members, all of whom are present at the gathering not just to honor the memory of a fallen colleague but to make sure that similar injustices are not visited on other reporters.

And yet, as eulogizing letters are read from the likes of actors Jack Lemmon and Ed Asner, and financier Malcolm Forbes, and as tears are shed by those who remember, the mystery of what really happened to John Sullivan three years earlier in the dark and lonely jungles of El Salvador persists.

"Even now," the *New York Times* reports in a March 13, 1983, article on the memorial service, "the family said, after thousands of telephone calls and letters to United States and Salvadorian officials, after poring through documents and notes and anonymous letters filed in everything from bureau drawers to disposable diaper boxes, little is known for certain about how and why Mr. Sullivan died."

Sometimes forensic science can do nothing to solve a crime. It can only bring a sense of completeness to the events of a death, and to some humble extent, provide a feeling of "at least we *know*" to those who would otherwise spend the remainder of their lives in a state of constant and painful wondering.

CHAPTER 11

Bungled Cases, Ingenious Methodologies, Forensic Curiosities

The field of forensics is so filled with so many morbid fascinations, weird side shows, esoteric testing methods, brilliant autopsies, dumb calls, horrible and occasionally funny situations, that I'd like to write a ten-thousand-page book on the subject of the curiosities I've witnessed in forensic pathology through my many years.

—A COLLEAGUE AT THE ROCKLAND MEDICAL EXAMINER'S OFFICE, WHO PREFERS TO REMAIN ANONYMOUS

IN COMPENSATION

Now that you have read through ten forensic studies with their moments of shock and complexity, their inventive and sometimes breathtakingly ingenious techniques, and their often ghastly, though occasionally heroic views of the human soul, it is my hope that your interest in this remarkable system of maintaining social justice is piqued and that your understanding of what forensic pathologists and medical examiners do both for the living and the dead is enhanced.

Now, a few words about what are arguably the two most widely reported and least satisfactorily resolved homicide cases of the second half of the twentieth century: the JonBenét Ramsey strangulation and the O. J. Simpson trial. And lastly a look at how forensic facts can be distorted by popular entertainment and popular superstition, as well as in the crime lab.

JONBENÉT BOONDOGGLE

As all of us know, sometimes to our edification, occasionally to our chagrin, whenever a sensational murder takes over the headlines for more than a day or three, legions of law enforcement specialists populate television news shows, providing endless insights, theories, and especially I-would-have-done-it-a-better-way rebuttals concerning the methods being used to solve the crime.

Perhaps because I have been the forensic examiner in many high-profile crimes, or perhaps simply because there is a limited pool of medical examiners to draw on in this country—only about 500 practice in the United States—I have frequently been one of these professional talking heads, giving my forensic two cents' worth on a number of tabloid homicides. It can be, I blush to admit, agreeable to give one's opinions on another person's errors.

One of the most notorious homicides I have been called on to Monday-morning-quarterback is the strangulation of a six-year-old child pageant star, JonBenét Ramsey, the daughter of a wealthy Boulder, Colorado, businessman and his socialite wife.

JonBenét's dead body is found on Christmas day, 1996, wrapped in a blanket on the basement floor of her home. After a great deal of investigative frenzy going nowhere and solving nothing, her official autopsy report is given over to the press in August of the following year. A few days after it is released, MSNBC sends me a copy and asks me to review it and offer my evaluation in a TV interview.

In preparation for the interview, I study the Ramsey autopsy and related forensic papers for almost a day. Up to this time I have taken only a general professional notice of the Ramsey investigation; now, as I pore over the records, I find it difficult to believe what I am reading.

"Tell us how well you think this case has been handled so far," the MSNBC commentator asks as the interview opens. "And if you would, Dr. Zugibe, let our audience know how you might have done things differently if you'd been the original forensics guy on this case."

"It is always easy for a doctor to second-guess the work of another physician," I reply. "But in going over the autopsy and police report of this little girl's homicide, my experience, my textbook knowledge, and my gut reaction come to the same conclusion: this investigation and autopsy have been botched beyond belief."

To begin, I point out that a ransom note demanding $118,000 for the return of JonBenét Ramsey is found by her mother at 5:52 A.M. She calls 911. The police arrive at 6:00 A.M. and a detective at 8:00. The police set up wiretap and recording equipment, and perform a cursory canvass—but, amazingly, they do not check the entire house. JonBenét's body remains undetected in the basement for many hours.

Finally, at 1:30 in the afternoon, at the suggestion of a friend, the cellar is searched and the missing child is found by her father. The child's mouth is taped and a nylon rope is knotted tightly around her neck. A massive blow has been struck to the side of her head, leaving an eight-and-a-half-inch crater and fracturing her skull. The Boulder coroner-pathologist, Dr. John Meyer, is immediately contacted.

But now the police do another baffling thing: they bar the coroner from the scene of the crime. Dr. Meyer may not enter the Ramsey residence, they insist, until a search warrant is issued. It is thus not until *8:20 that evening* that the coroner is allowed to enter the house and examine the child's corpse. More than six hours have been allowed to elapse from the time the body is discovered to the time it is examined—a period that, as you have seen in this book, is inestimably critical for, among other things, establishing the all-important time of death.

How could this happen? I ask the MSNBC interviewer. Even police cadets in their first year at the academy know that coroners and medical examiners have the legal authority to enter a crime scene at any time without a warrant, and that, in fact, it is the essence of their job to take over the body and the scene as quickly as possible, and to oversee the investigation until the corpse is removed from the premises. To bar a coroner from a murder site is not only an outlandish breach of protocol, it is illegal.

And that, I tell the interviewer, is just the beginning

Once the coroner is finally allowed access to the body, he examines it for less than fifteen minutes, far too short a period of time to perform an effective forensic analysis. It is no surprise, then, that during this super-accelerated once-over the most rudimentary forensic procedures, routinely performed at any homicide scene, are left undone. The coroner performs not one of the following must-do-to-solve-the-crime, Forensics 101 procedures:

1. Note the condition of the body as to any postmortem changes.

2. Note whether the body is in or out of rigor mortis. If it is in rigor, determine the state of the rigor and the phase.

3. Check the corneas of the eyes for clearness or cloudiness.

4. Take a rectal temperature. Check the ambient temperature of the basement and of the upstairs rooms. Record this information, along with the time the readings are taken.

5. Take a vitreous humor sample from one eye, recording the time taken.

6. Examine the victim's fingernails. Place vinyl gloves over the fingers for protection.

7. Interview witnesses and record their accounts of when the victim was last seen alive and the nature and time of her last known meal, as well as a chronology of the victim's predeath activities plus any information they may have bearing on the case.

I am further dumbfounded, I tell the interviewer, to learn that the Boulder coroner then tells the press that the estimate of time of death in a homicide is an opinion that should be reserved for court proceedings.

It is simply not the coroner's responsibility to announce this figure when examining the body, he insists.

I point out that such an attitude runs counter to the current practice of forensic investigation.

Immediately after hearing my interview, I should add, officials of the Boulder Police Department counter my remarks by claiming that forensic methods for determining time of death are too inexact to be of value. From reading the cases in this book, you know that this is patently incorrect; in many and perhaps most homicides, especially when the victim has been dead for twenty-four hours or less, we can learn the approximate and on some occasions the exact time of death. As we have seen many times, determining time of death in a homicide is the first and arguably *the* most important job a medical examiner must attempt.

The list of the Boulder coroner's lapses goes on. I point out to the interviewer that he also failed to have photographs taken of the body, and of the scene in general, other than those taken by the police. These photos should include wide angles of the crime site, working down to close-ups of the body. You have seen how important photographs are in court, and how critical their presence can be for creating subsequent reconstructions.

Nor does the coroner query witnesses at the scene of the crime concerning where and how the body was found. He does not take note of the exact position of the body when discovered. This last factor has a direct effect on the rate at which a body's temperature decreases, and can sometimes play a major part in establishing time of death.

Finally, JonBenét's body was discovered in the basement by her father. He then carried her upstairs, thoroughly contaminating evidence on the body and in the area around it. If a medical examiner had been overseeing the scene, as he should have been, moving the body before it was examined and photographed would have been strictly forbidden. And since the body was discovered and moved by the father, it was the coroner's obligation to take a full report from him concerning where he found his daughter, what the exact position of her body was at the time he located her, the degree of rigor mortis noticed, and so forth, and to record all this information.

I likewise tell the MSNBC interviewer that during autopsy JonBenét's genitals revealed external and internal abrasions, with a small amount of bleeding, which is evidence of sexual molestation despite the coroner's insistence that these findings are commonly seen in young girls. Methylene blue should have been applied to her genital area at this time to show whether additional abrasions invisible to the naked eye were present. Such studies would definitively establish the extent of vaginal damage and help investigators reach a more thoroughly considered opinion as to whether JonBenét was sexually molested.

Next, I point out to the interviewer that when her body was found, JonBenét's hair was tightly tied in ponytails secured by rubber bands at top and bottom. She was also wearing a spangled shirt and a sequined gown with a silver star emblem on the front. Usually, the person putting a child to bed will undo her ponytails and dress her in pajamas or a nightgown. This regalia seems unusual sleepwear for a six-year-old. Even if, as the family claims, JonBenét was tired from her long day as a beauty contestant, and was laid down asleep wearing her competition gown, the way she is dressed seems suspect.

Finally, when discovered in the basement JonBenét was wearing panties with "Wednesday" printed on them. Since she was found on a Thursday morning, this suggests that she may have been killed before going to bed Wednesday night.

Why were all these essential forensic measures not taken? Why were they overlooked and even derided by the very authorities who are normally the first to employ them? Why did the coroner perform such an absurdly short and incomplete on-site exam?

"It is no wonder that the killer has not been hunted down so far," I tell the interviewer in closing. "In my opinion the mistakes that were made during the first twenty-four hours after JonBenét's killing now make it extraordinarily difficult to *ever* solve this terrible homicide. If not downright impossible."

THE O. J. SIMPSON PLOYS

During the trial of O. J. Simpson, the prosecution made countless procedural mistakes. But there were several key forensic errors that are rarely mentioned when this case is discussed. These errors were, I believe, a principal reason why Simpson beat the rap.

There is little need to remind anyone that the 1995 trial of O. J. Simpson, unquestionably the most famous in the history of American jurisprudence, revolved around the June 1994 homicides of Simpson's wife, Nicole Brown Simpson, and her friend Ronald Goldman.

The defendant, we know, was a Football Hall of Fame running back, a successful film actor, a national spokesman for a popular car rental company, and a much lionized celebrity.

I was often called by TV and radio stations to solicit my opinions on this trial, which was televised across the world on a daily basis, but my schedule at the time was so hectic that I was—somewhat reluctantly—forced to turn down these requests. Later on, when the trial was over and leisure time became available, I examined the Simpson records in depth—the autopsies, the evidentiary findings, the DNA data, the defendant's possible motives, and his history of domestic abuse.

As I read this material it seemed increasingly clear that Simpson was guilty as charged, and that given the quality and quantity of evidence against him, he should have been convicted in weeks. But never underestimate the power of a good lawyer.

Let us start at the beginning of the trial, when O.J.'s "Dream Team" begins the proceedings with little or nothing substantive in their client's favor, while the prosecution boasts a mountain of forensic and circumstantial evidence against the defendant.

The defense responds to this David and Goliath duel in a way that is so brilliant and so subtly undermining of the truth that it goes largely unnoticed. Indeed, the O.J. trial shows how it is possible for smart attorneys to manipulate forensic information in such a way that night becomes day, guilty becomes innocent, science becomes science fiction.

The defense's plan was a simple one: keep the jury confused. More important, keep them *scientifically* confused. Constantly introduce into their minds reasonable doubt concerning the competency of the police and of the forensic experts on the case. Frequently accuse the police of gross incompetence, particularly in the collection and preservation of blood samples from O. J. Simpson, Nicole Brown Simpson, and Ron Goldman. Repeat over and over that the results of lab tests, *particularly* the all-important DNA test, are unreliable, primarily because the police in their haste and incompetence corrupted the blood samples. Finally, add a bit of smear to the mix, frequently implying to a predominantly black jury that certain key members of the L.A. police, particularly Detective Mark Fuhrman, are racists plotting to frame and ruin Simpson. Do not suggest any reasons why the police would attempt such a vendetta against a man many of them admired.

Now, of all the evidence that the prosecution has in its war chest, its star proofs are bloodstains found on the center console and driver's side carpet of O.J.'s famous white Bronco. These droplets apparently contain DNA from Nicole Simpson, Ron Goldman, and O.J. himself. In addition, blood found on the Aris Isotoner glove once worn by O.J. and found on O.J.'s estate also bears the DNA of Ron Goldman. There is a bloodied sock at the foot of O.J.'s. bed that contains Nicole's DNA.

In court, several DNA experts testify for the prosecution that the odds are in the range of several billion to one against these samples' belonging to anyone but O.J. Simpson, Nicole Simpson, and Ron Goldman. The evidence is overwhelming and is based on solid science.

But though the data is indisputable, the defense keeps hammering away at their theme to the highly inexperienced jury: the L.A. police have contaminated the DNA evidence. Therefore, all these tests are invalid.

The prosecution makes five crucial errors in the face of this relentless pounding.

First error. At trial, Richard Rubin, a glove designer and a former vice president of Aris Isotoner Gloves, examines the defendant's hands and testifies that his glove size is extra large. He also identifies a pair of Aris Isotoners that O.J. is wearing in a videotape and photo as the same make and model as the bloodied glove in question. It is further known that in 1990 Nicole Simpson purchased two pairs of these gloves for her husband at Bloomingdale's in size extra large. Only 300 of this model glove in extra large were ever made. Sixty of them were never even sold.

Gotcha!

But then the prosecution, instead of leaving well enough alone, proceeds to shoot itself in the foot by suggesting that O.J. *try on* the glove. When this test takes place, at Johnnie Cochran's cunning insistence, O.J. is allowed to slip on a latex covering under the bloodied mitt. Another mistake.

Why? Because everyone knows—including Richard Rubin, who testifies to same—that a leather gloves shrinks a good deal when it is wet, whether from blood or any other substance, and that wearing a latex covering beneath a regular-size glove makes the fit substantially tighter.

The prosecution's best strategy in this case would have been to allow an expert to identify the make and size of the bloodied glove, then to ask O.J. to try on a *new* Aris Isotoner glove of the same size and model.

But no. The "tight glove syndrome" prevails. Even though the prosecution has initiated the glove-fitting fiasco, once the test is over and the glove proves too tight and small to belong to O.J., Johnnie Cochran proudly announces that "the prosecution would do anything to contort and distort the fact. If the glove doesn't fit, you must acquit."

Second error.   Bloody footprints found behind Nicole Simpson's condominium and bloody shoe impressions discovered in the white Bronco are identified as having been made by Italian Bruno Magli brand shoes in a style called Lorenzo. The identification is made by an FBI agent and shoe print expert, William Bodziak. Only 300 pairs of these exclusive shoes were ever sold in size 12, O.J.'s size.

Three years before the trial, it turns out, an AP photographer named Harry Scull, Jr., took a picture of O.J. wearing the very same shoes. Scull's photograph is duly entered into evidence. But by the time the prosecution presents this critical piece of evidence—in a lackluster and almost irrelevant way, it should be mentioned—the jury is uninterested and unimpressed.

Third error.   During the trial, the prosecution allows scientists to waste entire days providing the jury with extremely complex and sophisticated information on DNA testing—information that is far beyond the grasp of nonscientists.

This barrage of technical formulas and equations confused the jury, then loses them, and finally puts them to sleep, in some cases literally. Thus, many valid reasons given by experts as to why the DNA tests offered conclusive proof of O.J.'s guilt sail far above the jury's heads. "I didn't understand the DNA stuff at all," one juror famously stated after the trial. "To me, it was just a waste of time. It was way out there and carried no weight with me."

Fourth error. The prosecution team would have been well advised to educate the jurors concerning the basics of DNA. But they should have done so on a very simplified level, say, the way teachers explain basic principles of physics to a fifth-grade class.

Fifth and final grand error. The prosecution should have let down its hair and admitted to the jury that yes, the defense was correct: some errors were made by police in handling and preserving blood samples collected at the various crime sites.

Yes, the prosecution should have admitted, sometimes rubber gloves were not used, and sometimes unclean gloves were used.

Yes, samples were sometimes collected in the wrong containers.

Yes, some of the blood samples were improperly stored.

Yes, unsanitary tools were used in the collecting process.

Yes, yes, and yes.

But here, they should then have made clear with fists slamming on tables, is the *really* important point to note. DNA testing, even of contaminated DNA, *does not give false positives; it only gives false negatives.*

If the results of the DNA testing had come back negative, the prosecution should have told the court, if the images had shown DNA profiles that clearly did not belong to Simpson and the victims, then yes, Simpson might have been innocent of bloodshed.

But if on the other hand, regardless of the alleged sloppy work, the samples returned positive for the two victims—and if this positive reading occurred *even though the samples were contaminated*—is this not *stronger* proof that the blood belonged to O. J. Simpson? And to his victims?

Again: DNA testing, even of contaminated DNA, does not give false positives; it gives only false negatives.

THE PASSION OF THE CHRIST: THE MOVIE AND THE FORENSICS

When the controversial film by Mel Gibson, *The Passion of the Christ,* was first released it was touted as being not simply another Cecil B. DeMille Pan-Cake makeup fairy tale about the life of Jesus.

It was, claimed Gibson and the film's publicity machine, a scientifically accurate depiction, down to the smallest, most accurate anatomical detail, of how Jesus of Nazareth was done to death, and the ways in which he physically suffered, both before the crucifixion and during the terrible hours he hung on the cross.

Having studied the scientific and medical aspects of crucifixion for fifty-two years, I went to the theater with high expectations. Before long a string of forensic inaccuracies in Gibson's portrayal of the Passion made it clear to me that someone did not do his homework—or, at least, did not do his homework correctly. To my knowledge, none of the many errors made in this movie have been discussed or debated at any length, either by friends of the film or by its severest critics.

The Scriptures, for example, tell us that after Jesus was taken into captivity, Roman soldiers scourged him.

In Gibson's cinematic version we watch Jesus being caned thirty-two times with wooden rods. This beating is followed by almost ten minutes of upper-body scourging with a *flagrum,* a vicious Roman weapon consisting of octopuslike leather thongs with razor-sharp bits of bone or metal attached to the ends. In the movie, the strokes of this flail are delivered by burly soldiers, swinging full force.

In the revelations of Catherine Emmerich, the beatified Roman Catholic mystic on whose visions Gibson based much of his movie, the scourging of Jesus causes large pieces of flesh to be torn from his body at every blow. Medically speaking, few human beings could suffer such flesh- and organ-destroying excoriation and remain alive, let alone conscious. Remember also that Jesus had already been beaten at the house of Caiaphas, the high priest, and was severely weakened before the serious scourging began.

In a homicide I investigated and autopsied a few years ago in Rockland County, the victim was a young, healthy man who was beaten across his back several times in a row with a belt and a lamp cord. These blows were enough to collapse both lungs, to cause massive hemorrhages in the chest cavity, and finally to kill him. Given that this beating was relatively mild compared to the one Jesus is shown receiving in the film, most medical examiners would shake their head at the notion that any human being could walk away from such an ordeal.

For the sake of argument, though, let us suppose that Jesus did survive the beatings depicted in the film.

After being struck severely and often around the chest and stomach, Gibson's Christ shoulders a 200-pound wooden cross and carries it for some distance.

If you have ever received a sharp punch to your chest or a blow to your ribs, you know that afterward it is practically impossible to take a deep breath. This condition is known medically as splinting. Supposing that Jesus did not pass out from the brutal whippings delivered by his cinematic flagellators, he would nonetheless be gasping for air so desperately that just leaning a heavy piece of wood against his chest or shoulders would produce unbearable pain. Carrying it would be out of the question. It is interesting, too, that in Gibson's film Simon of Cyrene, the bystander forced to carry the cross after Jesus collapses, is portrayed as a big, powerful man; and even he has trouble dragging it.

But much of Gibson's cross-carrying scene is historically awry anyway. For example, the cross that Jesus carries is depicted as a complete cruciform structure, with the upright and crosspiece joined. But according to Roman records, a prisoner destined to be crucified was forced to carry only the crosspiece, or *patibulum.* The other section of the cross, the upright or *stipes,* was waiting for him at the execution grounds outside the city gates. The Romans instituted this practice out of necessity, one supposes, rather than mercy. Few men on earth can lift a 200-pound object and drag it hundreds of feet, perhaps thousands of feet, and remain standing, especially if they have been beaten for several hours first. Indeed, how many of us can carry 200 pounds at all? How many of us can even lift 200 pounds off the ground?

Now segue to the film's crucifixion scene.

To begin, the *suppadenum* or foot rest shown in the film at the bottom of the cross is an invention of latter-day artists. The Romans never heard of such a thing.

Then there is the critical event of the nailing of the hands and feet.

Here we know from studies of soldiers wounded during World War II that when shrapnel pierces the median nerve on the palm of the hand or the plantar nerve on the soles of the feet—the places where the nails enter Jesus's body—a pain known as causalgia takes place. This pain, even when just one hand or one foot is pierced, is so excruciating that even morphine is ineffective as an analgesic. During the war, surgeons treating such cases were forced to sever the corresponding nerve near the spinal column to prevent patients from going mad with agony, falling into shock, and dying.

Imagine now that all four of these tender spots, the median nerve on both hands, the plantar nerve on both feet, are penetrated by massive iron spikes. Such cruelty would surely cause a victim to shriek and writhe in the most indescribable agonies, passing out finally from shock and probably dying soon thereafter.

But not in our movie.

Jesus, who the Scriptures tell us voluntarily accepts the physical sufferings wrought on him to redeem humankind, takes his punishment in the film with a minimum of yelling or fainting. Even after receiving flesh-tearing whippings, dragging a 200-pound cross, and wearing a crown of thorns, he remains relatively placid as he hangs.

And speaking of the crown of thorns, the long, hatpinlike needles that the film shows perforating Jesus's forehead would soon cause the wearer to develop trigeminal neuralgia, a nerve condition characterized by unbearable lancinating pains across the face.

Still another forensic error that any medical examiner would immediately notice is the fact that Mary and the Magdalene are busy at the bottom of the cross cleaning up the vast quantities of blood that spill from Jesus's wounds. Considering the methods of penetration involved in this execution—nailing with spikes and piercing by a narrow-pointed blade—only small amounts of blood would, in fact, be shed, far less than the large red pools shown soaking the ground beneath Gibson's cross. In the hundreds of homicide scenes I have investigated, I have only seen such blood accumulations in cases of multiple stabbings with a knife, or in massive injuries where wide and gaping wounds are visible.

Then there is the lurid scene when the Roman centurion pierces Christ with a spear, and a spray of blood and water shoots out, covering the face of Mary and the soldier. This physical reaction to stabbing is both scientifically and scripturally inaccurate. Biologically speaking, after the scourging, fluid would have slowly built up around Jesus' lungs. Once the spear penetrated the chest cavity, both lungs would collapse from the loss of negative pressure in the chest cavity due to the influx of the atmospheric pressure. After the spear was withdrawn, blood and water would emerge, yes, but they would flow out gently owing to this drop in fluid level.

Last, there is the perennial question: What caused Jesus's death?

In my personal studies of crucifixion through the years, I have conducted a large number of experiments to determine what actually happens to a human being suspended on the type of cross the Romans used. I worked with a full-sized Roman-style wooden cross, multiple volunteers, sophisticated blood studies, and forensic reconstructions.

The results demonstrated to me and to a majority of my colleagues that the cause of death under such circumstances is hypovolemic shock due to low blood and fluid volume, and traumatic shock due to the multiple injuries that were inflicted. Asphyxiation, heart attack, rupture of the heart, and even drugs, which have sometimes been suggested, must all be ruled out as a cause of death.

And yet, all such studies and observations of the crucifixion are academic if we are to trust in the logic of this movie. For given the extreme punishments that the film's Jesus endures even before reaching Golgotha, it would take a physical specimen of Superman-like proportions simply to stay alive long enough to reach the cross.

And Jesus of Nazareth, we know—at least, according to the Scriptures that have come down to us—willingly chose not to show off his divine strength and immortality during his ordeal, but to die on the cross as an ordinary mortal would, suffering as an ordinary mortal would when subjected to the indignities visited on him by his many persecutors, both in Jerusalem—and in Hollywood.

USING PSYCHICS TO SOLVE HOMICIDES

Although the public is not generally aware of the fact, psychics are occasionally asked by the police to use their supposed powers to locate kidnapped children or find bodies of homicide victims.

I am ambivalent concerning such an approach to crime solving. Although I do not categorically deny the possibility of extrasensory perception, and although there are cases in which, I am told, psychics have accurately described murder scenes and the physical characteristics of an assailant, from my personal experience psychic identification of both killer and killed remains questionable.

In the murder of the fashion student discussed in chapter three, for example, a well-known psychic was consulted by the Rockland District Attorney's Office. There was hearsay that other victims had been killed and buried on the Rockland County property owned by the family of the self-admitted killer, Bernard LeGeros.

The psychic walked the length of this well-tended estate, indicating all the while that she was receiving strong signals from buried corpses. She stopped at several places on the property and told my forensic team to dig.

A great deal of shoveling followed. At the end of the day, not a trace of human remains had appeared, despite copious sweat and a number of blisters.

Not long afterward, police authorities were informed that Andrew Crispo, a witness to this crime, had the bodies of his own murder victims buried all over his estate in Southampton, on Long Island. A crew was dispatched there with backhoes and other construction equipment. They dug up most of Crispo's elegant lawn and driveway, even burrowing under large and expensive outdoor works of art. No remains were discovered.

No matter what opinion one may harbor of the notorious Mr. Crispo, I cannot but feel sorry for him, standing there in front of his million-dollar dream house, gazing wistfully at his flower beds and green Long Island vistas reduced to mounds of churned-up earth. "If we'd kept on digging," one police officer was quoted as saying, "we'd have to have repaved half of Southampton."

When I discussed this case with several medical examiners from other jurisdictions, they all told me of similar experiences.

The jury remains out on the use of psychics in criminal detection.

But for my money, in forensics, give me science every time.

© Cheryl Jenkins

FREDERICK ZUGIBE, M.D., Ph.D., is the former chief medical examiner of Rockland County and remains one of the nation's most respected forensics experts. DAVID L. CARROLL has cowritten thirty-one books and produced twelve network television films. Both men live in Rockland County, New York.

Printed in the United States
by Baker & Taylor Publisher Services